Literacy,
Bible Reading,
and Church Growth
THROUGH THE AGES

By Morris Watkins

William Carey Library

533 HERMOSA STREET • SOUTH PASADENA, CALIFORNIA 91030

Library of Congress Cataloging in Publication Data
Watkins, Morris, 1923-
    Literacy, Bible reading, and church growth
through the ages.

    Bibliography: p.
    Includes index.
    1. Missions--History. 2. Church growth.
3. Bible--Reading. 4. Illiteracy. I. Title.
BV2105.W33   270   78-15315
ISBN 0-87808-325-1

Copyright © 1978 by Morris G. Watkins

Published by the William Carey Library
533 Hermosa Street
South Pasadena, California 91030
Telephone (213) 798-0819

In accord with some of the most recent thinking in the academic
press, the William Carey Library is pleased to present this
scholarly book which has been prepared from an author-edited
and author-prepared camera ready copy.

PRINTED IN THE UNITED STATES OF AMERICA

Contents

Figures

vi

Foreword

Because time is a priceless possession, it is important to choose carefully the books you read. It is my conviction that you made a wise decision when you chose to read this meaningful book by Dr. Morris Watkins.

As you read, I sincerely trust you will experience three things: first, an increased admiration for God's pioneers world-wide who laid the foundation for world evangelism -- which we must complete in our generation. Second, an overwhelming gratitude that you are a Christian today -- with global opportunities to communicate the gospel of Jesus Christ to vast multitudes. "I sent you to reap that whereon ye bestowed no labor; other men labored, and ye are entered into their labors" (John 4:38).

Above all I pray that you allow the Holy Spirit to underline the great importance of your involvement in providing God's Word for literally millions of hungry people who live in areas of the world where there is a famine for it.

This informative volume speaks for many generations of the human race -- they all testify to the inherent hunger for the truth which alone can liberate and which is found only in God's Holy Word. Please remember we are debtors to all Bible-less people. Our lives have meaning as we make installments on the payment of that debt.

Jack McAlister, *President/Founder*
World Literature Crusade

Preface

The subject of literacy, Bible reading, and church growth has been of particular interest to me for many years. I was first involved in literacy and literature as a missionary in Nigeria (1959-1964). Since that time I have directed two mission organizations involved in literacy work. From 1959 to 1962 I worked in Ogoja Province where there are some forty different ethnic groups speaking as many different unwritten languages. It was during this time I became aware that there were another five hundred languages in Nigeria and perhaps two thousand tongues spoken throughout Africa, most of which had never been reduced to writing. Believing that no strong church could exist in any society unless it has a good (dynamic equivalence) translation of God's Word in its own language, I set myself to recruit and train Bible translators, as founder and director of Lutheran Bible Translators (1964-1972).

In that capacity I found myself becoming increasingly sensitive to the fact that even when the Bible is available in a people's language, the majority of the people are often unable to read it. There are hundreds of millions of those who already have Scripture in their mother tongue, who are not able to read it. Furthermore, I became painfully aware of the fact that though the percentage of illiterates in most countries is decreasing each year, the rapid population increase in developing countries means that the actual number of illiterates is greater today than ever before.

Because of the fact that some eight hundred million adults (over fifteen years of age) are illiterate, I decided in 1972 to leave the Lutheran Bible Translators in the hands of others and begin a new organization, the All Nations Literacy Movement. The main aim of this organization is to help teach all Christians to read and to equip them with a literacy and evangelistic tool (the Christ-centered primer) with which they can lead their illiterate friends and relatives to Christ. We also seek to promote Bible training for new literates and leadership training for the church, through extension courses. This is the work in which the writer has been engaged for the past six years.

I am indebted to more than a hundred missionaries whom I interviewed here in the States and from Mexico to Ecuador, especially those members of the Wycliffe Bible Translators who have had many years of field experience. I am also grateful to those many missionaries and agencies that have been involved in literacy and literature production and distribution as well as those who have written about their accomplishments. We hesitate to mention them by name for fear of overlooking some. I am also indebted to my wife, Lois, who has been a constant source of help, inspiration, and encouragement to me. My grateful appreciation goes to Miss Margaret Frick for her careful typing of the final manuscript and to all members of the All Nations staff for their assistance. Finally, I am indebted to Dr. Charles Kraft, my mentor, for his patience, guidance, and encouragement.

Introduction

In 1978 there are 2.8 billion non-Christians throughout the
world and more than eight hundred million adults who are blind
to the printed page. Teaching all these people to read is such
a staggering task, I have often wondered if there is not an
easier way to make disciples of all nations and thoroughly teach
them all that Christ has commanded (Matthew 28:18-20). Certainly people can be won to Christ through hearing the Good News
alone. There is no question about that. It happens all the
time. But can a body of believers grow spiritually and numerically if there are few or no literates among them? Can they remain faithful to the Word? Can they effectively witness to
people in their own communities, much less reach out to peoples
in other lands and tongues? Is literacy and Bible reading
really of any value in Church growth? Do people come to faith
in their Savior solely through reading? Do they grow in their
faith solely through reading God's Word? Do literacy programs
help indirectly by opening doors for the Gospel of Jesus Christ?
Does literacy among church members help keep the church doctrinally sound? Can the church grow faster and be stronger where
people are literate than where they are not literate? In what
other ways might literacy be of value for church growth? Does
literacy pose any dangers to church growth?

To answer these and related questions precisely--to the satis-
faction of all concerned--is probably not even possible. Perhaps the only way we could be absolutely certain that literacy
can help any particular group of people become a numerically
larger and spiritually stronger church than they could become if
they were illiterate, would be to observe that group of people

for a number of years--first without any literacy among them,
and then with literacy.

Or, perhaps a missionary could go to a totally illiterate
ethnic group where the Gospel was never proclaimed before, and
work in two villages. He could work orally in one village, but
translate Scripture, teach people to read, train authors, prepare Bible courses for new literates, etc., in the other. But
even in this situation, if the church grew faster where literacy
and literature work was done, this fact would not necessarily
"prove" that literacy contributes to church growth. It could
still be argued that this particular village was simply more
responsive to the Gospel. Even if this procedure did prove that
literacy has value for church growth, the time required for such
an undertaking would be prohibitive.

METHOD OF RESEARCH

Since time did not permit the above approach to the problem
in even one ethnic group, it was decided to send a questionnaire
to several missionaries in various countries around the world.
I also decided to interview as many as possible on a trip
through Mexico, Central America, Colombia, and Ecuador. This
survey was made during the four months ending November 15, 1975.
Upon our return from Latin America, I also wrote to twenty-five
organizations engaged in literacy and in literature distribution
for stories of church growth through reading. Almost all of
them responded with helpful information.

While a lot of valuable material was gathered in these ways,
I became increasingly interested in the part that literacy and
Bible reading played in church growth down through the centuries.
I came to feel that a study of this history would help to put
the contemporary materials in their proper perspective. In
gathering information for this aspect of the study, books and
articles were consulted not only on church history and mission
history, but also on such subjects as the history of education,
history of languages, paper, writing systems, printing, history
of translations, colportage, influence of the Bible, and related
subjects. A search was made through many libraries in Southern
California, including McAlister Library, Fuller Theological
Seminary in Pasadena, and libraries at the University of California at Los Angeles, Biola in La Mirada, Azusa Pacific College
in Azusa, Chapman College in Orange, Pacific Christian College
in Fullerton, Southern California College in Costa Mesa, California State University at Los Angeles and California State
University at Fullerton, and the public libraries in Pasadena,
Los Angeles, and several in Orange County.

SCOPE OF THE STUDY

When it comes to the influence that literacy and Bible
reading have had on church growth over a period of nearly
two thousand years, there is no limit to what could be written.
This dissertation, therefore, is not an exhaustive study of
Bible reading and church growth in every age. It does, however,
trace the major developments in church history, from the beginning of the synagogue down to the present day, showing the
results of Bible reading or the lack of it. The same is
especially true regarding the influence of Bible reading in
our own time. There is literally no end to the number of
stories of church growth as a result of Bible reading in the
present century. An exhaustive presentation of these stories
was felt unnecessary and beyond the scope of this present work.

1

The Fulness of Time

The Bible tells us that when the fulness of time was come, God
sent forth His Son, made of a woman, made under the law, to re-
deem them that were under the law (Gal.4:4). The fulness of
time had indeed come for the advancement of the Gospel of our
Redeemer. God's timing was perfect. The Jewish people were a
people of the Book, and these Bible-reading Jews were scattered
throughout the Roman Empire. The Greek language, with its simple
writing system, was spoken throughout the Mediterranean world and
even further to the East. The Septuagint, the Greek translation
of the Scriptures, was read in synagogues from one end of the Empire to the other, and there was a high rate of literacy among
the Gentiles as well as among the Jews. There was also a large
amount of apocalyptic literature, occupied to a considerable extent with the coming Messiah. In addition to all of this, there
was relative peace throughout the world, and travel by land or
sea was comparatively safe. Everything was ready for the proclamation of the greatest message the world has ever known.

THE PEOPLE OF THE BOOK

In the eighth century B.C. the Kingdom of Israel was conquered
by the mighty Assyrian Empire and its inhabitants taken captive
into Assyria and the cities of the Medes (2 Kings 15:29;17:6).
Apparently there were no prophets among the exiles and no written
Word of God. These ten tribes completely lost their identity.
They were completely swallowed up by their conquerors.

A little over a century later, the downfall of the Southern
Kingdom followed the same pattern. But the outcome was very
different. The end of the Jewish state did not mean the end of
Judaism. The practice of "orthodox Judaism" actually had its
beginning in these events. Why? What made the difference?
Why was it that the exiles from Judah did not assimilate in the
Babylonian world as the exiles from Israel had assimilated in
the Assyrian Empire? For one thing they had the written Word
of God with them, and they began to read it themselves and/or
to hear it read and expounded on a regular basis (Bamberger
1959:33).

Many of the exiles, no doubt, intermarried and otherwise
disappeared from the Jewish group. Those that remained, however, had a deeper conviction than ever had been seen among
the masses of Israel. They were the servants of the great God
who had punished them, but He had the power to restore them to
their land, and this He had promised to do. This conviction
grew out of the teaching of the great prophets which had been
preserved from the catastrophe, and also out of the living
prophetic Word that was still preached among them (Bamberger
1957:34).

The Synagogue

Many of those who went into captivity took with them their
cherished Scriptures, copies of the Law and the Prophets. Some
of the best educated and most devout Jews had been taken to
Babylon (Tenney 1953:51). Far from their homeland, they probably felt the need of having special meeting places for common
prayer, especially on the Sabbath. From the Book of Ezekiel
we learn that the exiles met from time to time in the house of
the prophet himself, for instruction and inspiration (Ezekiel
8:1; 14:1; 20:1). It may have been in such meetings that the
synagogue had its origin. At any rate, most authorities believe that the synagogue did have its origin during the
Babylonian captivity (Metzger 1965:56). Whether they built
special houses of worship during the exile, we cannot say. But
after the Jews returned from exile, and during the pre-Maccabean
period (before 167 B.C.), they built for themselves religious
meeting places in addition to the rebuilt temple at Jerusalem
(Metzger 1965:56).

At the beginning of the Christian era, synagogues were to be
found in almost all Palestinian cities and towns as well as in
many centers throughout the Mediterranean world and at least as
far east as Babylon. They were probably found also in Parthia,
Elam, and Media (present day Iran), for we know that Jews and
proselytes from these places were present in Jerusalem on the
day of Pentecost (Acts 2:9), and the Apostle James tells us that

for many generations Moses was read in the synagogues every
Sabbath day in every city (Acts 15:21). We also know that in
order to organize a synagogue only ten men (heads of families)
were required (Pfeiffer 1959:60). In larger cities there were
many synagogues. According to Talmudic tradition, Jerusalem
had 480 synagogues. While this is probably a gross exaggera-
tion, there must have been a large number of these places of
worship in that city (Metzger 1965:56).

The central feature of the synagogue service was the reading
of Scripture. The Torah (the five books of Moses) was divided
into 154 lessons to be read in a definite period of time. The
Palestinian Jews read through the Pentateuch every three years,
whereas the Babylonian Jews completed the entire cycle in one
year. Every Israelite, even a minor, could take part in the
public reading of the Law. On the Sabbath day at least seven
readers were chosen. If priests were present, they were called
on first, followed by the Levites, and then by lay members of
the congregation (Pfeiffer 1959:62). No one was to read fewer
than five verses. After the reading of the Law came a lesson
from one of the prophets, chosen at the discretion of the
reader (Luke 4:16-21).

The need for a translation of the lessons must have arisen
early, perhaps as soon as the institution of the reading
itself. The language of the Bible (classical Hebrew) had not
been the vernacular of the Jews anywhere for a long time. In
Palestine and Babylonia and in interior Syria they spoke distinct dialects of Aramaic. In Egypt, Aramaic had given way
to Greek, which was the speech of almost all the Jews in the
western Dispersion after the conquests of Alexander the Great.
In the more remote provinces of the Parthian Empire (east of
Babylon) they spoke the languages of their surroundings, perhaps in addition to Aramaic. However greatly the Jews rever-
enced the 'sacred tongue', they had no superstition about it.
Understanding was more important than sentiment (Moore 1946:
303).

In the Palestinian synagogues the lessons were read in
Hebrew, and an interpreter standing beside the reader, translated them into Aramaic. In Luke 4:16 ff. there is no mention
of translation. But Luke no doubt was better acquainted with
the Hellenistic synagogues where there was no need for an
interpreter. The reading was from the Septuagint, the Greek
translation dating from the third century B.C., which was
understood by everyone in Nazareth which was in "Galilee of
the Gentiles" (Is. 9:1; Matt. 4:15).

Worship services were held in the synagogue, not only on the
Sabbath day but also on other holy days. Since farmers, many
of whom lived at some distance from villages and towns, could
not travel on the Sabbath, portions of the Torah were read on
market days--Monday and Thursday--when the country people could
be present (Bamberger 1957:46).

The Schools

The synagogue was just one of two great institutions of
religious education in Judaism. The second was the school.
In some form or other the school is as old as the synagogue,
if not older, and the synagogue was always dependent upon it.
The reading of the Scriptures in the ancient language, the
vernacular interpretation, the homiletical exposition drawing
out of the Scripture its religious and moral lessons, the instruction in the peculiar observances of Judaism and their
significance, all required a considerable measure of education.
Futhermore, to fulfill its possibilities as a school of re-
vealed religion, the synagogue needed to have behind it a
higher learning upon which it could draw directly or indirectly
(Moore 1946:308).

The men who took the lead in this work in the last century
of Persian rule and the Greek period that followed are called
soferim, commonly translated 'scribes' or 'biblical scholars'.
The existence of many biblical scholars from the third century
B.C. down shows that there was regular provision for transmitting the learning of former generations and adding to it.

Great stress was laid upon the education of children. Philo
tells us that his people

> ...were from their swaddling clothes, even before
> being taught either the sacred laws or the unwritten
> customs, trained by their parents, teachers, and
> instructors to recognize God as Father and Maker of
> the world (Moore 1946:321).

For a long time elementary education was probably left to
parents or to private schools. But long before the Christian
era public schools were established to teach reading and
writing (Moore 1946:316).

Attendance at the elementary school began at the age of
five or six. The subjects taught were reading, writing,
arithmetic (in a very elementary form), and the Word of God.
The only textbooks were the rolls of the sacred Scriptures,
especially the roll of the Law, the opening chapters of

Leviticus usually being the first to be studied. After the
letters were mastered, the teacher copied a verse the child
had already memorized and taught him to identify the individual
words (Hastings 1963:231).

Schools of a similar kind existed in Babylonia before Christ
was born. Hillel was born and raised there. Philo, who lived
in Alexandria, Egypt, at the time of Jesus and Paul, testifies
that the Greek-speaking Jews had schools for the study of
Scripture. In these Hellenistic schools, the Septuagint was
used so the people did not have to learn to read the original
Hebrew (Hastings 1963:231).

As to the extent of education in Palestine, the edict of
Antiochus Epiphanes (about 170 B.C.) forbidding the possession
of Scripture on pain of death, implies that many people had the
Torah and were able to understand it and read it for themselves
(Hastings 1963:231). According to a tradition from the close
of the Maccabean period (about 75 B.C.) a famous scribe, Simon
ben-Shetach, had a law passed ordaining that "the children
shall attend the elementary school" (Hastings 1963:231). This
we understand to mean, not that these schools were begun at
this time, but that attendance was from then on compulsory.
The elementary school, termed "the house of the Book" (i.e.
Scripture), in opposition to "the house of study" or college
of the scribes was always closely associated with the synagogue.
In smaller places the same building served both (Hastings 1963:
231).

Wellhausen admirably describes the situation, saying:

> The Bible became the spelling-book, the community
> a school... Piety and education were inseparable;
> whoever could not read was no true Jew (Hastings
> 1963:230).

The Hebrews, with their life rooted in the Scriptures, were
probably as literate as any people of the ancient world
(Jeffries 1967:5). They were truly a "people of the Book"
(Russell 1960:41-57), a book that preserved their identity as a
nation and as the people of God.

THE JEWISH DISPERSION

When Cyrus permitted the Jews to return to their homeland in
537 B.C., a very small percentage of them took advantage of the
opportunity. The vast majority were comfortable and prosperous
in the land in which they were born or had lived since childhood and chose to remain in that land. Those Jews who remained

in the land of their captivity were held in high esteem by the
Jews of Palestine. According to one view, Babylonia, as well
as "Syria" as far north as Antioch, was considered part of the
land of Israel (Edersheim 1953:7).

It was between the Tigris and the Euphrates that the largest
and wealthiest settlements of the Jews were, to such an extent
that a later writer referred to them as "the land of Israel"
(Edersheim 1953:7). The oldest Jewish settlement was here on
the royal canal that connected the Tigris and Euphrates. A
synagogue was built there by King Jechoniah with stones said to
have been brought from the temple. In this fortified city the
Eastern Jews deposited vast contributions for the temple. From
there these contributions were conveyed to their destination by
thousands of armed men. Another of these Jewish treasure-cities
was Nisibis, in northern Mesopotamia. The fact that such great
wealth could be safely stored in these cities and then trans-
ported to Palestine shows how large the population of the Jews
must have been and also their great general influence. According to Josephus, with whom Philo agrees, millions lived in the
trans-Euphratic provinces. The number of those killed in popular uprisings (50,000 in Seleucia alone) bears this out. A
later tradition held that the Jewish population in the Persian
Empire was so great that Cyrus forbade the further return of the
exiles because he feared the country would be depopulated
(Edersheim 1953:8).

Theological Academies

There is good reason to believe that there were regular
theological academies in Babylon during the first period after
the exiles returned. We know that before the time of Christ
the authority of the Babylonian schools grew until they over-
shadowed those of Palestine. The proud Palestinians sneered
that the Babylonians were stupid, proud, and poor, but they had
to admit that it was Ezra, of Babylon, who restored the Law
when it had fallen into oblivion. The second time it had to be
restored by Hillel, another Babylonian. And it had to be restored a third time by Rabbi Chija, also of Babylon (Edersheim
1953:9-11).

Extent of the Dispersion

This dispersion extended in every direction--east as far as
India, north through Armenia, the Caucasus, and to the Black Sea
and through Media to the Caspian Sea, and south to the Persian
Gulf and through all of Arabia.

But the Jewish Dispersion was even greater in the West in
Egypt and Cyrene, Asia Minor, Italy, Greece, Cyprus, and Crete.

Much of this dispersion occurred after the conquests of Alexander the Great in the fourth century B.C. Under one great military power, much of the hostilities between kingdoms ceased and free travel became possible. Business opportunities increased and the Seleucid and Ptolemaic successors of Alexander offered citizenship and exemption from taxation of those who migrated to their lands. Many Jews took advantage of these offers and settled in the growing Hellenistic colonies. Some of them became only temporary residents of the Greek cities, but others became citizens and began new occupations. One whole section of the city of Alexandria was Jewish, with its own governor and officials who were practically self-governing. Its population was estimated at two million, and it was the largest single concentration of Jews in any one city of the world (Tenney 1953: 141).

In the Roman Empire the Jewish settlements increased rapidly. Ultimately, the slaves that Pompey brought back from Palestine were freed and settled near the docks on the right bank of the Tiber. In 4 B.C. there were about eight thousand of them in the city (Tenney 1953:141).

The Greek influence caused many of the Jews of the Dispersion to lose the distinctive characteristics that made them different from other peoples. Most of them, however, kept their Jewish allegiance. They held firmly to the law of Moses and their monotheistic faith. They went annually to the feasts at the temple in Jerusalem. They kept the Sabbath and conducted synagogue services wherever there were enough of them (a minimum of ten men who were heads of families) to form a worshiping group.

Two Kinds of Jews

There were two kinds of Jews within the Diaspora--the Hebraists and the Hellenists. The Hebraists or "Hebrews" retained the religious faith of Judaism and also the use of the Hebrew or Aramaic language and the Hebrew customs. A much greater number of the Jews, however, were Hellenists. They had taken on the Graeco-Roman culture and were no longer Jews except in matters of faith. They spoke Greek or the language used in the land where they lived. They adopted the customs of their neighbors and were hardly distinguishable as Jews. The Jews in the Roman Empire at the time of Christ, including both Hebraists and Hellenists, numbered about half a million (Tenney 1953:142).

Throughout the Roman Empire there were large numbers of Jews attending synagogues where they heard the Word of God read every Sabbath day. It was read in Greek, which they understood, or in Hebrew with an Aramaic interpretation. This large Dispersion of the "people of the Book" with its prophecies of the Messiah, scattered as it was throughout the length and breadth of the Roman Empire, was one very definite way in which the world had been prepared for the coming of Jesus Christ and for the rapid expansion of the Christian Church.

A COMMON LANGUAGE

In the rapid conquests of Alexander the Great, many colonies were formed throughout Asia Minor, Syria, Egypt, Persia, and even as far east as the Indus River. He encouraged the marriage of his soldiers to oriental women and he began the education of thirty thousand of the Persians in the Greek language. When he died, his successors kept up his Hellenizing policy throughout the Near East, especially in Asia Minor, Syria, and Egypt. Many of the cities in Palestine became bilingual, especially in Galilee (Tenney 1953:48-49). One recent piece of evidence shows the extent to which the Jews became Hellenized or at least bilingual. In a Jewish cemetery of the first century, near Jerusalem,80% of the epitaphs are in Greek (Bouquet 1953:157).

Alexandria for several centuries, before and after the birth of Christ, was the intellectual capital of the world. It had the largest and one of the most famous libraries with some 500,000 books (papyrus rolls). It was created as a part of the Museum (an academy of arts and sciences) about 300 B.C., and together they were one of the cultural wonders of the ancient world (Standard Education Corporation 1975:s.v.) In the days of Christ this great intellectual center had a population of some 600,000 to 700,000 people of many nationalities, mostly Greeks and Jews (Davis 1956:26). It seems likely that at least 100,000 of them were Jews (Pfeiffer 1959:72). It is not surprising that Alexandria with its large population of Greek-speaking "people of the Book" became one of the three great centers of Christendom during the first three centuries.

The other great centers of Christianity, after the destruction of Jerusalem in A.D. 70, were Antioch and Rome. Antioch also had a large and famous library. Another was to be found in Pergamon in Asia Minor, where there was also a large number of Greek-speaking Jews (Pfeiffer 1959:84). Christianity made rapid gains in both of these places.

There were also Greek colonies along the seacoast of Gaul and Spain, in the island of Sicily, and on the mainland of the lower Italian peninsula. Greek slaves, many of whom were more learned than their Roman masters, became part of Roman households. Many were employed as teachers, physicians, accountants, and overseers of farms and businesses. Aristocratic young Romans learned to speak Greek and attended Greek universities of Athens, Rhodes, Tarsus, and other cities. The Greek culture so thoroughly conquered the victors that Rome itself became a Greek-speaking city (Tenney 1953:46).

A SIMPLE WRITING SYSTEM

The fact that there was a common language spoken throughout the empire was of tremendous significance for the rapid spread of the Gospel. Another factor of major significance, however, is the development of the Greek alphabet. This development, in which each sound of the language is consistently expressed by means of consonant and vowel symbols, is the last important step in the history of writing. In *A Study of Writing*, I. J. Gelb distinguishes three types of alphabets in use in the world today, of which type I, which includes Greek and Latin and Slavonic, is the simplest (Gelb 1952:184). From the Greek period up to the present, nothing new has happened in the inner structural development of writing. Generally speaking, we write vowels and consonants in the same way as the ancient Greeks did (Gelb 1952: 184).

More will be said about writing systems and their relationship to church growth in a subsequent chapter. Suffice it to say that there seems to be a close relationship between the two. Among peoples who have the Greek or Roman type alphabet there has been considerable church growth, but there are many other factors to consider.

THE SEPTUAGINT

The translation of the Hebrew Old Testament into Greek was, without question, the greatest monument of Alexandrian Judaism. The translation was probably made at the impulse of Alexandrian Jews who wanted their Greek-speaking children to be able to read Scriptures. The mother tongue (Hebrew) was forgotten by the younger children and some provision had to be made for preserving the Hebrew literature in the popularly spoken Greek. The Torah, or Pentateuch, was translated sometime around 250 B.C. The remaining canonical books of the Old Testament and the apocryphal books were translated later (Pfeiffer 1959:85).

No doubt a copy of the Septuagint was placed in the famous Alexandrian library. Although it had been translated by Alexandrian Jews for their own use, it did serve as a means of acquainting the non-Jew with the principles of Jewish faith and practice. In New Testament times there were many "God-fearers" among the Gentiles. In a real sense the Septuagint helped pave the way for the ministry of the apostle Paul and others who

took the message of Christ to the non-Jew as well as to the
Greek-speaking Jews. In the Greek-speaking world, Biblical
preaching was based on the Septuagint text. Many of the quotations from the Old Testament which are found in the New Testament are taken from the Septuagint, although others are translated from the Hebrew. The writers are apparently paraphrasing
Scripture which they assume to be known to their readers (Pfeiffer 1959:85-87).

After the beginning of the Christian movement the Septuagint
became so widely used by the Christians and was used so freely
in their controversies with the Jews that the orthodox Jews
grew skeptical of the translation and had other translations
made. But the Septuagint continued to be the Bible of the
Christians down to the Middle Ages. It was frequently quoted
by the New Testament writers, especially the author of Hebrews.
The early church fathers used it almost exclusively. For a
hundred years after the birth of Christ it was the only Bible
of the Christian world (Dana 1937:53).

APOCALYPTIC LITERATURE

In addition to the twenty-four books of the Hebrew Old Testament (which are the same as the thirty-nine books which are considered canonical by Protestants), and the fourteen apocryphal
books written between the first and third centuries B.C.
(which were included in the Septuagint), another species of
literature developed among the Jews during the last two centuries before Christ and the first century of our era. Much
of this literature is apocalyptic in nature and is occupied
to a considerable extent with the coming Messiah.

Perhaps the best known of these writings is the *Book of
Enoch*, written in the first and second centuries B.C., containing revelations supposed to have been given to Enoch and
to Noah. In the earliest Christian literature we find it
highly spoken of. The church fathers even quote it as Scripture. Jude, who wrote one of the epistles in the New Testament
also quoted from it (Jude 14 and 15). The *Book of Enoch*,is a
very long book, one part of which is known as the Similitudes.
Its peculiar feature is: The Day of Judgment is coming, and
this will be the day of deliverance and reward for those who
suffer for God. The Lord's Anointed, the Son of David, will
bring that day. And He is on the way. The signs of His coming
are clear and unmistakable (Gregg 1908:73-74).

This book, together with other apocalyptic writings, helped
create the expectation of the immediate coming of the Messiah.
This body of literature helped prepare the people for Christ
and the Kingdom which He preached. It helped pave the way for
the planting of the Christian Church and the advance of the
Gospel (Gregg 1908:75).

The amount of apocalyptic literature must have been very
large; and only fragments of it have come down to us. These
fragments have been preserved for us by their having been used
by Christians and included in the Canon of various Christian
Churches--Syriac, Ethiopic, and Latin (Grant n.d.:139).

For generations the apocalyptist represented the protest of
spiritual religion against the formalism of the Scribes and the
secularism of the Sadducees. He kept alive the Blessed Hope of
Israel, even while he seriously mis-shaped it. Except for him,
the church of Moses might have dropped down to the depth of an
unresisted legalism, and to worship of the "letter" which the
highest authority has told us "kills". And so, he too had his
work to do in making "ready a people prepared for the Lord"
(Grant n.d.:141).

LITERACY

A large number of people at the beginning of the Christian
era were able to read and write. As far back as the fifth
century B.C. most Athenian citizens were literate. Apparently
even uneducated people could read, and when an Athenian wanted
to describe a complete ignoramus, he used the proverbial phrase,
"He can't read, he can't swim." The Spartans were alleged to
be not as literate as the Athenians, but, contrary to an old
legend, many Spartans were able to read.

Rome inherited this tradition and disseminated it throughout
the West. Roman society appears to have been tolerably literate
and the Roman legionary was not uncommonly a literate soldier.
In Roman towns, laws were posted on boards in public places and
it was assumed that the majority of citizens would read them
(Cipolla 1969:38).

There is unmistakable evidence that in Ptolemaic Alexandria
(before Christ) literacy was widespread. Estimates as high as
60% of the middle class men and 40% of the women are quoted
(Sullivan 1933:513). Graffiti scrawled on rocks in Transjor-
dania show that a significant percentage of the population was
in some measure able to read and write (Bouquet 1953:156).

We have already seen that in Palestine there were schools in
every town and that there was compulsory education in them for
every child over six years of age. In fact, it is said in one
of the tractates of the Talmud that it was unlawful for parents
with school-age children to live in a place where there was no
school (Bouquet 1953:156).

Outside of Palestine, in the first century A.D., in urban
centers, not only state schools and municipal schools were to
be found, but there were schools for girls as well as for boys

and a variety of subjects was taught.   Also in Italy by the
beginning of the first century, the Romans had already had
schools for a long time.   Even the slave class was not illiterate, and there were some schools on the university level,
at places like Carthage and Marseilles as well as at Athens,
Rhodes, and Tarsus (Bouquet 1953:158).

Under Augustus (27 B.C.-A.D. 14) there was a literary
revival in Rome. Vergil, the poet, became the prophet of the
new era. In his writings the hope of a golden age to come was
reflected, and at least one of Vergil's Eclogues (The Fourth)
seems to show that he had some knowledge of the Old Testament.
The Augustan age was also graced by Horace, who cast Latin
poetry in Greek molds, and by Ovid, whose stories of Greek and
Roman mythology reveal the contemporary moral attitudes of the
Roman people (Tenney 1953:82).   Writing was extensively carried
on in all the more enlightened centers, and books in vast numbers were produced. Scribes who had been specially trained for
the task devoted themselves to the reproduction of manuscripts
as a profession.   In fact, not until the eighteenth century do
we find more intellectual activity and enlightenment than there
was in the Graeco-Roman world in apostolic times (Dana 1937:
183-184).   In the opinion of some scholars it was the age of
the widest literacy for about 1800 years to come (Bouquet 1953:
156).

SUMMARY

When we put all this together--the Dispersion of the
"people of the Book" throughout the entire empire, the common
language, the simple writing system, the Greek Old Testament,
the high literacy rate--and when we remember that there was
peace throughout the empire and excellent roads and sailing
vessels and travel was comparatively safe, we can see that the
fulness of time had indeed come. The stage was set for the
employment of literacy in the proclamation of the Gospel of
Jesus Christ in every land from the Atlantic Ocean to the Indus
River, and from the Danube River to the desert of Africa.

2

Rapid Church Growth
in the First Five Centuries

The Book of Acts begins with 120 timid disciples meeting
secretly for fear of their enemies. Within thirty years the
Gospel had been preached as far west as Rome, and there was a
thriving Christian Church in almost every city of any size in
the eastern part of the Empire (Kane 1971:7).

By the end of the third century the seed of the Gospel had
taken root in every part of the Roman Empire (Neill 1964:39).
Probably one-tenth of all the people who were subjects of Rome
at the accession of Constantine (A.D. 311) called themselves
Christian (Latourette 1970:Vol.1,169). By that time the
Gospel had been planted in many lands beyond the boundaries of
Roman rule. By the year 500, the overwhelming majority of the
population of the Roman Empire had become professedly Christian
(Latourette 1970:Vol.1,xviii).

REASONS FOR RAPID CHURCH GROWTH

Bishop Neill gives five reasons for the growth of the Church
during the first five centuries. First, there was the burning
conviction of a large number of the early Christians. Secondly,
the Good News that the Christians brought was in many ways welcome to their hearers. Thirdly, the new Christian community
commended themselves by the evident purity of their lives.
Fourthly, there was the sense of community and of mutual loyal-
ty in the Church, love for one another and charitable service.
And, finally, there was the effect of the persecutions themselves. The attitude of the martyrs, and particularly of the
young women who suffered along with the men, made a deep impres-

sion. There are a number of well-authenticated cases of conversion of pagans in the very moment of witnessing the condem-
nation and death of Christians (1964:39-43).

Edward Gibbon, in *The Decline and Fall of the Roman Empire*,
also gives five reasons for the success of the early Church:

> 1) the inflexible and...intolerant zeal of the
> Christians; 2) the doctrine of a future life; 3)
> the miraculous powers ascribed to the primitive
> Church; 4) the pure and austere morals of the
> Christians; and 5) the union and discipline of
> the Christian republic, which gradually formed an
> independent and increasing state in the heart of
> the Roman Empire (1960:144).

Kenneth S. Latourette offers several additional reasons for
the success of the early Church. First and foremost is the
uniqueness of Jesus Christ, his death and the conviction of his
resurrection and of moral and spiritual rebirth and immortality
through him (1970:Vol.1,168). We heartily agree that from our
Lord and Savior himself, and from beliefs about him, came the
main dynamic of the early Church.

Latourette hastens to point out, however, that Jesus and beliefs about him are not sufficient to account for the growth of
the Church during those first five centuries. In addition to
the reasons for Church growth given by Neill and Gibbon, Latourette adds 1) the disintegration of society, 2) the inclusive-
ness of Christianity, 3) Christianity's refusal to compromise
with paganism while at the same time being able to adjust to
many intellectual beliefs and practices, 4) the endorsement of
Constantine, 5) communities prepared for the Christian message
(Hellenistic Judaism), and 6) the authority of a long tradition
of the support of ancient sacred books (1970:Vol.1, 163-167).

This last point is of particular interest to us in this
present discussion. We would add several related factors without which the communication value of the factors listed above
would have been severely reduced. Among these were: 1) the
common language spoken throughout the empire; 2) the Jewish
dispersion with synagogues in every city where the Old Testament Scriptures were read; 3) the Greek translation of the Old
Testament, the Septuagint; 4) the fact that Apocalyptic writings
were in circulation and, like the Old Testament, prepared people
for the coming Messiah; 5) the relatively high literacy rate,
especially among the Jews, but also among the Gentiles; 6) the
writing and circulation of the New Testament; 7) the writings of
the Church Fathers and others; 8) the attitude of the Church Fathers toward the Scriptures; 9) Bible reading in the Church and
in the home; and 10) translations into the vernacular.

The King's Library

Rapid Church Growth in the First Five Centuries 15

We have already dealt with points one to four above, and to some extent with point five, the relatively high rate of literacy. Let us now look a little further into the rate of literacy in these early centuries, and then we shall take up points six to ten.

Literacy in the First Five Centuries

It is difficult to get statistics for this period of history, but we do have information regarding schools, literature, and libraries that shed some light on the subject.

The training of the child in the average Roman household began with the paidagogos, a slave who was charged with the responsibility of teaching the child his lessons and of conducting him to and from one of the private schools in the city where he lived. The curriculum consisted of reading, writing, and arithmetic. Later, he studied Greek and Latin poets, and memorized long passages that he had to recite with the proper expression. As the student progressed, he might learn the elements of oratory, how to compose a speech, and how to deliver it convincingly. Sometimes the wealthier youths went abroad to study in the Greek universities of Athens, Rhodes, Tarsus, Alexandria, or Marseilles (Tenney 1953:88).

Apparently each municipality within the bounds of the Roman Empire was responsible for its own educational system. The prevalence of writing, however, even in the poorest parts of Egypt, as attested by the papyri, indicate a fair degree of literacy was attained by the people of the first century. Moreover, the average attainment of the early empire would compare very favorably with that of the Middle Ages, or even with some parts of Europe in the eighteenth century (Tenney 1953:88).

The Writing and Circulation of the New Testament

I believe with Thiessen that all of the twenty-seven books of the New Testament were written before the end of the first century, all except the writings of John, before A.D. 70 (1943: 4).

The young Church realized the need to get the Gospel down in writing before the original eyewitnesses died, and before the message itself was forgotten or corrupted (Chirgwin 1954:13). Thus Mark is said to have written down the substance of Peter's conversation and public addresses, and Luke, to have written what he heard Paul say, and what he gathered from other sources.

The aim was not only to preserve the truth but to propagate it that others may be led to their Savior. The motive was evangelistic. Paul's epistles had the same evangelistic purpose as

his addresses, "to preach Christ and Him crucified". The New
Testament writers were not just writing history; they were writing for a verdict (Chirgwin 1954:14).

As the Gospel spread throughout the Roman world and multitudes were converted in almost every part of the empire, it was
impossible for new converts in every place to have an apostle
in their midst. They needed someone or something to keep
them from going astray. Some substitute for an eyewitness had
to be found. Written accounts were the substitute. As Luke
told his friend Theophilus, his purpose in writing was "that
you may know the truth concerning the things of which you have
been informed" (Luke 1:4 RSV). The new converts were the ones
who most of all needed accurate written accounts. How else
could they be sure of the facts? And how else could they hand
on the Word to others? The New Testament documents, as Canon
Herklots says, were propagandist literature of a widespread and
successful missionary movement (1950:15).

Just when it was that certain Christian writings began to be
generally accepted as of equal authority with the Old Testament
is not known. Presumably, as each Gospel was completed, it was
approved and used for public reading, first in the place where
it was composed. It was then copied and circulated to other
churches. The collecting of Paul's letters must have begun in
the apostle's lifetime. He himself prescribed (Col. 4:16) that
two churches interchange copies of two of his letters. From
that practice it was a natural step to their collecting copies
of his other letters as well.

At first a local church would have only a few apostolic letters and perhaps a Gospel or two. During the second century
most churches came to possess and acknowledge a canon which included the four Gospels, the Acts, thirteen letters of Paul, 1
Peter, and 1 John. Seven books still lacked general recogni-
tion: Hebrews, James, 2 Peter, 2 John, 3 John, Jude and Revelation (Metzger 1965:274). Some other Christian writings,
such as the first letter of Clement, *The Letter of Barnabas*,
The Shepherd of Hermas, and *The Didache* were accepted as scriptural by several ecclesiastical writers, though rejected by the
majority (Metzger 1965:275).

Probably the earliest document to quote any of the books of
the New Testament was 1 Clement, which was itself considered
canonical by some Christians. It was written from Rome to the
Church in Corinth, and is usually dated about A.D. 95 (Westcott
1864:74). In it there are plain allusions to Romans, 1 Corinthians, Hebrews, and the Gospel of Matthew (Tenney 1953:422).

Ignatius of Syrian Antioch (c. A.D. 116) knew all of Paul's
epistles and quoted Matthew, with a possible allusion to John.

Polycarp of Smyrna (c. A.D. 150) was also familiar with the Pauline epistles and the Gospel of Matthew. He quoted 1 Peter and 1 John. The short Epistle of Polycarp contains more clear references to the writings of the New Testament than any other work of the age (Westcott 1864:79).

The Didache, produced during the first half of the second century, referred to Matthew and Luke and many other New Testament books. *The Epistle of Barnabas* (c. A.D. 130) quoted Matthew. *The Shepherd of Hermas*, an allegory of the early second century (c. A.D. 140) alluded to James (Tenney 1953:422).

Justin Martyr (c. A.D. 100 to 165) referred to Matthew, Mark, Luke, John, Acts, and many of the Pauline epistles. He stated that the Gospels were read every Sunday in the worship of the Church along with the Old Testament. His pupil, Tatian, composed the first harmony of the Gospels, known as *The Diatessaron*, which became a standard harmony for the Church for many years (Tenney 1953:422). It seems that by A.D. 125 the chief part of the apostolic letters which are included in the New Testament were familiarly known and generally used by Christians (Westcott 1864:90).

With the age of Irenaeus (bishop of Lyons in southern Gaul, A.D. 175 to 200), all twenty-seven books of the New Testament were authoritative (Tenney 1953:423).

Origen, the great Alexandrian father (c. A.D. 185 to 250) divided the sacred books into two classes, the homologoumena, which were accepted by all the churches, and the antilegoumena, which were disputed and not accepted by all the churches. The former included the Gospels, thirteen epistles of Paul, 1 Peter, 1 John, Acts, and Revelation. The latter consisted of Hebrews, 2 Peter, 2 John, 3 John, James, and Jude (Tenney 1953:423).

Eusebius of Caesarea (c. A.D. 325) followed Origen's lead. He placed in the category of accepted books the Gospels, fourteen epistles of Paul (including Hebrews), 1 Peter, the Acts, 1 John, and Revelation. Among the disputed books were James, Jude, 2 Peter, 2 John and 3 John. He rejected *The Acts of Paul*, *The Revelation of Peter*, *The Shepherd of Hermas*, and others, and drew a sharp line between the canonical and apocryphal books (Tenney 1953:422-423). This is virtually the canon as we know it today (Metzger 1965:275).

Writings of the Church Fathers

Besides the New Testament itself, a great deal of other Christian literature was produced during the first four centuries of the Christian era.

Clement of Rome wrote extensively. In addition to his epistle to the Corinthians mentioned earlier, he wrote the earliest law books of the Church. His *Homilies and Recognitions* contain great depths of thought and wisdom (Westcott 1864:74).

Papias, bishop of Hierapolis in Phrygia about A.D.100, gives us the earliest account of the Gospels. His work, *An Exposition of Oracles of the Lord Based Upon the Teachings of the Elders*, was an explanation of some of the sayings of Jesus (Westcott 1864:95).

The *Epistle of Polycarp* to the Philippians was written about A.D.110. Polycarp, bishop of Smyrna, had been a pupil of John. This epistle contains far more clear writings of the New Testament than any other work of the age (Westcott 1864:79).

Ignatius, bishop of Antioch, was also a pupil of John. On his way to martyrdom he wrote seven epistles--six of them to churches and one to Polycarp. The phrases he uses could not have been used unless it had been assumed that those for whom they were written were familiar with the Gospel of John (Westcott 1864:79).

The great defender of the Christian Church during the second century was Justin Martyr (A.D. 100 to 165). His writings are by far the most extensive literary remains of the period (Westcott 1864:92). He wrote books in defense of Christianity and founded a school in Rome where many pagans received instruction in the Christian religion (Thiessen 1969:16).

The *Epistle of Barnabas* was probably written at the beginning of the second century. This is a general epistle addressed to all Christians, containing a sort of outline interpretation of Scripture (Westcott 1864:1-80).

The *Didache ton Dodeka Apostolon* ("Teaching of the Twelve Apostles") was written between A.D. 80 and 120. Not a composition of the Apostles, this was a statement of an unknown author of what he understood those teachings to be. This book, together with the *Shepherd of Hermas*, the *Apocalypse of Peter*, and the *Epistle of Barnabas*, was used in public reading as though it belonged in the canon (Latourette 1953:117-118,121,134,215).

The book, *Shepherd of Hermas*, was written in the first part of the second century. It has been called the *Pilgrim's Progress* of the primitive church. The writer saw visions which he wrote in this book, emphasizing repentance, spiritual life, and the imminent return of Christ. The book was read in many churches down to the time of Jerome (c. 400).

In the last quarter of the second century we emerge into the full light of Christian history. From this time the Church

stands in open strength and challenges the power of the empire.
From this time, Christianity leaves its stamp on the schools of
heathen thought. It had won the heart of men. It now was ready to conquer their minds. From this time on, Christian writers made good their claim to stand in the first rank among the
teachers (Westcott 1864:117).

The three great writers at the end of the second century or
beginning of the third represent three great divisions of the
Church. The traditions of Asia Minor, Egypt, and North Africa
find worthy exponents in Irenaeus, Clement of Alexandria, and
Tertullian (Westcott 1864:118).

Irenaeus, who had been trained under Polycarp in Asia Minor,
became bishop of Lyons in Gaul. Of his numerous writings only
one has been preserved--his *Refutation of Knowledge, Falsely
So-Called*. In this he deals in passing with the inspiration
and authority of Scripture. He makes it very clear that the
Old Testament writings are of equal dignity. He speaks of the
permanent spiritual value of every part of them and of their
supreme power as "the rule of truth" (Westcott 1864:122). Irenaeus wrote in Greek (Latourette 1970:Vol.1,98).

Clement of Alexandria (c. 155 to c. 215) was also a very
learned writer. About the year 190 he became a teacher of the
great Christian school in Alexandria and was later president of
this school for about ten years (Westcott 1864:126).

Origen (A.D. 185 to 254), who succeeded Clement as head of
the catechetical school in Alexandria, was an even greater
scholar. He is said to have written six thousand works (Kane
1971:23). He produced commentaries or homilies on practically
every book of the Old Testament (Herklots 1957:118). Twenty
years' work lay behind the production of his *Hexapla*, a six-
fold version of the Old Testament, comparing the Hebrew text
and its transliteration in Greek characters with four Greek versions in adjoining columns (Schwarz 1955:26). Origen was considered by Erasmus, that great scholar of the sixteenth century
(d. 1536),to be the best expositor of the Bible (Schwarz 1955:
130).

Tertullian of Carthage (c. 150 to 222), a lawyer of great influence, was another voluminous writer. He wrote in Latin and
his writings laid the foundation for Latin theology (Thiessen
1943:23).

One of the most saintly leaders in the Church during the
third century was Cyprian (A.D. 200 to 258), the bishop of Carthage, who had been greatly influenced by the writings of Tertullian.

Eusebius of Caesarea (c. 265 to 340), the "Father of Church
History", was bishop of Caesarea at the time of the emperor Constantine's conversion. He had great influence upon Constantine
and had fifty copies of the Bible made for him. He wrote an
Ecclesiastical History...from Christ to the Council of Nicea
(A.D. 325) (Westcott 1864:154). He was also the author of two
apologetic works, one showing that Christians were justified in
rejecting the religion and philosophies of the Greeks and in
accepting the Hebrew Scriptures; the other upholding the general
thesis that Christians were right in regarding Jesus as the Messiah (Latourette 1970:Vol.1, 188).

One of the greatest writers of the early church was St. Augustine, bishop of Hippo in North Africa. He is perhaps best
known for his unfinished masterpiece, "City of God", consisting
of twenty-two books. In the first ten books he presents an outstanding defense of Christianity against paganism. In the last
twelve books he contrasts the secular state with the kingdom of
God. His vision of the gradual extension of the City of God
over the world is truly magnificent. Unfortunately, this book
formed the religious background for the theology of medieval
papacy (Qualben 1955:126). Augustine was also a prolific writer
of apologetic and dogmatical works.

Other illustrious Christian writers of this period include
Athanasius (300-373), Ambrose (340-397), and Chrysostom (347-
407). Athanasius, called the Father of Orthodoxy, was a bishop
at Alexandria. The Athanasian Creed has its name from him.
Ambrose, a bishop of Milan, was a great champion of Catholicism
against Arianism, the belief that Christ was neither true God
nor true man. Chrysostom, known best perhaps for his oratory,
was also a great writer and one of the foremost champions of
the truth in the early church. He was a presbyter at Antioch
and later a patriarch at Constantinople (Qualben 1955:125).

We must not overlook the Cappadocian Fathers—Basil (c. 330-
379), Gregory of Nazianzus (329-389), and Gregory of Nyssa (c.
330-395). Stephen Neill tells us that they had received the
best education of their time and that they were perfectly familiar with the works of Homer, Plato, and Demosthenes. They wrote
in a Greek that was not classical but which was easily understood and admirably adapted to the purposes for which they used
it (1964:47).

Mention must also be made of Jerome (A.D. 343-420), the most
learned of the Latin Fathers, who translated the Old Testament
directly into Latin from Hebrew and prepared a conservative Latin revision of the New Testament with the aid of the "Itala"
and other existing translations. His completed Bible, the Vulgate, became the Bible of the West for a thousand years. In
France, Italy, and Spain, the supremacy of the Vulgate continues
to this day.

The Vulgate, however, was not without error. One of its greatest weaknesses was that the term "repent" was translated "do penance". This corruption of the thought has been a source of prolific error in the Roman Catholic Church. Instead of an internal process, it makes repentance an external affair (Boyd 1933:64).

It is interesting to note that all of the great writers either worked in areas where the Church was strong, or, like Ireneaus, they came from areas where the Church was strong, namely, Asia Minor, Antioch, Alexandria, North Africa and Rome.

Neither Spain nor Gaul, where the Church was weak, produced any great writers during the first five centuries of the Christian era. Spain was more thoroughly Romanized than any other province of the empire. Consequently there were very few people in Spain who could have read Greek in the latter part of the first century when the Gospel and the epistles were written. No Latin translations were available to them until the last quarter of the second century, and no translations of the Scriptures were ever made into any of the indigenous languages of the Iberian peninsula until the fifteenth century. It is not surprising, then, that not a single author is to be found in Spain before the time of Constantine (Harnack 1907-1925:Vol.V,436-439).

It is difficult to determine which was cause and which was effect. Were the great writers of Asia Minor and North Africa, for example, largely responsible for church growth in those lands? Or was it because of the strength of the Church in those lands that great writers were produced? One thing is certain. Where the Church was strong, we find great writers. Where the Church was weak and corrupt, we find few writers or none at all!

Bible Reading

Another reason for the growth of the early Church, we believe, is that the laity had access to the Bible and either read it themselves or heard it read in their homes as well as in the church services.

In Judaism the Bible was the book for every Jew. He heard it read in the synagogue, but he was also expected to read it at home. Among the Jewish Christians, the private use of Scripture continued. The fact that they had become believers in the Messiahship of Jesus increased this practice. For it was now necessary to study the Prophets and the Psalms which provided prophetic proofs of the Messiahship of Jesus (Harnack 1907-1925:Vol.V,31).

This use of Scripture easily passed over from the Jewish to
the Gentile Christians, for the Scriptures in the Greek translation (the Septuagint) were accessible to, and were read by,
the Jews of the Dispersion (Harnack 1907-1925:Vol.V,32).

It is an indisputable fact that in Apostolic times the Old
Testament was commonly read (John 5:47; Acts 8:28; Acts 17:11;
2 Tim.3:15). This reading was not restricted in spite of its
abuse by Gnostics and other heretics (Jackson 1958:85).

At first the private use of the Sacred Writings among the
Gentile Christians was limited because of the lack of copies.
Thus Timothy is exhorted to "attend to the public reading of
Scripture..." (1 Tim. 4:13 RSV). It was from this reading in
public that the community gained most of its knowledge of the
Bible in Apostolic times (Harnack 1907-1925:Vol.V,33). Justin
Martyr, when describing the Christian service, informs us that
"the Memoirs of the Apostles or the Writings of the Prophets
are read as long as the time admits (Westcott 1864:101).

We know, too, that it was possible for a person to buy
separate parts of the Sacred Word. This obviously was much less
expensive than buying the entire Scriptures (Harnack 1907-1925:
Vol.V,35).

The writings of the Apostolic Fathers make it quite clear
that the Scriptures were known to a large number of Christians,
and that this knowledge could not have been derived solely from
what they heard in public worship. The writings had to be also
in their own hands. Even in the days of the Apostles Peter and
Paul (probably in the early sixties) it seems that the writings
of the latter were quite well known. For Peter refers to them
as Scripture in his second epistle, saying that they that are
ignorant and unstable twist Paul's writings, as they do also
"the other Scriptures", to their own destruction (3:15,16 RSV).

There was also other literature that presented all that was
most important in a shorter form. Among these were *The Didache*
and collections of sayings from the Old Testament focusing on
doctrines such as the uniqueness and unity of God, future judgment, or on ethical matters. It seems to have been the object
of Christian teachers to conduct and lead as many as possible
of the members to the reading of the Holy Scriptures themselves.
It is safe to assume that the practice of the Jewish converts
of Berea of daily searching the Scriptures (Acts 17:11) was encouraged by the missionaries and carried out in other communities (Harnack 1907-1925:Vol.V,38).

Toward the end of the first century, Clement of Rome testifies of the Corinthian Christians: "You know the Holy Scriptures, yes, your knowledge is laudable, and you have deep

insight into the oracles of God" (Harnack 1907–1925:Vol.V,39).
Such an acquaintance with the Scriptures is not likely, except
through personal study.

The publicity, the wide circulation, and the easy accessibil-
ity of the Scriptures of the Old Testament are presupposed in
the writings of all the apologists of the second century.
Their demonstrations, their exhortations to read the Scriptures,
would be incomprehensible if the use of the Holy Scripture
among the Christians had been confined to public worship (Harnack 1907–1925:Vol.V,41).

In all probability the Old Testament was first translated
into Latin, not by Jews, but by Christians. These translations
began to be made before the time of Irenaeus and Tertullian
during the last quarter of the second century. The Gospels
were probably translated into Syriac about the same time (Harnack 1907–1925:Vol.V,46).

During the time of Irenaeus and Tertullian (about A.D. 200)
we begin to receive abundant evidence of the extent of the private and domestic use of Scripture. Irenaeus writes:

> Let a man take refuge in the Church. Let him be
> educated in her bosom and be nourished from the
> Holy Scriptures. The Church is planted like Paradise
> in this world; of every tree of this Paradise shall
> you eat; that is, eat from every Scripture of the Lord
> (Harnack 1907–1925:Vol.V,55).

Tertullian and Clement of Alexandria (c. A.D. 200) both ad-
vised that married people should read the Scriptures together.
Clement believed it was impossible for one without learning to
comprehend fully what has been made known in the Christian
faith (Latourette 1953:148).

Numerous passages in the Christian literature of the third
century attest to the fact that the Holy Scriptures were constantly found in at least the more wealthy Christian homes
(Harnack 1907–1925:Vol.V,58).

From the pseudo-Clementine epistle "De Virginitate" we learn
that into those homes that possessed no Bible, fellow Christians would come and read the Sacred Word. In addition to the
central services for public worship, smaller informal groups
would gather where, among other things, the Sacred Writings
would be read. We are told that the central worship service in
a special room grew out of the less formal services in private
homes (Harnack 1907–1925:Vol.V,63–64).

There was also a very wide circulation of Christian literature other than the books of the Bible. This literature was

written for the layman. It was intended for all Christians.

As time went on, it apparently was considered unwise to
launch immature Christians upon the wide sea of the Scriptures
without guidance. It was this that led Cyprian to publish his
Testimonia, a systematised collection of Biblical quotations
for the use of beginners. This book quickly gained wide circulation and had immense influence. But Cyprian had no intention
that this book should take the place of the Bible. Rather, he
intended that, as soon as his book had served its purpose, it
should give way to the Bible itself. The *Testimonia* was valuable also for those who had advanced to independent Bible reading, for every Christian was supposed to have in concise form
the Scriptural proof for the clauses of the Baptismal Creed
(Harnack 1907-1925:Vol.V,66).

Origen (A.D. 185 to 254) speaks frequently of reading the
Scriptures at home. He strongly recommends that the Bible be
read every day, even one to two hours per day seem too little
to him (Chirgwin 1954:18).

As for the understanding of Scripture, Origen holds to the
principle that the Scriptures are quite understandable to the
simple believer (Harnack 1907-1925:Vol.V,71). We also learn
from the writings of Origen that the Bible was the principle
textbook of education. The chief aim in the whole training of
a child was that he should be taught to understand the Bible
(Harnack 1907-1925:Vol.V,75).

Although the Bible is difficult in places, and heretics de-
rive their godless doctrines from it, nevertheless, the Sacred
Word must be made available to all Christians and they must become well acquainted with it through daily reading. This was
the conviction of the early Church. And the Church acted according to this conviction as we see from the persecution under
Diocletian (A.D. 284-305), which was a persecution of the Bible
as well as a persecution of Christians. The State tried to
destroy the Church by destroying its buildings, its officials,
and its sacred writings. This is the best proof of the important position that the Bible held among Christians, and of the
publicity that it had already gained in the non-Christian world
(Harnack 1907-1925:Vol.V,79-80).

But the Church not only regarded the Bible as a necessary
source of its life and faith. It also considered the Sacred
Word an indispensible tool for its expansion. In their efforts
to persuade the unbelievers to accept Jesus as their Savior and
Lord, the Apostles were constantly appealing to Scripture
(Chirgwin 1954:20).

This appeal to the Scriptures seems natural enough when
speaking to Jews who were brought up on these Holy Writings,

but it seems somewhat strange to appeal to them when the hearers were pagans. We would not expect people unfamiliar with the Scriptures to be moved by arguments based on such documents. But this is what was done. Aristides (c. 125) for example, one of the earliest apologists, addressing pagans, urged them to turn to the Bible and read it for themselves (Chirgwin 1954:21).

The method proved to be a good one. The Bible did win converts. Its constant use by Christian preachers and advocates led inquirers to read it for themselves. This led to conversion so often that the belief came to be widely held that "the regular way to become a convinced Christian was to read the Holy Scriptures".

There was a serious decline in learning during the fourth and fifth centuries (Thompson 1966:1-2). But in spite of this, Bible reading was still fairly widespread, especially in the East.

Countless passages from the writings of the Greek Fathers of the fourth century commend the practice of private Bible reading. But the attitude of the Latin Church was quite different. The Latin Church made no effort to translate the Sacred Word into the "barbarian" tongues. There never existed a Punic Bible for North Africa, nor, for many centuries, a Frank, a Celtic, or an Anglo-Saxon Bible. Furthermore, the Roman Church never did really make itself at home with its own Latin Bible. Even Jerome's translation of the Bible, of which we shall hear more later, made little difference in this respect. The more educated Latin could take no pleasure in the vulgar idiom of the old translations.

Uneducated Latins were more numerous than uneducated Greeks, and the number of those who could not read continually increased. Under such circumstances, exhortations to read the Bible are much less frequent in the West than in the East. Nevertheless, even in the West it seems that Bible reading continued to be fairly widespread.

In A. D. 359, a catalogue was drawn up by a publisher of Bibles, in which the cost is given for each book. These lists were evidently drawn up to meet the demand of private customers (Harnack 1907-1925:Vol.V,94). In every important city, the Bible and books of the Bible were on sale. (Harnack 1907-1925: Vol.V,98).

Many poorer Christians who were able to write copied portions of the Bible for themselves. Hilarion, whose biography was written by Jerome, is one who acquired the Scriptures in this manner.

During the fourth century it was the hearing of the Bible read aloud that continued to give the greatest impetus to the practice of Bible reading. In addition to the lections in the principal worship services, there were the lections in subsidiary services, in family worship and in private Bible classes. We know also that libraries were attached to many churches and were accessible to laymen, who could either read the Bible for themselves or hear it read (Harnack 1907-1925:Vol.V,112).

Chrysostom (347-407) never grew tired in his endeavor to plant the Bible in every home. He was convinced that if he could establish regular reading of God's Word in the family and among individuals, he would thus lay a solid foundation for a truly Christian life (Harnack 1907-1925:Vol.V, 117).

The Church Fathers direct that children in Christian homes should be introduced to the Scriptures from a very early age. Many Fathers state that they themselves, from their earliest childhood, were made familiar with the Book of Books.

Several Fathers also insist that women as well as men should study the Scriptures. They say that every Christian ought to read a portion of the Sacred Word every day, and that those who have completely surrendered to Christ and his service should spend several hours every day in quiet meditation, alternating prayer with reading. Others should follow their example as much as possible (Harnack 1907-1925:Vol.V,123).

We see, then, that Bible reading was strongly urged by the Church Fathers during the first four centuries at least. The Bible was as accessible to the layman as it was to the clergy, and many laymen were ardent students of the Word. This is particularly true of the Eastern Church.

Bible Translations

Syriac. The experience of the evangelistic value of the Bible led to the translation of the Scriptures into several languages. The entire Bible, except for five of the smaller books of the New Testament, was translated into Syriac as early as the second century. Syriac was the form of Aramaic spoken in Syria and much of what is now Iraq. It was, therefore, a sister Semitic tongue to Hebrew (North 1938:315). The influential Greek Septuagint, in the dominant world-language of the day, did, however, exercise some influence upon the Syriac translation. All educated Syrians also knew Greek. Thus the translators must have been at home as well in the language out of which the New Testament was translated. Under these circumstances, it is not surprising to hear high praise of this version from competent judges. In its standardized text it came to be called *Peshitta,* that is, "the simple" (North 1938:315).

Such was the Bible that the missionaries of the Syrian churches carried with them on their long journeys. With them it went out as far as Ceylon in the sixth century and to China in the seventh (Nida 1972:412).

One remarkable feature of the Syriac New Testament was the widespread use of what the Syrians termed "the Gospel of the United". This was a harmony of the Gospels, or rather a continuous narrative of the life and words of Jesus, formed by interweaving our four Gospels. It was made by Tatian, who, as we have seen, had been converted through reading. The Gospels also existed separately in the Syriac language. They were termed "the Gospel of the Separated", to distinguish them from Tatian's work (North 1938:316).

Not so long after the Scriptures had been translated into Syriac, a new Christian Church grew up in Baghdad on the Tigris River, and the language of its worship was Syriac, the native tongue of Nestorius, its founder. Nestorius had been Patriarch of Constantinople early in the fifth century. He insisted upon the separate natures of Jesus, the son of man, and Christ, the son of God. Condemned for heresy in 431 by the Council of Ephesus, he was driven into exile in Egypt. But his doctrine, carried by his disciples and manuscript copies of his sermons, spread widely. It went first down the Euphrates from Antioch or Edessa (now Urfa) to Baghdad, which became the world headquarters for the Nestorian Church (Mathews 1951:67).

From Baghdad, merchant caravans wound their way along trade routes through cities of Central Asia to China. Others went through Afghanistan and the Kyber Pass into India. With these Nestorian merchants went missionaries, trained in their monastic schools (Mathews 1951:68).

We cannot help but wonder, however, how strong this Nestorian Church could have been spiritually. We have no evidence of any Scriptures having been translated into the vernacular in any of the above lands east of Syria. We know, too, that the Muslims conquered this entire area within twenty years after the death of Mohammed in 632 (Aberly 1945:22). Perhaps if they had had the Word of God in their mother tongue, they would have remained firm in their faith in the face of the Muslim advance.

Coptic. By the end of the second century there was a strong church in Egypt (Kane 1971:10). The Greek language was widely used in Egypt, from the Mediterranean coast to the borders of the Roman Empire on the Upper Nile, especially in the cities. However, the farther up the Nile the larger the proportion of the population that did not know Greek--at least, not well enough to be able to read the Scriptures. Therefore, the earliest Coptic version (perhaps in part as early as the third

century) was that made in Upper (southern) Egypt--the so-called
"Sahidic" dialect. This language was the descendant of the
ancient Egyptian tongue, as spoken around the old capital,
Thebes (now Luxor), with a large admixture of Greek elements
especially in all that belongs to Christian life, doctrine, and
worship.

Next to the Sahidic, the Bohairic dialect of the Delta has
played the most important role in the history of the vernacular
Bible in Egypt. It eventually drove out the other three dialects into which all, or a part, of the Scriptures had been
translated (North 1938:100).

We have no record as to how the Gospel spread in southern
Egypt, but by the end of the fifth century there was hardly one
city of any importance without a bishop (Edman 1949:76). Could
it be that this advance of the Gospel in southern Egypt was
made possible as a result of the Coptic translations of Scripture, which were made during the third century?

Latin. The Church of North Africa was, for the most part, a
Latin-speaking Church, and there seems to have been at least
two translations into the Latin language toward the end of the
second century. Augustine refers at times to the Punic language
which Carthagian settlers had long ago brought with them from
Phoenicia. There apparently were areas where a knowledge of
Punic was a necessary qualification for a priest. Below the
Punic level were the village and desert dwellers of Berber culture and language. The church seems to have paid very little
attention to them. No translations of Scripture were made for
the Punic or Berber speaking peoples. The Church was only established among the Roman colonists. It was this foreign character of the Christianity there that assured that Christianity
would disappear with the disappearance of the Roman colony itself (Neill 1964:38).

Gothic. The Goths were the first of the Teutonic peoples
north of the Danube to accept Christianity in significant numbers. The systematic evangelization of the Goths was the work
of Ulfilas (c. 311 to c. 380). His most outstanding work was
the translation of the Bible into the Gothic language. Before
he could do this he had to reduce the language to writing (Kane
1971:13). Unfortunately, Ulfilas was an Arian, and Arianism
denies that Jesus is either true God or true man. It must be
regarded as un-Christian, because it reduces Christ to the
level of the highest of His creatures (Neill 1964:55). Possession of the Scriptures in their own tongue, however, may have
made it easier for them to be won to the orthodox Christian
faith later, than if they had continued to worship their pagan
gods with no Scriptures in their mother tongue and without even
a written language.

Armenian. Armenia was the first country of any size that may be called a Christian land (Latourette 1970:Vol.1,105). Christian missionaries came from Antioch, Edessa, and Cappadocia. As a result, the Armenians got both Greek and Syrian Christianity, as well as the literature of both of these peoples. At the end of the third century the king, Tiradates, was baptized a Christian. He had large numbers of heathen temples destroyed, and he declared Christianity to be the State religion.

The conversion of the land is said to have been the work of Gregory the Illuminator, but Christianity seems to have entered the land long before his day (Latourette 1970:Vol.1,105).

In A.D. 406 the scholar Mesrob, a descendant of Gregory, invented a new alphabet for the Armenian language, and took part in the translation of the New Testament which was completed in 410 (Neill 1964:54). A quantity of religious books were also translated from Greek and Syriac (Latourette 1970:Vol.1,106).

Bishop Stephen Neill tells us that:

> The close identification of race, language, religion, and political organization has given to Armenian Christianity an extraordinary resilience and pertinacity. In the face of endless wars and persecutions the Armenians have held on, and can rightly claim that theirs is one of the most ancient churches in the Christian world (1964:55).

Ethiopic. Ethiopia was another land which received the Scriptures at an early date. Early in the fourth century, two young men of Tyre, Aedesius and Frumentius, having been shipwrecked, were taken to the court of the king of Axum (now Eritrea and Ethiopia). The king and others may already have been Christians. The two men were given full freedom to preach the Gospel. Converts were won and the Church was strengthened by other Christians who came from Egypt.

After some years, Aedesius returned to Tyre, but Frumentius went to Egypt to seek help. There he was consecrated bishop by Athanasius (c. 296-373), the patriarch of Alexandria. The date seems to have been 341. Frumentius returned to Ethiopia and served the rest of his life as head of the Ethiopian Church (Neill 1964:53).

One tradition suggests that Frumentius translated the Bible into Ethiopic. According to another tradition, it was a group of nine men from Egypt, known as the Nine Saints, who did the translating during the fifth century. Study of the oldest extant manuscripts reveals its early origins. This Bible was

the only version known to Ethiopians until 1840, when the
Amharic Bible was published (Nida 1972:132).

Although the Ethiopic Church has had the Word of God in
Ethiopic from an early date, only a very select few were able
to read it. Even today that country is one of the most illiterate in the world. Only about five per cent of the adults can
read (Time Magazine 1975). Could this be the reason that the
Church of Ethiopia has never been very aggressive in the evangelization of Africa?

Centers of Learning

Egypt. Perhaps the best known of all the Christian schools
of the early Church was the catechetical school in Alexandria,
founded about A.D. 180 by Pantaenus. He was followed by Clement
and Clement was followed by the brilliant Origen (Kane 1971:10).
Its primary purpose was the instruction of candidates for Church
membership in the principles of the Christian faith. But it
also became a center for advanced and creative thought and extensive literary activity (Latourette 1953:147).

Palestine. In the second half of the first century, Palestine became more Greek than Jewish. In the cities along the
coast there lived many Christians. Caesarea rivalled Alexandria
in theological learning and activity. A great library was
founded there by Pamphilus (Westcott 1864:138). In spite of
this, at the beginning of the fourth century Palestine was predominately non-Christian. Such Christians as there were however, were mostly Greek-speaking and were living along the coast,
in or near Caesarea (Latourette 1970:Vol.1,87).

Edessa. Christianity probably came to Edessa in the Tigris-
Euphrates Valley in the first century, for it was right on the
caravan route, and a Jewish population provided it a natural
foothold (Latourette 1970:Vol.1,80). We know that early in the
second century there was an important Christian school there
(Westcott 1864:132). We know, too, that missionaries were sent
from Edessa to Armenia at the beginning of the third century
(Latourette 1970:Vol.1,105). At the dawn of the third century,
few if any cities contained a larger percentage of Christians
than Edessa. By the beginning of the fourth century, Edessa may
have been predominately Christian (Latourette 1970:Vol.1,102).
It seems that Edessa was a point from which Christianity was
carried farther into Mesopotamia and to the edges of Persia
(Latourette 1970:Vol.1,103).

Monasticism began in Egypt in the third century and spread to
Asia Minor and from there to the Western Church where it took on
a more practical character. The cloisters and monasteries

founded in Italy, Gaul, Britain, Ireland, and Scotland became important centers of learning.

Western Europe. Martin of Tours (A.D. 316-400) was the first great exponent of monasticism in Gaul (Edman 1949:78). Martin seems to have inspired Ninian to establish monasteries as a means of propagating the Gospel among pagans. The "White Hut" (Casa Candida), therefore, was built among the native tribes north of Hadrian's Wall in what is now Scotland. This was a training school for monastic missionaries and monastic founders (McNeill 1974:27).

The monastic ideal was soon to lay hold of the British Church so strongly that a century after Ninian, all British churchmen of note were monks (McNeill 1974:35).

In Wales the most eminent figure of the fifth century was St. Illtud (c. 425 to 505). He founded the long famous Llantwit (Llanilltud) Major on the shores of the British Channel. This was a seminary and trained numerous able monastic leaders and founders in the sixth century (McNeill 1974:35).

From Casa Candida, Christianity went northward among the Picts of Scotland, southward to the border of Wales, and westward across the sea to Ireland (Edman 1949:98).

Ireland. St. Patrick, having escaped from Ireland where he had been taken captive as a boy, seems also to have been influenced by Martin of Tours. Some authorities believe that he spent several years in the monastery of St. Honoratus (founded in 410) (McNeill 1974:62) at Lerins (Latourette 1970:Vol.1,218), an island off Cannes (Latourette 1970:Vol.1,205) in the Mediterranean (McNeill 1974:62), but this allegation has been generally abandoned.

Patrick returned to Ireland where he served the Lord untiringly for thirty years, beginning about 432. He speaks of baptizing thousands and ordaining clergy and travelling through many perilous regions where none before him had ever gone (Latourette 1970:Vol.1,219). By the time of his death in 461, Ireland was largely a Christian country (Neill 1964:56).

In Patrick's writings we find the reason for his great success. In the first place, he was a preacher of the Word of God. His *Confession* abounds with references to Scripture. He was a man of the Book. His quotations of Scripture show his familiarity with both the Vulgate and the Old Latin version (McNeill 1974:64). For centuries after him, the Irish Church held forth the light of God's Word in contrast to the traditions and superstitions of the Church of Rome. Patrick's writings show that he taught the essentials of Nicene Trinitarianism (McNeill 1974: 66). We find nothing in the writings of Patrick about the Virgin Mary or the veneration of relics and holy places. He was a Bible-reading, Bible-believing, Bible-preaching missionary (Edman 1949:101).

Patrick established an indigenous church. He established the schools from which missionaries were sent forth for four centuries after his death. He opened schools everywhere and taught boys and girls the alphabet which he is said to have invented (Smith 1897:64-65). He laid the foundation for the learning and scholarship of the Irish Church. In the fifth century, a monk who could read Greek was obviously from the Irish Church, for that learning had ceased in the Church of Rome (Edman 1949:101).

Patrick laid a firm foundation for the growth of the Church of Ireland after completing the evangelization of that land. On that foundation he erected a missionary church that sent the Gospel light throughout Scotland and England and to the Continent across the channel, a continent which by this time was languishing under Roman superstition and ignorance (Edman 1949: 102).

THE ADVANCE OF THE GOSPEL IN ASIA

India

If it is true that the Apostle Thomas was the founder of the Church that bears his name in South India, he apparently did not translate God's Word into the vernacular. When Claudius Buchanan, Chaplain of the East India Company, visited the Mar Thoma Church in 1806, he found that they were using the Syriac Bible, which no one could understand. It is doubtful that even the priests, who read it occasionally in the worship services, could understand what they read (McGavran 1947:220).

Whether Thomas was the founder of the Church in India or not, we cannot be sure. We do know that Christianity came to that country at least by the second century. About A.D. 180, Pantaenus, founder of the catechetical school in Alexandria, was sent by the Bishop of that city to India, and there he found Christians and the writing of St. Matthew in Hebrew (Sinker 1953:9). However, the land referred to as India might well have been southern Arabia, since the term "India" was used to designate a much larger area than it does today.

According to a Greek Christian traveller named Cosmos, who lived in the sixth century, there was a church in Malabar, the southwest coastal region, and there was a large number of Christians there. The Thomas Christians received bishops from the

Nestorian Patriarch in Baghdad. But there seems to have been another Church consisting of Persian traders originally, but who married Indian women and the original Persian element diminished as the percentage of Indian blood increased. Unfortunately, as far as we know, no one born in India was ever consecrated to the episcopate until the seventeenth century, and divine services were always conducted in Syriac. As time went on, the people understood less and less of the Syriac service, and many could do little more than recite the venerable words (Neill 1970:19). What a tragedy that they were not given the Word of God in their own language and taught to read it for themselves! There are some 700 languages in India and no attempt was ever made to translate the Good News of Jesus Christ into any of them for 1700 years (Kane 1971:106). Is it any wonder that so few people in India are Christians today?

Mesopotamia, Persia, Central Asia, and China

The adoption of Christianity as the official religion of the Roman Empire hindered church growth in Mesopotamia. The fate of Christianity was affected by the relations between Rome and its perennial enemy, Persia. It is amazing that Christianity survived in Mesopotamia at all. Its persistence apparently was due to its close association with Syriac-using peoples. Although Christianity won some adherents from those of Persian blood and language, its strength was primarily among those whose mother tongue was Syriac. These were usually politically subject either to the Romans or to the Persians and later to the Arabs. Many of them, however, were merchants, and some accumulated considerable wealth. Partly under the tutelage of their priests and monks, they developed men of education who rose to prominence in the service of the State. As merchants they established communities in the cities of Persia and Central Asia which became centers for the propagation of their faith (Latourette 1970:Vol.1,226).

The Christianity which sprang from these sources, however, never achieved complete independence from Syrian culture. Mediterranean Christianity became identified with the dominant Graeco-Roman culture, and in that association was triumphant among the peoples of Northern Europe who saw it as an integral part and the vehicle of the only civilization they knew. But, as Latourette points out, this did not happen in Mesopotamia and further east. In that part of the world, Christianity spread only in connection with the Syriac-using peoples. Without them it might not have spread as far as it did. But being a politically subject people, their faith nearly always faced far more severe competition from other religions with their associated cultures than did Christianity in Northern Europe. While it attained a wide geographic expansion in Asia, Christianity never enjoyed the practical monopoly that it did in much of

Europe. Eventually, in severe political vicissitudes of later
centuries, it was all but stamped out (1970:Vol.1,226).

SUMMARY

While there are a good many reasons for the growth of the
Church during the first five centuries, it appears that the Sacred Scriptures in the language and in the hands of the laity
had a good deal to do with it. Where the people had the Word
of God in their own language and could and did read it, the
Church was strong spiritually as well as numerically. In lands
where the Scriptures were not translated into the vernacular
and where people were unable to read the Sacred Word, such as in
Spain and in Gaul, the Church grew numerically due to political
pressure or compulsion. But the Christianity of such lands was
very superficial. Superstition and corruption among the clergy
as well as the laity was rife. Scripture in the mother tongue
and the ability to read it did not guarantee a strong, healthy
Church. Heresies were perpetrated by scholarly men. While this
is true, and while it is also an incontrovertible fact that
large numbers of illiterate people became Christians, it is also
true that there is no record of the Church in any land becoming
strong spiritually where the leadership was illiterate or where
laymen were not encouraged to read the Bible.

3

Light in Dark Ages, A.D. 500-1000

These were some of the darkest years in the history of the Christian Church. From the middle of the third century onward, the Roman Empire was troubled by northern peoples beyond its borders and found the work of defense increasingly difficult. The pressure continued until the old civilization of the Western Roman Empire had been almost completely destroyed, and the long period of destruction and chaos, known as the Dark Ages, set in (Neill 1964:61).

THE DARKNESS ON THE CONTINENT

These were years of little education and of widespread poverty in Europe--years of superstition and corruption in the Church. And these were years when Islam overran Southwest Asia, North Africa, and Spain, all but stamping out the Christian Church in these lands and blocking the way to the East for 700 years.

And yet, as we shall see, the lamp of learning was kept aglow in some areas, and where there was learning, there was a strong, pure, and aggressive missionary Church. But to help us fully appreciate that light, let us first look at the darkness that prevailed on the European continent during this half millenium from A.D. 500 to 1000.

Education

Literacy during the Middle Ages may be measured almost entirely by the extent of the knowledge and use of the Latin language. Illiteracy of the common people is not open to question (Thompson 1966:1-2).

By the end of the sixth century, Europe had reached a very low ebb intellectually and spiritually. During the seventh and eighth centuries the condition grew even worse (Thompson 1966: 1-2).

The last public schools of the Roman Empire, except those in Italy, expired in the seventh century. In the seventh and eighth centuries education in Western Europe reached its lowest ebb. The vast majority of the people of Merovingian Gaul (A.D. 486-752) must have been illiterate. Even in cities like Marseilles, where the cultural influence of Roman civilization may be supposed to have been preserved, the mass of the population seem to have been unable to read Latin. Illiteracy was prevalent even among the lower clergy (Thompson 1966:8-11). Even such rulers as Pepin the Short were illiterate, and Charlemagne did not learn to read until late in life (Thompson 1966:5).

Under the magnetic influence of Charlemagne and a multitude of brilliant scholars and teachers whom he gathered around him, there was a definite advance in the knowledge of Latin among the laymen of the royal court. But this influence apparently was not widespread. The lower classes were for the most part unaffected by the cultural developments known as the Carolingian Renaissance. Most people were still able to understand only the Vulgar Latin or the Teutonic vernacular, German. But they were not able to write either language. The ability to write was less widespread among the laity in Carolingian times than in the preceding age (Thompson 1966:27,29). After the time of Charlemagne, laymen who had an interest in scholarly pursuits disappeared completely.

There was a brief period of intellectual brilliance at the court of Charles the Bald (d.877), but it was short-lived. By the year 900, secular learning north of the Alps was almost extinguished (Thompson 1966:38).

By that time the Vulgar Latin had separated into a number of different Romance languages including Old French. Even after Vulgar Latin was no longer used as a spoken language, Classical Latin was maintained as the language of learning, and it was cherished as the vehicle of a great religion and a great literature (Prosner 1966:30-52). But there were very few who could read it.

In Germany lay learning was practically non-existent at the end of the ninth century, and illiteracy of the masses seems to have become even worse in the late tenth and early eleventh centuries (Thompson 1966:82-87).

The best learning available in Europe during the ninth century was probably in England, but Alfred the Great (847-901)

paints a dark picture of the cultural conditions of his time.
He says:

> ...there are very few on this side Humber who would
> know how to render their service book into English or
> to read off an epistle out of Latin into English.
> (Thompson 1966:88).

Monasteries and cathedral schools became almost the sole centers of learning during the Middle Ages. Monasteries established along the pagan frontier or in heathen territory became centers of missionary activities, as we shall see in the following
pages. The Church owed her victory over the barbarians mainly
to the zeal and devotion of the monks. A number of monasteries
gradually accumulated libraries and became celebrated for their
literary and intellectual activities. These monasteries became
the "publishing houses of the Middle Ages" because the monks
copied and transmitted manuscripts and preserved books. Monastic schools became teaching institutions of great importance
(Thompson 1966:12).

Even so, it seems that many of the clergy were illiterate in
almost every period of the Middle Ages, both in England and on
the Continent. The lower clergy, mostly identified with the
peasantry, could hardly have had much learning of any kind.
But even the higher clergy were not all well trained (Thompson
1966:182).

We have said nothing yet about Eastern Europe. It is probably safe to assume that the literacy rate in the Slavonic languages was no higher than in the languages of Western Europe.
As late as 1850, Tolstoy estimated that no more than one percent of the Russian people were able to read and write (Jeffries 1967:8).

Bible Reading

Because of the high percentage of illiteracy during the Middle Ages, it is not surprising that few laymen ever read the
Bible. But there were other reasons, one being the high cost
of the Scriptures.

The Bible of the Middle Ages could not be bound in one volume. It needed at least two large folio volumes—or even as
many as four. All of the Scriptures had to be hand produced,
and this necessarily made them very expensive. The cost of a
Bible in the Middle Ages might easily amount to a priest's entire annual income (Herklots 1957:44).

Even if laymen could read the Bible and could afford a copy
of the Sacred Word, it was in Latin. Not only was it in a

strange tongue, but down through the centuries, the copies had
become less and less accurate. We have seen that Jerome used
the word "penance" in place of "repent". By the middle of the
sixth century the text of the Vulgate was showing signs of becoming corrupt. The errors and interpretations of copyists
were having their effect (Herklots 1957:54).

Study of the Bible in the Middle Ages was confined almost
entirely to the cloister and the clerics and was largely artificial and allegorical. A scholar would take a passage of
Scripture and interpret it according to his own presuppositions
or those of his school without attempting to find what the original writer intended to say (Chirgwin 1954:26).

Besides being corrupt, the Vulgate also contained Apocryphal
books. In the Middle Ages many people were more familiar with
some of the incidents that they contained than they were with
much in the Gospels themselves (Herklots 1957:53).

Corruption in the Church

Together with the corrupted Biblical text and the allegorical
interpretation of Scripture and an illiterate society, there
was a corrupt Church. The Church of Rome was extremely corrupt, especially from the middle of the ninth to the middle of
the eleventh century, from Nicolas I (858) to Leo IX (1049).
This period has been called by historians the Midnight of the
Dark Ages. Bribery, corruption, immorality, and bloodshed make
it just about the blackest chapters in history.

This was an age when the Church of Rome substituted fable
for faith in Jesus Christ. Edman lists eight major substitu-
tions for Biblical truth:

> ...the substitution of tradition and the authority
> of the Church in the place of the Scriptures; Church
> membership for membership in the body of Christ; sacra-
> mental grace for saving grace; works for faith; the
> Virgin Mary and the saints for the mediatorship of
> Christ; superstitious reverence for relics for the
> worship of God; the establishment of a temporal king-
> dom on earth for the spiritual kingdom of God; and the
> monastery for the Great Commission to preach the
> Gospel to the ends of the earth (1949:127).

We said earlier that the monastic schools became the only
centers of learning during the Middle Ages. Some of them became great missionary training centers. But generally speaking,
the monastery became a substitute for the missionary program.
The monastic outlook on life was inward rather than outward to
the unreached. Most monks had no assurance of their own salva-

tion. Consequently they saw no need for helping others. They
presented a false idea of salvation, one of earning merit to
appease an angry God (Edman 1949:136).

IRISH LEARNING AND MISSIONARY ZEAL

Where the lamp of learning had gone out, the Church was also
in a state of spiritual decay. But in Ireland it was a different story. Ireland was the center of learning during the early
Middle Ages. In fact, Ireland was the most learned country of
Western Europe from the sixth to the eighth centuries (Edman
1949:165). Here the Church was doctrinally sound, spiritually
alive, and full of missionary spirit.

From Ireland there spread abroad a vast effort of evangelism
that reached all the way to northern Italy. The sixth and
seventh centuries were the golden age of Irish evangelism, when
missionary effort was "the one all-absorbing national thought
and passion". Aldhelm (A.D. 639 to 709), partisan of Rome and
critical of the Irish, had to confess that the number of monks
who went to study in Ireland, later to go abroad, seemed like a
swarm of bees. Trained in the Sacred Scriptures in the missionary schools and dedicated to the cause of Christ, the Irish became strangers and pilgrims in the earth, in order that they
might bring the saving message of Jesus Christ to many lands.

How can we explain this missionary zeal of the Irish? For
one thing, the isolation of Ireland, cut off from the rest of
Christendom by Anglo-Saxon paganism, gave opportunity for the
development of a Christianity which was little affected by the
superstitions and secularism of the continental churches. Dec-
adent Christianity in Southern Europe fought a losing battle
against the barbarian invaders, and found itself at a lower
spiritual and intellectual level when the migrations became
less severe. Ireland, on the other hand, was free from invasion
and had opportunity to provide the education and the evangelization needed to combat paganism in England and nominal Christianity on the Continent.

The two basic factors for Scriptural evangelism--the Word of
God and the Spirit of God--had been fundamental in Irish Christianity from the start, because of the ministry of Patrick. We
have seen what a large part the Scriptures had in Patrick's
preaching, and in the schools established in Ireland.

Great Missionary Training Centers

Many great monasteries were founded in Ireland in the sixth
century. One of the first was that founded by St. Enda on an
island off Ireland's west coast. About the same time, St. Boite
founded the important monastery of Monastirboice. Ciaran (d.

548?) reputed to have been a disciple of St. Enda, was founder
of Clonmacnois. Building a primitive shelter, he soon found
himself at the head of some thousands of volunteer learners of
the monastic way, and Clonmacnois maintained a front-rank position in Irish monasticism to the age of the Vikings. Finnian,
abbot of Clonard in Meath, seems to have established that monastery about A.D. 520. Until his death from the plague in 549,
Clonard was regarded preeminent in learning. Through some of
his disciples, known as "the 12 Apostles of Ireland", Finnian's
influence was great throughout the century (McNeill 1974:75-76).

Included among these "Twelve Apostles" are St. Columba of
Iona, St. Ciaran of Clonmacnois, St. Brendan of Birr, and St.
Brendan of Clonfert (McNeill 1974:78).

As early as A.D. 536, no fewer than fifty continental students at once are said to have been on their way to a single
monastery in Ireland, and we are told that seven shiploads of
foreign scholars came up the Shannon to pursue their studies at
Clonfert in Brendan's time (McNeill 1974:121), about A.D. 550.

A generation later, Comgall founded the great monastery of
Bangor which was unmatched as a nursery of scholars and missionaries. Even before Comgall's death in 603, many of these
men had become distinguished in service on the Continent (Mc-
Neill 1974:78).

Hardly less renowned was St. Coemgen (Kevin), who established a monastery at Glendalough.

Characteristic in the rise of Irish monasticism is a modest
beginning with a small company followed by an unforeseen inrush
of recruits from which a community of hundreds or even thousands
was soon formed. We read of 4000 monks at Bangor and 3000 at
Clonmacnois (McNeill 1974:80-81).

GREAT MISSIONARIES OF THIS PERIOD

For more than 500 years a stream of educated and dedicated
men poured from the monasteries of Ireland to go on pilgrimages
for Christ wherever they might feel divinely led. Some came
from Wales and Cornwall, but the distinguished names are almost
entirely Irish. Most of them entered this service on their own
initiative.

Columba (521 to 597)

The pioneer missionary of the Picts of western Scotland was
Columba, an Irishman. He was educated in the famous school of
Finnian at Clonard (McNeill 1974:88). When he was forty-two

years old (A.D. 563), he crossed the sea to bring the Word of
Life to the Picts and the Scots. With twelve companions he
established a monastery on the island of Iona, which became the
spiritual lighthouse of Scotland and England. For two hundred
years this monastery stood as one of the chief bases for the
church's missionary operations. It was an indigenous work, completely independent of Rome. Its first field of labor was among
the Picts of Scotland. This was extended later to Britons in
what is now Wales, and even to the Saxons (Aberly 1945:23).

Aidan (died c. 651)

After the evangelization of Scotland, the next advance of
the Irish Church was into the kingdom of the pagan Angles of
Northumbria (now northern England). The fierce invaders of
Britain--Angles and Saxons--had been ignored and untouched by
the remnant of the British Church that had survived the invasion. British Christianity had persisted after a fashion in
Cumbria, Wales, and Cornwall; but the antagonism of Briton to
Angle and Saxon was so bitter that no effort was made to give
the Gospel to these cruel worshipers of Woden and Thor.

It was to the savage Angles and Saxons, untouched by British
Christendom and unreached by emissaries from Rome, that the
successors of Columba brought the glad tidings of great joy.
It appears that Aidan (died c. 651) was sent from Iona to Northumbria in the year 635. He chose as his base Lindisfarne, an
island (at low tide) off the coast of Britain. Many missionaries came to help Aidan, with the result that multitudes were
converted, churches were erected, and monastic seminaries were
established as training centers for an indigenous clergy, and
the Message of Salvation was taken into the realm of Mercia
(Middle England), as well as to other Angle and Saxon kingdoms
(Edman 1949:154).

The spirit of Aidan's devotion to the Savior was perpetuated
in the labors of his followers. Finan from Iona, who was consecrated as bishop in his place, sent out many missionaries,
southward and westward to pagan kingdoms that knew only their
ancient Teutonic gods. So the Middle Angles, East Saxons, and
West Saxons had begun to bow the knee to Christ because of the
faithful evangelization of Irish missionaries. By 655 the Light
from Ireland, Iona, and Lindisfarne had penetrated into the last
stronghold of heathenism in northern England (McNeill 1974:108).

Columbanus (c. 543 to 615)

One of the great Irish missionaries who swarmed to the Continent during the sixth and seventh centuries was Columbanus,
who was born in Ireland and educated in the famous monastery at
Bangor, Wales (McNeill 1974:158). From his writings it appears

that he was learned in Latin, Greek, and Hebrew (Aberly 1945:23).
23).

With a band of twelve fellow laborers, Columbanus set out
for the Continent in A.D. 590 when he was in his mid-forties
(McNeill 1974:158). The reports of his ministry came to the
ears of King Sigibert of Austrasia (the eastern Frankish kingdom), who persuaded Columbanus to establish a monastery in the
Vosges Mountains in Northeastern France. Two other monasteries
were later established and the ministry of Columbanus was alter-
nated between these three centers with great success. One of
them, Luxeuil, became the community of thousands (McNeill 1974:
159). For at least a century the houses founded by Columbanus
and his immediate disciples multiplied and drew numerous recruits. By the end of the seventh century there were approximately sixty of these monasteries in Frankish territory (McNeill
1974:166). Later he went to Switzerland and then to northern
Italy where he founded the monastery of Bobbio in the Apennines
(about thirty miles from Genoa on the Mediterranean). This
monastery became famous for its school and library, and was a
citadel against Arianism and superstition (Edman 1949:160).

One of Columbanus' companions, St. Gall (d. 645), is the
founder of the monastery in Switzerland that bears his name.
He was the chief agent of the conversion of the Alemanni and
the greatest figure in the founding of the Swiss Church. When
he died in 645 the whole territory of the Alemanni had adopted
Christianity (McNeill 1974:168-169).

Through the energy of the Christian movement in Britain and
Ireland, Celtic paganism was exterminated. But Germanic paganism took root in much of Britain as a result of the invasions
of Angles, Saxons, Jutes, and smaller tribal units, to whom
Christianity was unknown. Their conquests left Christian
Britain reduced mainly to Wales, the Cornish peninsula, and
parts of Scotland. The British Christians, defeated by the
invaders, were in low morale and incapable of an effective mission to their conquerors. It was from other sources that Angles, Saxons, and Jutes were to receive the faith.

THE CHURCH OF ROME IN THE BRITISH ISLES

In 596, Pope Gregory the Great (590-604) commissioned Augustine and forty other monks to evangelize England (Mathews 1952:
30). This is one of the very few examples of papal promotion
of missions and, as we shall see, it was an event of world historic significance.

Augustine baptized King Ethelbert of Kent in 597, and this
virtually meant the winning of all his people (Qualben 1955:
142). But it was the Iro-Celtic Church which did most of the
mission work in England (McNeill 1974:102).

By 663, the greater part of England had become permanently
Christian under the influence of the Celtic mission and was being served by preachers and bishops trained under Irish teachers at Lindisfarne. The tiny island had become in just thirty
years the capital of Christian England. "Not St. Augustine,
but Aidan," wrote Bishop J. B. Lightfoot in 1890, "is the true
Apostle of England" (Bulloch 1968:72).

But at the Synod of Witby in 664, differences between the
Iro-Celtic Church and the Roman Church were settled in favor of
Rome, and the Roman practices rapidly replaced the Iro-Celtic,
even in Ireland. In time the Iro-Celtic Church was swallowed
up by the Church of Rome.

ROMAN ADVANCE IN CENTRAL EUROPE

Numerous English missionaries to the Continent got their
higher education, and probably their missionary purpose, in
Ireland or at Iona or Lindisfarne.

Wilfrid

Wilfrid of Northumbria (634-709), who had been trained at
Lindisfarne, carried the Gospel to the pagan dwellers by the
Zyder Zee and instructed them in the Word of Truth. Later he
returned to England and completed his service of forty-five
years for Christ.

Egbert

The burden of Frisian evangelism fell upon Egbert of Northumbria, who had been trained in Ireland. He was a teacher of
missionaries at the famous training center at Iona (Edman 1949:
188).

Willibrord

The evangelization of the Frisians became the responsibility
of a student of Egbert. Willibrord or Wilbrord (658-739) spent
twelve years in Irish monasteries (McNeill 1974:115). In 690
he went to Frisia with eleven companions to work among the
pagans along the south shore of the North Sea. We know little
about his missionary methods, but it is clear that the monastery was the center of the whole work. During his forty years
of service among the Frisians, Willibrord founded four monasteries. By the time of his death, Frisia had a well-establish-
ed Church (Neill 1964:74).

By the eighth century there had been some evangelization of
western Germany, but Christianity in those areas was more superstition and idolatry than faith in Jesus Christ. Missionaries

began to appear along both sides of the Rhine, but their evangelism was not followed by church organization (Edman 1949:189).

Boniface (d. 754)

It was St. Boniface who effected the Christian organization
of Western Europe and built a structure of ecclesiastical government. Although regarded by many as the greatest missionary
of the Middle Ages (Neill 1964:74), Boniface was much more an
administrator than a preaching missionary (McNeill 1974:172).
In 719 he received the Pope's commission to evangelize Germany
and to bring the labors of the Irish monks under the control of
Rome (Aberly 1945:24). His general attitude toward the Celtic
missionaries who remained aloof from the tightly organized hier-
achical Church system he earnestly fostered was one of suspi-
cion and hostility. They were regarded by Boniface and the ter-
ritorial bishops as a serious menace to unity and order.

Boniface was consecrated bishop in 722 and archbishop of
Mainz in 732. In 741 he was made special legate to reorganize
the whole Frankish Church (Aberly 1945:24).

In a real sense, Boniface was the successor of the Celtic
pioneers. The Celts had already introduced Christianity to
those Germans whom he brought under hierarchical control. As
Philip Schaff says, "He reaped the fruit of their labors and
destroyed their further usefulness, which he might have secured
by a liberal Christian policy (1910:4, 98).

We know more about Boniface than any other missionary of
this period. When a group, often under the influence of a ruler,
decided to become Christian, it was customary to baptize the
catechumens without any long delay. Then followed the long and
patient process of trying to make Christians indeed out of those
who had become Christians in name (Neill 1964:77).

For the permanency of his work, Boniface established nunneries and monasteries in centers such as Utrecht, Fritzlau, Fulda,
Amoneburg, and Ohrdruf. English monks and nuns were used as
teachers. Fulda was perhaps the greatest and most famous of his
monasteries. It still plays a special part in the Roman Catholic Christianity of Central Germany (Neill 1964:75).

SOME BRILLIANT SCHOLARS OF THE EIGHTH AND NINTH CENTURIES

Bede (c. 673-735)

A contemporary of Boniface was the Venerable Bede, probably
the best educated man of his day. He studied amid all the existing sources of learning in the West--the Irish, the Roman, the
Gallic, and the Canterbury learning. He had a rare knowledge

of Greek and Hebrew, and seems to have read all the literature
preserved up to that time. This enabled him to help in the
foundation of the great missionary school at York, from which
the light of the West was rekindled over England and Europe.
He also translated portions of Scripture (Smith 1897:89).

The flow of Irish clerical migration across Europe continued
throughout the eighth, ninth, and tenth centuries. But about
the middle of the eighth century, the stream of missionaries
gives way to a large extent to a troupe of professors. Reinforc-
ing the educational activities of the Irish professors were a
large number of persons from the Continent who were trained in
Irish schools. The monastic schools of Ireland were everywhere
regarded as offering the best opportunity for the acquisition
of scholastic knowledge (McNeill 1974:177).

But the largest number of scholars were the Irish themselves,
teaching in Frankish domains and beyond, both southward and
eastward. One writer about 870 exclaimed, "Almost all Ireland,
despising the sea, is migrating to our shores with a herd of
philosophers". By philosophers he means men of sound learning.

Decade after decade the stream of learned immigrants flowed.
They brought with them what in Ireland was sometimes called
"divine and human wisdom", a comprehensive knowledge of the Bible and its chief interpreters supplemented by a knowledge of
Latin classical poets and prose writers. The scheme of studies
known as the Seven Liberal Arts had entered the Irish schools
and was employed by them. The Seven were divided into the
Trivium (Grammar, Rhetoric, and Dialectic) and the Quadrivium
(Arithmetic, Astronomy, Geometry, and Music). Irish scholars
wrote textbooks on one or another of the seven (West 1912:5-27).

Alcuin (735-800)

One of the greatest figures in the history of the Church and
of the world was Charlemagne, sole ruler of the Kingdom of the
Franks from 771 to 814. A wise and a powerful ruler, he also
had a real interest in learning and in theology. He loved the
Irish scholars who began to frequent the courts of kings and
emperors (McNeill 1974:179-180). But it was an English scholar,
Alcuin, whom Charlemagne made head of his Palace School at
Aachen (Aix-la-Chapelle). Although English, Alcuin had been
trained by Irish scholars at York (McNeill 1974:180).

After holding his position as head of the Palace School for
fifteen years, Alcuin retired in 796 to become abbot of the famous monastery at Tours. Here he put to advantage the writing
skill he had acquired from the Irish at York to develop the
much admired "Carolingian minuscule" which would be a standard
script for centuries (McNeill 1974:180).

John Scotus Eriugena (c. 810-877)

The most illustrious Irishman of the ninth century was John
Scotus Eriugena. He had a knowledge of Greek unmatched in the
world for centuries, and translated many famous works from
Greek into Latin. He also produced numerous original works,
the greatest of which was *On the Division of Nature*, in which
philosophy embraces and transforms theology (McNeill 1974:187).

Andelm

Another famous Irish scholar, a contemporary of Eriugena,
was Andelm. He may have been a brother of Scotus (McNeill 1974:
187). In the same generation, St. Gall Abbey in Switzerland
flourished under Irish leadership. Eminent among the teachers
there was Moengall of Ulster (McNeill 1974:187).

The Irish brain drain to the Continent came to an end in the
tenth century, but Irish monks continued to come in large numbers (McNeill 1974:188).

THE DECLINE OF THE IRISH CHURCH

The results of the Irish movement of the sixth and seventh
centuries, along with the resultant missionary surge of the
English Church of the eighth and ninth centuries, compares
favorably with the evangelism of the first century. But with
the passing of time, its energy slackened and its dynamic de-
creased. Why? For one thing, the Irish were individualists.
Although courageous and effective, they were not given to team-
work or organization (Edman 1949:162). Another reason for the
Celtic Church's inevitable decline was the fact that its growth
took place simultaneously with the rise of the papacy. Popes
of great talent were instrumental in the enlargement and inten-
sification of the papal sway. It was inevitable that the
strongly organized Roman system with its universal claims would
eventually absorb the relatively uncoordinated Celtic communities (McNeill 1974:193). Then, too, its evangelism was dulled
by controversy with Rome and by its increasing stress on peni-
tential systems in the place of true repentance and faith in
Christ. Another major factor in the decline of the Irish
Church was the raids of the Northmen which began late in the
eighth century, with piracy and plundering and destruction of
monasteries. Lindisfarne was destroyed in A.D. 793 (McNeill
1974:206) and after years of siege, Iona was all but extinguished in 825 (McNeill 1974:207). The monasteries and churches with
their treasures of artistically wrought vestments and metalwork
invited the attention of the Vikings. Early in the ninth century they laid waste to such venerable monastic communities as
Comgall's Bangor, Finnian's Moville, Brendan's Clonfert, Bri-
gid's Kildare, and Ciaran's Clonmacnois. Armagh's buildings

were repeatedly looted and burned to the ground in A.D. 840
(McNeill 1974:213).

THE "CONVERSION" OF THE SAXONS

Although Charlemagne had a real interest in learning and in
theology, he was also brutal and cruel in the conquest of his
enemies. From 772 until 798 he was at war with the Saxons.
The savagery of the conflict was reflected in the beheading, by
personal command of Charlemagne, of 4,500 Saxons in a single
day in 782, and the wanton destruction of women and children in
burning villages. Anyone who harmed a church or a priest or
refused baptism was put to death. For generations after their
professed conversion, the Saxons were understandably inwardly
attached to their pagan practices (Neill 1964:78-80).

WORK AMONG THE SLAVS

In the latter part of the eighth century, about 763, Celtic
monks played a pioneer role as missionaries in Slavic lands.
About the middle of the eighth century, unnamed Irish and British missionaries penetrated in some numbers into Moravia (Mc-
Neill 1974:174).

Meanwhile, two Byzantine brothers, Cyril (d. 869) and
Methodius (d. 885) were apostles to the Slavs. Cyril gave the
Slavic people an alphabet based on the Greek. He also translated Scripture portions and the liturgy into the language of
the people. This linguistic work accomplished more for the
Slavic peoples than all the Romanist swords or the baptism of
untaught, illiterate heathen (Edman 1949:212).

The translation of the liturgy into the vernacular was a
normal course of action for these Byzantine missionaries, for
that was the practice in the East, in contrast to that of the
West, which used only Latin in its worship services. Consequently, the Slavic peoples had a liturgy that they could understand, rather than a religious ritual sung in an unknown tongue,
as was the case in the Roman West. This was very significant in
the Middle Ages when almost everyone was illiterate.

Cyril died in 869, but Methodius continued his missionary
labors, devoting most of his time to the translation of all the
canonical books of the Bible. After his death, papal support
of the use of the vernacular was withdrawn, and slowly a liturgy understood by the people ceased to be used in the church services. But the disciples of Methodius, with his translated
works, went to the Balkan Slavs and the Bulgarians, and there
the Slavonic literature persisted (Edman 1949:213).

Bulgaria

Between 800 and 850, barbarians of Hunnic (Turkish) origin
repeatedly came into conflict with the Byzantine armies. When
they returned home to what is now Bulgaria, they took thousands
of Christian captives as slaves. Some of these captives were
priests who worked to convert their pagan masters, often with
success. Because the Bulgars had no literature or arts, the
Christian faith with its higher culture came to dominate. This
story has been repeated over and over again throughout the history of the Church. Wherever people have not had any written
Scriptures of their own, as among the animistic peoples of Africa and Latin America and the South Pacific, Christianity with
its Sacred Scriptures has enjoyed its greatest growth when
people were given those Scriptures in the vernacular and were
taught to read.

About 864, the Byzantine army marched into Bulgaria and
seized control. They made the king, Boris, accept the lordship
of the Emperor of Constantinople and be baptized by Greek
priests of the Orthodox Church (Mathews 1952:60-61).

Boris sent his younger son, Simeon, to Constantinople to a
Slavic college where disciples of Methodius had by this time
trained hundreds of missionaries in the use of the written Slavonic Word. Boris resigned his throne and entered a monastery
which he founded, to make it a center of Slavonic Christian
culture. He sent a splendid missionary, Clement, to Macedonia
where he founded a college for the translation of Christian
books into Slavonic and for the training of a missionary priesthood. By the time of his death in 907, King Boris had lifted
his previously pagan illiterate people to a golden age as the
first cultural Christian leaders of the Slavonic world.

Russia

About the year 860 the ruler in Kiev asked the Patriarch of
Constantinople to send them a bishop. The request was granted,
and several missionaries were also sent. By the time Igor ruled
in Kiev (913-945), a church existed, and his widow, Olga, in 954
became a Christian. Their grandson, Vladimir (c. 956-1015) was
a pagan who persecuted Christians. But in 986 he became an Orthodox Christian. He destroyed idols and ordered his subjects
to be baptized. He built churches and founded monasteries.
Above all, he sent missionaries to the half-nomadic, half-pas-
toral countryfolk. We shall hear more about the growth of the
Russian Church and the influence of Christian literature and
learning in a later chapter.

THE RISE AND SPREAD OF ISLAM

We now come to what might well be the most tragic story in Christendom—the failure on the part of Christians to translate the Word of God into Arabic.

Mohammed (570-632), in the prime of life, was regarded by his countrymen as an upright and trustworthy man. He heard of the one true God, whom Jew and Christian worshipped. Some spoke about a Word from God, but they had no Scriptures in their possession.

Mohammed's wife Khadija's aged cousin Waraka knew something of the Scriptures of the Jews and Christians. Some of his own people had embraced the Christian faith. There were also those who professed the Jewish faith within the boundaries of Arabia and spoke the Arabic language, but there were no Scriptures (Sweetman 1953:8-10).

There had been preachers who went to the remotest places to proclaim the Good News of Jesus Christ. But there were no Scriptures in a known tongue and probably but few who could have read it. The Arabic language had not yet been reduced to writing. Its first letters were to be derived from Syriac, and the first great book was the Quran—when it might so easily have been the Bible.

But it was left to Mohammed to learn by hearsay from uninstructed or imperfectly instructed Christians what those Scriptures contained. It seems that Mohammed believed he was putting Biblical truth into language which could be understood by his own countrymen. He felt that his mission was to bring the Arabs to forsake their idols and to worship the one true God.

It is evident to anyone who reads the Quran that Mohammed had some knowledge of what was contained in the Bible. He must have thought that what he heard from Jews and Christians was indeed that which was contained in the Bible. But, sad to say, the Christians seem to have neglected the Bible and to have been content with romantic tales of the Lord.

The translation of Scripture of the Old and the New Testaments had to wait at least another hundred years after the experience of Mohammed on Mount Hira, when he thought he heard a voice saying, "Cry" (Quran) (Sweetman 1953:12).

The Quran commends reading the Bible. But when Muslims read it, they find that it doesn't agree with what they have heard. So they conclude that these writings are not the original Scriptures, but that the Jews and Christians have corrupted them. Some, like the Spanish Muslim, Ibn Hazm, in the eleventh century,

attack the Bible as a forgery and fraud. How tragic that the
Word of Christ was not translated into Arabic in those early
centuries. Not only have the Arabs themselves been kept from a
saving knowledge of Jesus Christ, but they soon overran north
Africa and western Asia, conquering even Persia within twenty
years after the death of Mohammed. And they tied up the trade
routes to India and China for centuries to come, keeping missionaries from Europe from reaching these lands.

In 642 Alexandria was captured. It was not long before the
whole of Egypt was added to the Muslim domain. The advance
westward across Africa continued, and in 697 Carthage fell into
their hands. By 715 the greater part of Spain had fallen to
Islam. The Muslim advance was finally checked by Charles Mar-
tel at Tours in the very heart of France in 732 (Neill 1964:63).

Although loss of life was small, the Muslim conquest was a
major disaster for the so-called Christian world. The tragedy
is that there may never have been any such religion as Islam if
the Scriptures had been translated into Arabic and the people
had been able to read those Scriptures for themselves. Then,
too, if the Berbers of North Africa had been given the Scriptures in their mother tongue, perhaps a much larger percentage
of them would have been won for Christ and would not have suc-
cumbed to the Muslim advance. But the Berbers not only offered
little or no resistance; they actually became allies of the Muslims in their conquest of Spain (Mathews 1952:43).

CHINA

As far as we know, it was not until the seventh century that
Christianity came to China. In the first third of the seventh
century a bishop and a young monk started eastward from their
home in Persia. They were received in the palace of T'ai Tsung,
the emperor of China, in the year 635. The Chinese gave the bishop the name Alopen, which means, "the man who was sent by God"
(Mathews 1952:68). The emperor commanded that a monastery be
built for these men and for twenty-one monks at his own expense,
and that they be permitted to preach anywhere in China.

Alopen never returned to Persia, and we would know nothing
about him if it had not been for the discovery of the "Nestorian Monument" in 1625, on which this story is recorded. Engrav-
ed in the year 781 in Chinese characters, the tablet informs us
that Christian monasteries were built in different parts of China and that Christian literature had been produced (Broomhall
1934:17).

The list of translations of Christian books in Chinese suggests that the monks learned the language and made themselves
at home in China. But we cannot help but wonder to what extent

they made their presence felt. Were their translations printed
and circulated? If so, to what extent were they read? It is
doubtful that more than five percent of these Chinese people
could read and write. It is known that as late as 1950, only
twenty percent of the population of China was literate (Latourette 1964:14). In his book on *Nationalism and Language Reform in China*, J. de Francis (the main authority in English)
tells us that only one or two percent of the people throughout
most of Chinese history have been able to read the ideographic
script (1950:222).

Chinese characters, called ideographs, have no relation to
the sound of the word. In a large dictionary there are forty
or fifty thousand characters, while the telegraphic code book
contains nearly ten thousand. A Chinese child learns to read
about two thousand characters by the time he is ten, but it
takes two or three times as many to be able to read a novel or
a newspaper (Katzner 1975:210). This being the case, even in
this twentieth century, we find it difficult to believe that
even five percent were literate back in the seventh and eighth
centuries when the Nestorians made their translations. One or
two percent literacy, as suggested by de Francis, would probably be more accurate.

It should be pointed out, however, that it was possible for
the Nestorians to print their translations and circulate them.
One of the major developments under the T'ang dynasty was printing, first developed perhaps as early as the Sui dynasty (589-
618). From the T'ang, however, comes our first example of a
printed book--a Buddhist sutra. It may be that printing was a
gift of Buddhism to the world, the result of an attempt to make
widely available the literature of that persuasion. This first
printing was by wood blocks, not by movable type. Movable type
and other methods of printing were devised in China, but it was
by wood blocks that the finest work was done (Latourette 1946:
126). If the translations were printed, however, there is no
trace of them today.

In 845 the Emperor Wu Tsung, an ardent Taoist who opposed
monasticism in all its forms, issued a decree proscribing Buddhism, dissolving monasteries, and ordering the monks to return
to private life. Since the Nestorians were monks, the decree
applied to them also.

It is unlikely that the Christian Church was exterminated,
but its power was apparently broken. In 987, a monk and five
other men were sent to inquire into the state of the Church in
China. They returned to report that they could find no trace
of Christianity in the Empire (Neill 1964:97).

SUMMARY

As in earlier centuries, the expansion of the Christian Church was the result of the tireless efforts of well-educated, Bible-reading, Bible-preaching missionaries. There is no record of any mission work by illiterate people, although it is quite possible that many illiterate laymen did witness for Christ with some success. As far as we know, however, all church growth was either the result of well-educated missionaries or by coercion, and we can hardly justify coercion as a God-pleasing means of bringing people into the Church. While church membership by compulsion added to the numerical strength of the Church, it could not but weaken the Church spiritually. It is impossible to say how many of those people who became church members by coercion ever became true followers of Jesus Christ. Those who did become true believers did so because of the teaching of Bible-reading, Bible-believing, Bible-preaching men of God.

4

Years of Uncertainty, A.D. 1000-1500

During the second half of the Middle Ages, Christianity made some gains in Europe, but because of losses to Islam in the seventh century and following, it may be that there were fewer Christians in A.D. 1500 than there had been a thousand years before (Latourette 1970:Vol.2,2).

But there were some important developments for Church growth during the period under consideration, especially toward the end of the period when there was a return to the study of Hebrew and Greek, the original languages of Scripture. These languages were practically unknown, even by scholars, during the Middle Ages (Schwarz 1955:11). A few of the Schoolmen did know Greek and knew that the Latin Vulgate had been corrupted, but they were afraid to make the necessary corrections for fear of being branded as heretics.

EDUCATION

As in the first half of the Middle Ages, so in the second half of the millenium, practically all formal education in Western Europe north of the Alps was carried on through ecclesiastical agencies or in institutions which were the outgrowth of such agencies. Even in Italy, where the collapse of secular learning was not so extensive, lay schools were reduced in number. The gap was filled by monasteries, bishops, and sometimes by secular parish priests. The monastery and the bishop found it necessary to have education if the Bible and the writings of the Church Fathers were to continue to be read and if the services and the organization of the Church were to be maintained. The Benedictine rule, whose emphasis upon work could be satis-

53

fied by literary pursuits, encouraged them in their continuance
of learning (Latourette 1970:Vol.2,386).

In the twelfth and thirteenth centuries came a great awakening in the intellectual history of Europe. Its most marked
manifestation was perhaps the rise of the universities. In
Northern Europe, these were largely religious in origin. The
first and most influential of them all was the University of
Paris which grew out of the cathedral school and whose major
subject was theology (Latourette 1970:Vol.2,389).

The Franciscans and Dominicans (founded in 1209 and 1215,
respectively) made major contributions to the universities in
their formative period, and in the ranks of these mendicant
orders were found such outstanding scholars as Roger Bacon,
Thomas Acquinas, Bonaventura, Albertus Magnus, Alexander of
Hales, Duns Scotus, and later, William of Occam. It seems
probable that the religious dynamic back of these orders stirred these great minds to the intellectual achievements which
have made their names memorable. The impulse back of the
scholarship of Roger Bacon, for example, was at least in part
his Christian faith. He maintained that scholarship should be
used to promote such a knowledge of God as would save man (Latourette 1970:Vol.2,390).

It is significant that from these northern universities, in
which the Christian tradition was so strong, came some of the
outstanding leaders of religious awakening. Wycliffe, Hus, and
later Luther, Calvin, and Loyola, and still later, Wesley,
studied in them (Latourette 1970:Vol.2,390).

While there was an increase in intellectual activity during
this period, few laymen benefited from it. Conditions in lay
society were not very favorable to study, and very few laymen
found time or opportunity to learn to read. All the French
kings from A.D. 900 to 1300 were probably illiterate (Thompson
1966:123). Apparently as late as the thirteenth century, a
person was considered well educated even though he might be
illiterate. In a section of the municipal statutes of Marseilles, the qualifications required of a good lawyer are enum-
erated, and it is added: "litteratus vel non litteratus" (whether literate or not literate). If one could become a lawyer
without knowing how to read, this is further evidence that
there were very few people who could read and write (Pernoud
1950:134).

In Germany, people thought it a waste of time to instruct
anyone who did not intend to enter the ministry. With the
political dissolution of Germany in the thirteenth century, and
the decadence of the monasteries, education in Germany suffered
more than in any other country. Even the noble laity of Germany

was, for the most part, illiterate (Thompson 1966:88-100).

In England, in the times of the Norman kings (A.D. 1066-1154), as in other European kingdoms, the ability to read and write was confined almost entirely to the clergy. It must be pointed out, however, that the term "clergy" covered numbers of people of minor orders, as well as priests, who carried out all the necessary legal, financial, secretarial, and other paper work for the rulers, the nobility, and the merchants, most of whom were illiterate.

References to literate laymen in England do not begin to appear until the end of the fourteenth century, and it was not until about two centuries later that a literate middle class came into being to meet the needs that could no longer be adequately served by churchmen (Jeffries 1967:5).

Lest we give the impression that only the laymen were illiterate and that all of the clergy were highly educated, let us hasten to add that even the clergy of this period were none too well versed in the language of learning. Hardly any of the priests of Leon, for example, knew even the rudiments of Latin, which continued to be the language of the church (Thompson 1966:123-136). As we mentioned earlier, hardly anyone had any knowledge of Hebrew or Greek, so were completely ignorant of the Scriptures in the original languages (Schwarz 1955:11).

In the East, as in Northwestern Europe, conversion began with the ruling classes and was very superficial among the masses. The cities were the centers of Christianity, and early were supplied with churches, monasteries, libraries, and schools. But, for centuries, the rural areas were Christian, for the most part, in name only. The rural clergy were hardly fit to do much to improve the religious knowledge of their flocks. The majority of the village priests were poorly trained. For many of them, the only preliminary education was obtained in the two weeks or so spent at the court of the bishop immediately before his ordination. It is not surprising that outside the relatively few cities, Christianity was long in gaining more than a superficial and formal hold. The East was much slower than the West in arousing indigenous religious movements such as the followers of Peter Waldo. In fact, none seem to have appeared until after 1500 (Latourette 1970:Vol.2,401).

BIBLE READING

Even if a layman were able to read, very few of them could afford a Bible. The cost of a Bible in the fourteenth century might easily amount to a priest's entire yearly income (Herklots 1957:44). Some laymen did possess at least some Scripture portions. But when sects began to appear, appealing to Scripture

to support their doctrinal positions and to show how far the
Church had departed from the teachings of Christ and the
apostles, the Church clamped down on the circulation and reading of the Sacred Word. The ecclesiastical authorities were
determined to put an end to Bible reading by the laity, or at
least to bring it under strict supervision. Pope Gregory VII
(1073-1085) ordered Bohemians not to read the Bible. Innocent
III (1198-1216) forbade the people reading the Bible in their
own language. This pope frowned upon unauthorized translations,
and after his day they were frequently forbidden, and the followers of Christ could not have copies of them in their possession. A few years later, in 1229, the Council of Toulouse made
the ban complete, demanding that "...no layman should be allowed to have any book of the Old Testament or of the New Testament, especially in translation, 'unless perhaps the Psalter, a
Breviary, or the Hours of the Virgin'" (Chirgwin 1954:28).

In Chapter Three it was mentioned that Bible study during
the Middle Ages was largely artificial and allegorical (Chirgwin 1954:26). Leading authorities like John Scotus in the
tenth century or Bernard of Clairvaux in the twelfth century
"took for granted that the Bible was to be read allegorically,
not literally" (Chirgwin 1954:27). A good illustration of the
prevailing method of Bible interpretation is found in the writings of Hugo, the principal of the school of St. Victor in
Paris. Referring to the statement in Genesis 6:15 that the ark
was fifty cubits wide, he says that:

> the width of fifty cubits signifies all believers,
> for fifty is made up of seven sevens, that is,
> forty-nine, a number that stands for the totality
> of believers, and one more, meaning Christ, who is
> the head of the Church and the consummation of our
> desires (Neill 1952:138).

It is easy to see that this kind of biblical activity did
more to obscure the Scriptures than to interpret them.

A FEW RAYS OF LIGHT IN A DARK AND DREARY AGE

Scandinavia

The Gospel of Christ was brought to Denmark and Sweden by
Ansgar and his successors beginning in the early part of the
ninth century, but met with very little success (Edman 1949:
226). It was not until the beginning of the eleventh century,
however, that their labors produced much of a harvest. Even
then, many of the "conversions" were by force (Aberly 1945:29-
30). But it wasn't entirely by force. Knut (Canute), who was
a Christian, was king of England and Denmark from 1019 to 1035
(Latourette 1970:Vol.2,122). He rebuilt monasteries in England

and sent bishops from that country to Denmark where the Seed of
God's Word gradually took root.

In Norway, most of the advance of "Christianity" was by compulsion. After their forced "conversion", however, by means of
patient instruction in God's Word, the Norwegians became exem-
plary medieval Christians (Edman 1949:225).

In Sweden, the advance of the Gospel was even slower than in
Denmark and Norway. But in the eleventh century, Christianity
spread throughout Sweden and even to the Lapps in the far north.
By the middle of the twelfth century, Sweden was nominally a
Christian land (Edman 1949:227).

Russia

After the death of Vladimir (1015), his son, Yaroslav, followed the example of Boris of Bulgaria by helping forward the
translation of literature into the Slavonic language which became Russian (Latourette 1970:Vol.2,255). In addition, Yaroslav
built churches, schools, and monasteries. Yet the knowledge of
the real meaning of Christianity for daily living was confined
to the comparatively few who could read. The higher clergy, including the heads of the Russian Church, for the first two or
three centuries, were almost all foreigners from Constantinople,
appointed by the patriarch. The Russian parish priests were
poorly paid and untrained except in the performance of the ceremonies of the Church (Latourette 1970:Vol.2,256). As a result,
the illiterate church members were very idolatrous and super-
stitious (Mathews 1952:64).

Early in the thirteenth century, the Mongol Golden Horde came
storming into Russia. Russian hermits and monks fled to the
forests of the north. This migration during three centuries of
Mongol dominance (13th to 16th centuries) created 294 new missionary monasteries (Latourette 1970:Vol.2,259).

Stephen of Perm, born between 1330 and 1346, is the most famous of these Russian frontier missionaries. In his later
teens he went to a Finnish people called the Zyrians, northeast
of Moscow. Learning their language from merchants, he invented
an alphabet and translated the service books into Zyrynian.
He baptized converts, taught them the Gospels and Psalms, founded monasteries, and trained a Zyranian clergy. By the time he
died in 1396, the majority of the Zyrans were Christians (Mathews 1952:65).

When the Russians threw off the Mongol yoke in the fourteenth
century, they set up their new capital in Moscow. The Russian
Church, with its Slavonic Bible, grew mightily so that, when the
Muslims captured Constantinople in 1453, the leadership of the

Orthodox Churches passed into the hands of the Russians, and
Moscow became the mother city of Eastern Orthodox Christianity.
There might well have been a complete collapse of Christianity
in Eastern Europe if they had not received the Word of God in
the Slavonic tongue, and if they had not had a literate church
leadership.

Wherever Orthodox Christianity confronted only animism or
polytheism, ultimately it prevailed, as did Latin Christianity
in Western Europe.

According to Latourette, the reason Orthodoxy spread no farther was due to the fact that on so much of its border it faced
advanced faiths—Zoroastrianism, Islam, and others—all of them
supported by strong political structures or by ardent racial
and national loyalties (Latourette 1970:Vol.2,262).

But perhaps there is another important reason. Christianity
advanced among animists and polytheistic peoples who had no
sacred writings of their own. On the other hand, Christianity
has never made much headway among peoples who had their own sacred writings, even though a very small minority (usually only
the religious leaders) were able to read those writings. Could
it be that the illiterate masses blindly follow their literate
religious leaders and will not be persuaded by outsiders, no
matter what approach is used? Or, could it be that they can be
persuaded to follow Jesus if they are taught to read and are
convinced of the truth of Christianity through reading the Bible
for themselves?

FORERUNNERS OF THE REFORMATION

As we have seen, by the twelfth century there was widespread
opposition in Western Europe to the corruption and the pretentions of the Church, and a growing desire of the people for
Biblical truth. Many different groups came into existence.
Two of the better known groups were the Albigenses and the Waldenses, both originating in southern France. The Church in
that area was unusually corrupt. Some of the clergy compiled
indecent books and permitted immodest songs to be sung in
church. Many of the priests were luxury-loving, indolent, pro-
fane, and illiterate, and they tolerated simony and clerical
concubinage (Latourette 1953:453).

The Waldenses

The Waldenses made a great contribution in preparing Christendom for the Reformation. Their first great leader, Peter
Waldo, was a merchant of Lyons in southern France. Late in the
twelfth century he came to such a sense of spiritual need that
only the Scriptures could satisfy his soul. He made a diligent

study of the New Testament through a translation into his native tongue. Inspired by it, he sold all of his possessions and began to preach in the city and in the countryside (Latourette 1953:451).

Waldo soon attracted many followers. His "Poor Men of Lyons" went everywhere preaching the Word. They spread throughout Western Europe as far as Naples, Bohemia, and England (Edman 1949:302). They taught that 1) the Church must return to the pure teaching of Scripture; 2) there is no purgatory; 3) the Church is not infallible; 4) Christian laymen are entitled to preach; 5) selling one's goods and giving the proceeds to the poor is an act of Christian consecration (Qualben 1955:182). They believed that all oaths were unlawful and sinful, that penance and confession to a priest were useless for the forgiveness of sins, and that the Church of Rome was the Synagogue of Satan and the Harlot of the Apocalypse (Edman 1949: 298).

With the dawning of the Reformation, the Waldenses became a part of that great movement. The early Lutherans, when asked where their faith had been before Luther nailed his 95 Theses to the door of the Wittenberg church in 1517, could reply, "In the Bible and in the valleys of the Piedmont" (Edman 1949:303).

John Wycliffe

Another ray of light in an otherwise dark and dreary age was John Wycliffe (1320-1384), called the Morning Star of the Reformation. In character and scholarship, he was one of the truly outstanding men of the fourteenth century. As a teacher at Oxford University, he became the leader of a strong reform movement that spread over England and certain parts of the Continent. He proclaimed the Biblical doctrine of justification by faith in Jesus Christ and acknowledged the Bible as the only source of truth (Qualben 1955:193).

To make the Bible accessible to all, Wycliffe had it translated into the English vernacular of his day. Portions of Scripture had been translated earlier, but England had to wait until 1380 for the complete Bible in the mother tongue (Látourette 1953:664).

Wycliffe also trained and sent out traveling preachers to instruct the people in the Word of God. He supplied them with tracts and sermon outlines and Scripture portions. In the beginning some of these itinerant preachers (known as Lollards) were university graduates. As time went on, they were drawn almost entirely from the poor (Latourette 1953:665).

Wycliffe's writings and the work of his preachers won a large
number of followers. They were outspoken in their denunciation
of the corruptions in the Church and of the clergy. Persecutions were sure to follow. In 1409, a synod in London condemned the doctrines of Wycliffe (who had died in 1384) and the unauthorized translation of the Bible. They also prohibited un-
licensed preachers. Some of the Lollards were burned at the
stake. Action against the Lollards continued, but Lollardry
persisted and seems to have enjoyed something of a revival in
the reign of Henry VII late in the fifteenth century and early
in the sixteenth century. Lollardry became one of the contributing sources of English Protestantism (Latourette 1953:666).

John Hus (c. 1373-1415)

The writings of Wycliffe also had a great influence on John
Hus, rector of the University of Prague in Bohemia (now Czecho-
slavakia). Those writings were being read in Prague at least
as early as the mid-1380s and Hus copied some of them with his
own hand (Latourette 1953:667).

Hus, and the writings of Wycliffe, attracted attention not
only in Bohemia but all over Europe. He was urged to present
his case to the Council of Constance, but although guaranteed
safe conduct to and from the Council, he was condemned by that
body and burned at the stake. That was July 6, 1415. But the
burning of Hus did not end the movement. Rather, it furthered
it. Hus became a national hero, and the demand for reform continued (Latourette 1953:669).

Other Writers and Reform Movements

There were many other reform movements during the fourteenth
and fifteenth centuries, and many great writers whose works were
to make a significant contribution toward a return to the Scriptures as the only source of Christian faith and knowledge.
While time does not permit a detailed account, or even a brief
survey, of all the writers of this period, we must at least make
mention of men like Marsilius of Padova and John of Jundun. The
latter's book, *Defensor Pacis*, which appeared in 1324, was the
most important contribution in the later Middle Ages on the relationship between Church and State. Among other things, the
book asserted the need for a reformation, religious individual-
ism, and the Bible as the only source of faith.

The writings of other men like William of Occam (1280-1349),
John Charlier of Gerson (1363-1429), and Thomas à Kempis (1380-
1471), to name but a few, had much influence in bringing about
church reform and the sanctified Christian life (Latourette
1953:648).

The Brethren of the Common Life (c. 1350-1500)

This was originally a society of pious clergymen founded in
the Netherlands by Gerhard Groot. The Brethren devoted themselves primarily to teaching and to preaching in order to reform the Church from within. The original association became
the nucleus of similar institutions throughout northern Europe,
also admitting lay people. The Brethren, moved by the desire
to give their pupils Christian training, were progressive educators, producing some of the best teachers, and conducted some
of the best schools of the fifteenth century (Latourette 1970:
Vol.2,393,435).

THE REVIVAL OF LEARNING

The Latin Vulgate was the authorized Bible of Western Christendom during the Middle Ages, even though not officially recognized. Whenever a translation into the vernacular was made,
it was the Vulgate which served as the original. The ignorance
of Greek and Hebrew in Western Europe helped establish this supremacy. Nearly all interpretations and commentaries were based
on the Latin text without referring to the original languages.
Only the Church had the right to decide whether any interpretation was correct (Schwarz 1955:45). There was no room for new
thought. The Bible translator was expected to preserve even the
order of the words which, according to Jerome, "contains a mys-
tery transcending human understanding." The word-for-word
translation paid little, if any, regard to the rules of the language into which the rendering was made. Medieval translators
up to, and including, the fifteenth century, generally speaking,
followed this method (Schwarz 1955:51). By so doing, they
thought that they were producing a faithful translation. This
method was believed to protect the translator from error and
from heresy (Schwarz 1955:51).

The Schoolmen, who knew only Latin, considered their ideas
to be in conformity with Scripture. No view was allowed which
did not conform with the interpretation of the Church Fathers
(Schwarz 1955:52).

The Schoolmen had to resist any change in the text of the
Latin Bible, for on this very wording their philosophical
thought was based.

At the end of the fifteenth century the belief in scholasticism was decreasing. Meanwhile, humanism was on the rise. The
humanists became expert in the great writers and philosophers
of pre-Christian Greece and Rome. They found pleasure in nature and sought to explore and understand it. They took joy in
challenging what had been accepted in the Middle Ages. They
poured scorn on scholasticism and the Schoolmen. They thought

of man as the architect of his own future. Many gave only lip
service to Christianity but tended to rule out God and the need
for redemption (Latourette 1953:604-605).

Many humanists, however were devout and sincere Christians
(Latourette 1953:606). In fact, all the early humanists were
good churchmen (Schwarz 1955:58). Their views toward the Scriptures and the interpretation of Scripture were virtually the
same as the Schoolmen, down to the end of the fifteenth century.

The Bible edition of 1498 was edited by Sebastian Brandt, a
humanist. His attitude toward the Bible was the same as that
of any humanist of the fifteenth century. He rejected any exe-
gesis of the Bible that did not conform to the doctrines of the
Church. He derided people who believed that they were able to
explain Holy Scripture in the light of their own reason. Even
as late as the 1520s, the humanist, Sir Thomas More, was opposed
to all modern Bible translations because the expressions used in
them were opposed to the traditions of the Church. He believed
that the personal view of an expositor is wrong and heretical if
it is contrary to the tradition of the Church (Schwarz 1955:59).

But it was humanism which led to the study of Greek and Hebrew and to new Bible translations from the original languages
(Schwarz 1955:62). It was not until 1506, however, when Reuchlin's *De Rudimentis Hebraicis* was published, that it was possible to learn Hebrew in Europe (Schwarz 1955:66).

Though there were translations of the whole Bible during the
fifteenth century--in German, Italian, French, Danish, Dutch,
Slavonic, Bohemian, and Spanish--they were all made from the
Vulgate rather than the original Hebrew and Greek (Schwarz 1955:
11). But many of these were in circulation in England and on
the continent long before Luther published his theses. The new
interest in the Bible, as far as translations are concerned,
preceded the Reformation and helped bring it about (Chirgwin
1954:32).

THE PRINTING PRESS

It is impossible to overemphasize the importance of the invention of printing by movable type in the mid-fifteenth century. The printing press spread widely and vastly increased
the circulation of books and ideas. Paper had already replaced
the more expensive parchment. Its manufacture in Europe became
common in the thirteenth and fourteenth centuries (Latourette
1953:606). The invention of the printing press, no doubt, had
much to do with increased translation of Scripture as well as
the publication of Scripture. After all, why translate the
Scriptures into the vernacular if they could not be published
in reasonably large numbers?

DISAPPEARANCE OF THE CHURCH IN CHINA

In the thirteenth century, Christianity had its greatest opportunity in China, at least until the nineteenth century.
Matteo and Nicolo Polo, the father and uncle of Marco Polo, arrived at the Imperial Palace in Cambaluc. They were received
with high honor by Kublai Khan, the most powerful ruler at that
time. His attitude toward Christianity was favorable. He even
dictated a letter to the Pope requesting a hundred missionaries.
The Polos traveled back to Italy, and in 1269 delivered the letter to the Pope.

But the Pope did not respond. After several years, the Pope
appointed two friars to go with the Polos to China. But they
had not gone far when the friars took fright and returned to
Rome. Later the Pope sent five more friars, but none of them
ever reached China. Twenty-five years after the Pope had received the letter, Kublai Khan died without having seen a
single missionary in response to his invitation. How tragic!
If the Pope had responded to this request in full obedience to
our Lord's command, it might have changed the history, not only
of China, but of the entire world (Mathews 1952:72).

Shortly after the death of Kublai Khan, however, in 1294, an
Italian Franciscan monk known as John of Montecorvino, arrived
in Cambaluc (Peking) with a letter from the Pope. After a five
year imprisonment because of false accusations against him by
Nestorian priests, John began his missionary work in China,
which was to continue for thirty years. He claims to have translated the New Testament and the Psalms into "the language and
character which is most in general use among the Mongols"
(Moule 1930:176). Although a letter of Pope Benedict XIII
(1335) mentions the finding of a Mongolian Bible in China, no
trace of these early versions has been found (Nida 1972:303).
John also claimed to have baptized some six thousand people in
a period of six years. We cannot help but wonder how well they
were instructed, for the work completely disappeared (Hudspeth
1952:10).

Three more bishops joined John in 1308. Others arrived in
1342, twelve years after John's death. But with the collapse
of the Mongol dynasty in 1368, Nestorian and Catholic Christians
totally disappeared from Chinese history for nearly two hundred
years (Hudspeth 1952:10).

We cannot help but wonder why the Church disappeared in
China. Apparently neither the Franciscans nor the Nestorians
made any great effort to train nationals for the ministry. We
also wonder about the New Testament that John claims to have
translated, of which there is no trace. If he translated it at
all, no doubt it was a word-for-word translation from the Latin

Vulgate, as were all the translations of the Middle Ages. Even if it had been a good translation, how many people would have been able to read it, or how many would have had access to it?

SUMMARY

We have seen that throughout this long period of five centuries the Church was planted in every part of Europe, from Ireland to Moscow and from the Mediterranean to the Arctic Circle. In some lands the Church was planted as the result of military force or political pressure, and the people were later instructed in the Christian faith. Often, however, this instruction was very superficial at best. Frequently the Word taught was the commandments of men rather than the Holy Scriptures which alone make us wise unto salvation through faith in Jesus Christ. The laity was at the mercy of the clergy, for they were almost all illiterate, or, if they were able to read, seldom had access to the Sacred Word. Because of this ignorance of God's Word, the Church was able to teach anything it wanted to teach. We also find that the Church was most corrupt at that period of history when the laity was the most ignorant of God's Word.

On the other hand, we do find evidence of physical Church growth and of the spiritual growth of individuals all the way through this period, in one part of Europe or another. But we find this growth only where there was a faithful literate leadership, and we find it most where the laymen were searching the Scriptures for themselves.

5

Three Centuries of Advance

We have seen that for several centuries there was a growing disgust with the corruption and the pretentions of Rome, and an ever increasing desire for a return to the Word of God. The Reformation did not suddenly burst upon the scene in 1517 when Luther nailed his theses to the Wittenberg church door.

THE STUDY OF GREEK AND HEBREW

In the fourteenth century there was much study of Greek, especially in Italy where many Greek refugees had come to escape the Turkish advance which culminated in the fall of Constantinople in 1453 (Herklots 1957:19). The study of Greek was pursued with great zeal. Later, Northern Europeans caught the infection. Some of them realized that knowledge of Greek would give them a powerful lever for Church reform (Herklots 1957:19). Church reformers were anxious to get hold of old manuscripts to find out what the New Testament really had conveyed to those for whom it was first written (Herklots 1957:20).

In 1496 one of these reformers, John Colet, began to lecture at Oxford on St. Paul's Epistle to the Romans. He spoke from the Greek text. He paid little attention to traditional interpretations. His only interest was to discover what St. Paul really meant when he first wrote. Colet won many followers. One of them was William Tyndale, of whom we shall hear more later (Herklots 1957:22).

Another scholar, the same age as Colet, was a Dutchman named Geert or Gerard, better known by his Graecized name, Erasmus. In 1498 he arrived in England to begin studying Greek. After some time he became Professor of Divinity and Professor of Greek at Cambridge University. While there he began work on a new edition of the Greek New Testament, accompanied by a fresh Latin translation. This was completed in 1516, and it became a best-seller. It is said that 100,000 copies were sold in France alone (Herklots 1957:25). It was Erasmus' Greek New Testament which was used by Tyndale in making his translation into English (Herklots 1957:26).

Meanwhile, Hebrew was also being studied more than it had been for centuries. Studies of Hebrew, like Greek, also developed in Italy, partly because of the exodus from Eastern Europe. But it was a German scholar, Johann Reuchlin (1455-1522) who became the founder of modern Hebrew studies (Herklots 1957:31-33). In 1506 he issued his *De Rudimentis Hebraicus* ("Rudiments of Hebrew"). In 1512 a number of Psalms were published in Germany with grammatical notes. But thirty-five years earlier, in 1477, a Hebrew Psalter with commentary was published at Bologna, and by 1487 the entire Old Testament had appeared in print (Herklots 1957:35). Official Rabbinical Bibles were published in 1516 and 1517. The first of these introduced the Christian chapter divisions (Herklots 1957:35).

THE REDISCOVERY OF THE BIBLE

Thus it is clear that the rediscovery of the Bible went hand in hand with the Reformation. In 1516 Erasmus published his Greek New Testament, and the next year Luther nailed his ninety-five theses to the church door. In 1522 Luther translated the New Testament into German, and within a few years, Germans began to call themselves Protestants. We must point out, however, that there were fourteen translations of Scripture into German before Luther's work. In 1525 Tyndale translated the Bible into English, and within two years Reformation doctrines were being advocated in that land. In 1535 Olivetan translated the Bible into French, and just one year later, Geneva went Protestant. Bible reading and the Reformation moved forward together, with Bible reading usually taking the lead (Chirgwin 1954:30).

The Reformers were not satisfied that there should be translations in the vernacular if they were only available to the scholar or the priest. They must be made available to everyone. Luther wrote:

> Would that this one Book were in every language,
> in every land, before the eyes, and in the ears
> and hearts of all men! Scripture without any comment
> is the sun whence all teachers receive their sight
> (Chirgwin 1954:33).

Erasmus wrote, in his Exhortation to his New Testament:

> I wish that even the weakest woman should read the
> Gospel--should read the Epistles of Paul. And I
> wish these were translated into all languages, so
> that they might be read and understood, not only by
> Scots and Irishmen, but also by Turks and Saracens...
> (Herklots 1957:26).

The Reformers wanted everyone to have the opportunity to
read the Bible, because they believed in its converting power.
Many of them had experienced that power themselves. Tyndale
was brought to a new understanding of Christianity through reading the Bible. Luther was convinced of the truth of salvation
through faith in Jesus Christ without the deeds of the law
through the reading of Romans and Galatians. Because of these
experiences, both of these men believed that they were called
to make the Bible available to others. They realized that if
God had spoken to them in Scriptures, it was their duty to give
others the same opportunity to read the life-giving Word (Chirgwin 1954:34).

Most of the leading Reformers did some Bible translating.
Some of them made it their top priority. They were convinced
that the Bible contained all that was necessary for salvation
and that it was meant for all men. This was their greatest
contribution to the growth of the Church (Chirgwin 1954:35).

In every land where the Bible was given a chance, it created
a kind of revolution. With the written Word of God in the
mother tongue, the weakest Christian knew more of God's redeem-
ing love and of the Great Commission to proclaim that love to
others, than the wisest teachers of the Middle Ages. When
Christians studied it, they began to send it forth to the rest
of the world.

The Protestant world, however, had little time to even think
about missions during the Reformation period. Until 1648 they
were fighting for their lives. Only the Peace of Westphalia in
that year gave assurance that Protestantism would even survive.
Moreover, Protestant nations could do little in the sixteenth
century to carry the Gospel Message to Africa, Asia, and the
New World, since Spain and Portugal controlled the sea routes
in both hemispheres, and these two countries remained Roman
Catholic (Neill 1964:222).

THE PURITAN AND PIETIST MOVEMENTS

While the Protestants could do little to carry the Gospel
outside of Europe in the sixteenth and early seventeenth centuries, they nevertheless made considerable gain in England as
well as on the Continent wherever the vernacular Bible had free
course and was regularly and diligently studied.

The Puritan and Pietist movements had their roots in the Bible. In Britain and in Germany, the Bible brought about a kind of revolution. In the words of J. R. Green:

> No greater moral change ever passed over a nation than passed over England during the years which parted the middle of the reign of Elizabeth (1558-1603) from the meeting of the Long Parliament. England became a people of a book, and that book was the Bible. The whole temper of the nation felt the change. A new conception of life superseded the old. A new moral and religious impulse spread through every class (1879:460-462).

The Puritans

The Puritans (late sixteenth and seventeenth centuries) took the Reformation seriously. They proclaimed its central truths and then put them into practice. They read the Scriptures, and they applied the Bible with all sincerity to personal and national affairs. They also responded to the missionary call. They granted charters for the planting of colonies which contained strong recommendations for the proclamation of the Gospel. The royal charter of the colony of Virginia (1606) specifically stated that one purpose of the enterprise was the propagation of "the Christian religion to such people as yet live in darkness and miserable ignorance of the true knowledge and worship of God" (Latourette 1970:Vol.3, 44).

In 1660 there was formed "The Corporation for the Promoting of the Gospel among the Indians of New England." This was probably the first missionary society of the Protestant era (Chirgwin 1954:37).

When the Pilgrim Fathers and their successors came to North America, they made the evangelization of the Indians a real part of their new life. John Eliot (1604-1690) is the first missionary that America produced. No sooner had he come in touch with the Indians than he realized that if he was to do any significant work among them, he must translate the Bible into their language. He translated the Scriptures into Mohican. It was one of the first books to be published in America. As soon as the Puritans came in touch with the non-Christian world, their first act was to translate the Bible. Why? Because they regarded the Bible as the best evangelistic tool (Chirgwin 1954: 38).

A name closely linked with Eliot's is that of David Brainerd (1718-1747), who also poured out his life in the service of the Indians, and left a story that has been the inspiration of countless others (Latourette 1970:Vol.3,220). He and Roger

Williams and John Eliot all saturated themselves in the Scriptures which was their source of missionary zeal and the essential tool of their missionary effort.

Pietism

The most striking phase of the religious awakening which followed the Thirty Years' War was Pietism. Profoundly influential was the *Wahres Christenthum* ("True Christianity") of the Lutheran, John Arndt (1555-1621), which appeared early in the 1600s and was translated into several European languages. It was a chief means of awakening Philip Jacob Spener (1635-1705), regarded as the founder of Pietism (Latourette 1953:894-895).

This movement was marked by a deep devotion to the Bible and a firm belief in its evangelistic power. It had a profound influence on the thought and life of European Christianity for more than a hundred years. It emphasized group Bible study, the priesthood of all believers, and the promotion of overseas missions.

Pietism found a focus in Halle where a zeal for studying and circulating the Bible combined with a passion for overseas missions (Neill 1952:195). The leader of the movement was August Hermann Francke (1663-1727), the professor of Oriental languages in the University. As a student at Leipzig, he and two others had launched a plan of Bible classes for students. The plan caught on, and Bible study grew to such an extent that the booksellers of the town could hardly keep up with the demand for Greek New Testaments. Many students became so absorbed in Scriptures that they hardly did any other reading. Because of this, Francke was eventually expelled from the University. He moved to Halle which soon became the headquarters of German Pietism. He started the Bible classes again, opened a hostel for students, and threw himself into the work of the Canstein House printing press which was producing Bibles and New Testaments and selling the copies for a few cents each. The press had been started by Baron von Canstein in 1710, and he left it in his will to Professor Francke. Before the British and Foreign Bible Society was founded, Canstein House had already printed over three million Bibles and New Testaments in many languages and dispersed them over Europe, America, and even parts of Asia (Canton n.d.:Vol.1,147).

Halle also became the first missionary training center outside the Roman Catholic Church since the Reformation (Clarke 1959:403). Its first two missionaries arrived in India in 1706. They were the first Protestant missionaries to that country. One of them, Ziegenbalg, began translating the New Testament. In a few years he was able to report that much of the Bible was in the Tamil tongue and that a little band of converts had been

won. Once again the Bible and evangelism went hand in hand
(Neill 1964:229).

Another Halle student to make missionary history was Count
von Zinzendorf (1700-1760). A number of refugees from Moravia
(Central Czechoslovakia) who were Bible loving peasants, took
refuge on his estate in Saxony (Southeast Germany). Under the
count's leadership the Herrnhut estate became the center of one
of the most remarkable enterprises in missionary work, and in
twenty years they had done more to spread the Message of Salvation than the whole Protestant Church had done in two hundred
years (Chirgwin 1954:42).

To summarize, Puritanism in Britain and Pietism on the Continent put the Reformation into practice. The Reformation made
the Bible available in the mother tongue. Puritanism and Pietism taught people to read it and meditate upon it and apply its
message to their daily lives. Pietism also began to print and
distribute the Scriptures in large numbers. Both movements
started pioneer missionary work--one in India, the other in
North America.

THE EVANGELICAL REVIVAL AND THE MISSIONARY ENTERPRISE

Throughout most of the eighteenth century, religion was formal and rationalist, and the Christian cause meant little in
the common life. Most people paid little attention to the
Church, while bishops and clergy were worldly and indifferent
(Chirgwin 1954:42).

The Evangelical Revival (1730s and following) was a return
to the Bible, or at least was accompanied by such a return, in
much the same manner that the Reformation was accompanied by a
rediscovery of the Sacred Word. In the years immediately preceding the Revival, the Bible was a neglected Book. Then a
little group in Oxford began to read together the Greek New
Testament and Law's *A Serious Call to a Holy and Devout Life.*
After a short time the group broke up, but the men continued to
read. In a few years, some of them were preaching to huge
crowds. There was a note of urgency in their preaching. A new
religious energy burst forth, expressing itself in the rise of
Methodism, the birth of the mission enterprise, the abolition
of the slave trade, and the first stirrings of a social
conscience. It can all be traced to a little meeting that took
place in London on May 24, 1738, when the heart of John Wesley
was strangely warmed when he heard the reading of Luther's
preface to the Epistle to the Romans. That incident was a mile-
stone in the history of the Church. For Wesley became the
greatest evangelist of his day. For fifty years he traveled
all over Britain, preaching everywhere. He averaged fifteen
sermons a week and 5000 miles on horseback every year (Chirgwin
1954:44).

At the center of all this evangelism was the Bible. It was the Bible that warmed Wesley's heart. It was the Bible that linked him with Luther whose preface to Romans was being read. There was a kind of Biblical succession linking Wesley through the Moravians, under whose auspices the meeting took place, not only with Luther but also with Hus and Wycliffe. Wycliffe pioneered in Bible translation, and Hus acknowledged his debt to him. Hus planted the Bible in the heart of Bohemia, where the Church of the Brethren, as the Moravians were called, grew up. About a century later, a treatise written by Hus made a deep impression on Luther, and two hundred years later a commentary by Luther, read at a Moravian meeting, inspired Wesley and started the Evangelical Revival (Chirgwin 1954:44-45).

The Evangelical Revival gave the Bible a central place. Wesley's preachers went through the land with the Bible in their hands and the flame of evangelism in their hearts. The Bible was the source of their evangelistic preaching. They familiarized the masses with the message of the Bible as the parish clergy had not done for a hundred years or more.

Men of substance also became evangelicals. They read the Bible diligently and launched organizations to make it more widely known. They helped start Sunday Schools whose aim was to teach the Bible. They encouraged Bible classes and often taught them personally. Above all, they founded societies for the printing and circulation of the Scriptures. The British and Foreign Bible Society was their foremost achievement. It was the clearest possible demonstration of the close connection between the Revival and the Bible. The hundred years following the Evangelical Revival have been called by Professor Latourette "the great century" (see the following chapter) in view of the fact that it witnessed the greatest expansion of Christianity since the days of the Apostles (Latourette 1953:1063).

BIBLE SOCIETIES AND THE MISSIONARY ENTERPRISE

The founders of the Bible Societies and the missionary enterprise were convinced that they were necessary to one another, and they started them almost simultaneously. In Britain the Baptist Missionary Society, the London Missionary Society, the Church Missionary Society, and the Methodist Missionary Society were born between 1792 and 1818, while the British and Foreign Bible Society came into being in 1804, right in the middle of that period. The Bible was at the heart of the newly-emerging missionary enterprise. The same thing happened in North America, where four of the largest missionary societies--the American Board, the American Baptist, the Methodist, and the Episcopal--were formed between 1810 and 1821, while the American Bible Society was founded in 1816, again right in the middle of the period.

On the European continent, in the twenty-five years between
1797 and 1822, the Netherlands Missionary Society and the Netherlands Bible Society, the Paris Missionary Society and the
French Bible Society, and the Danish Bible Society all came
into existence. Never was there a period in which so many missionary societies and so many Bible societies came into being.
It cannot be just an accident that the birth of Bible societies
is closely associated with the founding of missionary societies.
The instances are far too many, and they are drawn from far too
many countries to be written off as mere coincidence (Chirgwin
1954:47).

In his book, *The Bible in World Evangelism*, Chirgwin summarizes the influence of the Bible during these renewal periods
very well. He says:

> In all these renewal periods in the Church's life,
> the Bible played an important part. At the Reforma-
> tion, the Bible stimulated the Reformers by providing
> them with their message, while the Reformers stimula-
> ted the use of the Bible by providing it in a language
> the people could understand. In the Puritan and Pietist
> period, the Bible came into more general use than ever
> before, and from that sprang the first evangelistic
> and missionary ventures of Protestantism. In the
> period of the Evangelical Revival and the modern
> missionary movement, the Bible and evangelism once
> again acted and reacted upon one another. The Bible
> was the agency through which, in the heart of John
> Wesley, the Evangelical Revival began, while the
> Evangelical Revival produced the men through whose
> zeal and devotion the missionary societies were
> started for sending the Gospel to the ends of the
> earth, and the Bible societies for putting the Bible
> into the hands of all men everywhere (1954:49).

GEOGRAPHIC EXPANSION

During the sixteenth, seventeenth, and eighteenth centuries,
an unprecedented missionary movement carried the faith to every
continent and to many islands of the sea in both hemispheres.
The Roman Catholics were predominant, mainly because the Spanish
and the Portuguese, who were the leaders in overseas discovery
and conquest, were of that branch of the Church. Protestants
were later in developing missions in the newly discovered lands,
but whenever they came in contact with pagans, they did proclaim
the Gospel to them, and as time went on, their efforts were intensified. Russian Orthodox Christianity spread among the
pagans in European Russia and across Siberia into Alaska (Latourette 1970:Vol.3,452).

Through the missionary effort, the majority of the Indians
of Mexico, Central America, and South America became nominal
Christians. Hundreds of Indians in Canada, the Mississippi
Valley, and the English colonies were baptized. Strong churches
arose among the settlers in the colonies and many of the Blacks
who were brought to the Americas as slaves were led to adopt the
religion of their masters. In a few places along the coast of
Africa, Christian communities were established. Several hundred thousand in India became professedly Christian, and a large
number in Ceylon took the Christian name. Small Christian
groups arose in Burma and Siam and larger ones in Indo-China
and the East Indies. The majority of the Filipinos became
Christian in name, and promising beginnings were made in Korea
and Japan, though later checked by persecution. The Christian
faith was re-introduced into China (Latourette 1970:Vol.3,452).

But few of these Christian communities gathered from non-
European peoples displayed much initiative in propagating their
faith, and almost none of them developed truly indigenous, dy-
namic-equivalence churches, using their own forms of art, music,
worship, church government, etc. How could they, when in most
cases they were not given any Scripture in their own language?

South and Central America

In the New World, the Spanish and Portuguese missionaries
made no serious attempt to build an indigenous church (Neill
1964:173). In Lima, for example, not long after its foundation,
Spanish priests and brothers settled down to what has been des-
cribed as the life of a "select bachelors club" and showed no
enthusiasm for evangelizing the Indians of the interior. In
1555 the first Council of Mexico explicitly forbade Indians,
mestizos, or anyone not of pure European stock from entering
the priesthood (Neill 1964:175). There was a similar ban in
Lima, and this was not lifted until 1772. The first three
Indian priests were ordained in 1794 (Neill 1964:175).

Perhaps the most notable Roman Catholic enterprise was the
Jesuit mission in Paraguay, "the Republic of the Guaranís".
The area covered by this mission was in what is now Argentina
(Neill 1964:202). As was the custom throughout Latin America,
Indians were brought into Christian villages for protection and
Christian instruction. In 1623 there were twenty-three settlements with a population of 100,000, mostly pagan. Elementary
education was given and a small amount of literature was produced in the Guaraní language. But though the Jesuits were
there for more than a century, they did not produce a single
candidate for the priesthood. Finally the Jesuits were expelled
and everything crumbled. By the end of the eighteenth century
hardly anything was left.

The gravest obstacles to church growth in Latin America were the insistence of the Roman Church on the celibacy of the clergy and the use of Latin for the liturgy (Neill 1964:208). It was not until the twentieth century that the indigenous priesthood in the Roman Churches overseas began to overtake the foreign element, and the process is still far from complete (Neill 1964:209).

The only Protestant work in South America before 1800 seems to be that of the Moravians on the island of St. Thomas in the West Indies and in Surinam (Dutch Guiana). This work has continued to the present time (Neill 1964:238).

There is no record of a single Indian language of Latin America having been reduced to writing before the nineteenth century with the exception of Guarani in Paraguay. As mentioned above, the Guaranis received some literature, but no Scripture at all (Neill 1964:203).

Africa

Between 1500 and 1800, only the fringes of Africa were touched by Christianity, and then but slightly. Most of the missionaries were Roman Catholic, and most of them were under the auspices of the Portuguese.

The most spectacular of the Roman Catholic missions in Africa during this period were in the Congo, beginning in 1491. Missionaries of various R.C. orders appeared intermittently throughout the sixteenth, seventeenth, and eighteenth centuries, mostly from Portugal at first, later from Italy and other countries. But there were no Bible translations and so no Bible reading and no indigenous church, and in time the superficial Christianity that had existed for nearly three hundred years died out. The only trace that remained were some crucifixes and images of the saints which were kept as fetishes and used from time to time to dispel a drought (Latourette 1970:Vol.3,242-243).

There is no record of any languages of Africa being reduced to writing between A.D. 1500 and A.D. 1800 (Latourette 1970:Vol. 3,240-246), nor is there any record of any Scripture translations in any of the languages of that continent during this period.

Portuguese influence was especially strong in Angola. By the end of the sixteenth century, several chiefs and hundreds of their people had been baptized, and some districts were said to be completely Christian. But they were never given the Word of God in their own language. It is doubtful that their Christianity was anything more than superficial (Latourette 1970: Vol.3,244).

The strongest Protestant foothold in Africa before 1800 was
the extreme tip of the continent. The Dutch settled there beginning in 1652. When the English seized the colony in 1775,
the population was 21,000 whites, 25,000 slaves, and 14,000 Hottentots. In that year the colony had seven Dutch Reformed congregations and ten ministers. While some work had been done
among the slaves, we know of no effort to give them God's Word
in their mother tongue. As time went on, their zeal for the
conversion of the slaves cooled but the white population remained professedly Christian. Practically no mission work had been
done among the Hottentots before the last decade of the eighteenth century.

In A.D. 1800, as far as Christianity was concerned, Africa
was the Dark Continent. However, at several points on the
periphery, Christianity was present, and from these footholds
the faith made rapid expansion in the nineteenth century, as we
shall see (Latourette 1970:Vol.3,246).

India

Because of the conquest of Islam in the seventh and eighth
centuries, we hear nothing of the Church in India for hundreds
of years. The Muslims controlled the land and sea routes to
the Orient, making it impossible for Christian missionaries to
travel to the Far East. But a new era began when Vasco de Gama
discovered a sea route to India in 1498. The Franciscan priests
who accompanied him launched the missionary program of the Catholic Church in that part of Asia.

All of the large religious orders of the Roman Church were
represented in India, but the Jesuits made the greatest impact.
Francis Xavier, the first Jesuit missionary, arrived in Goa on
the southwest coast of India in 1542 and worked in that country
for three years. Goa, a Portuguese enclave, became the spring-
board for Xavier's work in Asia (Neill 1964:148).

In the short time that Xavier was in India he founded a college for the training of missionaries. Over a dozen languages
were spoken there by students from India, Africa, Malay, Siam,
China, Molucca, Ceylon, and Japan. In his later travels, he
regularly sent promising youths back to Goa for training. This
was the first college for developing Asiatic international
leadership (Mathews 1952:95).

Xavier worked for some time among the Parava fishing caste
along the Coromandel coast, and with the help of some students
from the school in Goa, translated the Creeds and prayers of
the Church into Tamil, the language spoken by the Paravas
(Mathews 1952:96). This seems to be the first translation of
creeds or prayers or anything else into an Indian language by

Christian missionaries. Another 170 years or more were to pass
before the New Testament would be translated into this or any
of the languages of that country.

Although the Roman missionaries translated no Scriptures
into Tamil, many thousands of people along the Coromandel are
said to have been converted (Mathews 1952:96). But since they
were not given the Word of God in their language, how closely
they were able to walk with Christ is certainly open to question.

The first Protestant work in India was that of Bartholomew
Ziegenbalg and Heinrich Plutschau who arrived in 1706. Within
seven years, Ziegenbalg had translated the New Testament into
the Tamil tongue (Neill 1964:228-229). This was the first complete translation of the New Testament into any of the languages
of India. It was published in 1715 (Nida 1972:418). It was
only the fifth language in all of Asia that received the Word
of God, the others being Hebrew, Syriac, Armenian, and Arabic
many centuries before (North 1938:321).

Ziegenbalg also began the translation of the Old Testament.
This was revised and completed by Benjamin Schultze in 1727.
This was only the fourth entire Bible to be translated into an
Asiatic tongue (North 1938:321). Other translations into Tamil
followed. Especially noteworthy was the translation by Philip
Fabricius of the New Testament in 1772 and of the Old Testament
in 1796 (Neill 1970:55-56).

We are told that Benjamin Schultze had also started translating the whole Bible into Telugu and the New Testament into
Hindustani (Urdu) (Mathews 1952:113). Apparently these translations were never published, for the first publication of any
portion of Scripture in Telugu, according to *The Book of a Thousand Tongues*, was in 1812, and the complete New Testament in
1818. The first publication of Scriptures in Hindustani was in
1805 (North 1938:925,974).

Towering in influence above Ziegenbalg and his colleagues
was Christian Friedrich Schwartz who arrived in India in 1750
and gave himself tirelessly to the work until he died in 1798.
By that time some twenty thousand Christians of varied caste
backgrounds were members of the churches that he and his prede-
cessors and colleagues had founded. The finest elements in the
Lutheran churches in South India today are descendants of their
converts, people who had God's Word in their own language and
whose leadership was literate (Mathews 1952:114).

Japan

We know of no Christian missionary work in Japan until 1549
when Francis Xavier arrived with two other Jesuits and a

Japanese convert. Other Jesuits followed him and continued the work (Kane 1971:61).

The political conditions at that time were favorable for the planting of Christianity. By 1581 there were two hundred churches and 150,000 professing Christians. By 1600 there were at least a quarter of a million converts (Robertson 1953:14), perhaps half a million (Kane 1971:61). In that year there were 109 Jesuit priests in Japan. They built elementary schools, high schools to train catechists, normal schools to train teachers, and seminaries to train the ministry (Mathews 1952: 102). We are told that by 1611 many books had been published, including twenty-seven different volumes, known as the Japan Jesuit Collection. This is still in existence. It includes: 1) The lives of the Saints; 2) a catechism; 3) an outline of Christian doctrine; and 4) a handbook of confession. Dictionaries, grammars, and other literature was also produced (Yanagita 1957:95).

In his book *The Bible Throughout the World*, Kilgour says that Xavier's interpreter, Anjino, made a version of St. Matthew's Gospel (1939:152). If this is true, there is no trace of it today (Robertson 1953:15).

At the turn of the century, the Tokugawa family seized power and were tolerant of the Christians at first. But in 1612 the new emperor started a persecution that in the end expelled all missionaries and threatened every Christian with execution. Many of those who refused to deny their Savior were hung head downward in agony for days. Others were crucified, burned over slow fires, or beheaded (Mathews 1952:102). In a single year, 1638, some thirty-seven thousand people were slaughtered (Kane 1971:61-62). For more than two hundred years Japan was a hermit nation, completely shut off from the rest of the world (Kane 1971:61-62).

China

For nearly two hundred years, from 1368 to 1552, Christianity seems to have disappeared completely from Chinese history (Hudspeth 1952:10). In 1552 Francis Xavier tried to enter China, but without success. The door of China had been slammed tight against missionaries of the Gospel due to the cruelty of Portuguese traders. Xavier died on an islet near Hong Kong while waiting for an opportunity to get into the country (Mathews 1952:107).

Xavier was succeeded by Valignano as superintendent of missions in Asia. At Macao (on the mainland not far from Hong Kong) Valignano was training something like a Christian "commando" group of young men to break through into China.

Matteo Ricci joined the group (Mathews 1952:107). After master-
ing the Chinese language, Matteo gained entrance to the country.
Eventually, he made his way to Peking, and, being a brilliant
scholar, was invited into the Emperor's palace. Within a few
years members of the Imperial family had joined a church whose
two hundred members included many others of the highest of the
land (Mathews 1952:108).

Ricci mastered the Chinese classics, especially the teachings
of Confucius. In these classics the names for the Supreme Spirit, Shang Ti and T'ien, meant something very impersonal. Ricci
used these words for God in Christian worship and in teaching
about Christianity. He also allowed converts to continue the
ceremonies in honor of ancestors and of Confucius. When he died
in 1610, he had called thousands into the Church. Forty years
later, the Catholic Church in China numbered over two hundred
fifty thousand, and by 1708 the number of Chinese Christians
had risen to a third of a million (Mathews 1952:109).

But then decline set in, due to a fierce controversy over
Ricci's policy. In 1704 the Pope forbade the use of the Chinese
terms for God that Ricci had used, and he ordered the Christians
to stop participating in the sacrifices to ancestors and to Confucius. The Emperor was furious that a foreign "barbarian"
like the Pope should disagree with him about the use of Chinese
words. The missionaries found themselves in quite a dilemma.
They had to obey the Pope and anger the Emperor or please the
Emperor and be excommunicated by the Pope. The debate continued until 1742 when the Pope ordered disobedient missionaries to
return to Rome for punishment.

Mathews gives four other causes for the decline of Catholic
missions in China as well as in other parts of the world in the
latter half of the eighteenth century:

> 1) The Spanish and the Portuguese empires were in
> decay; 2) The Jesuits were suppressed by the Pope in
> 1773, after having been expelled a few years earlier
> from French, Spanish, and Portuguese territories;
> 3) Persecution increased with the growth of the
> Church; 4) The French Revolution, followed by the
> Napoleonic wars, cut off the support of missionaries
> from Europe (1952:110).

Although there are many reasons for the failure of the Church
to grow in China, one of the greatest reasons may be the fact
that they were not given the written Word of God in their own
language until the nineteenth century, and even then, as we
shall see, it was a long, long time before many had access to
it and could read it for themselves.

6

The Great Century:
Europe and the Americas

The late Kenneth S. Latourette refers to the years 1815 to 1914
as "The Great Century" in the expansion of the Christian Church,
the greatest century that Christianity had ever known (1953:
1063). He devotes three out of seven volumes of his work, *History of the Expansion of Christianity*, to this period of one
hundred years (1970:Vols.4-6).

If there had been a general missionary conference in the year
1810 as proposed by William Carey, who would have been in attendance? Stephen Neill sums it up as follows:

> From Japan and Korea there would have been
> no one, and hardly a soul from China or South-
> east Asia, except for a few from Indonesia;
> a small group from the islands of the Pacific,
> and a rather larger group from India; no one
> from the Muslim world except members of the
> ancient Eastern Churches; a handful from Sierra
> Leone and other stations on the coast of Africa,
> but no one from the interior; a fair-sized
> group from the West Indies, but (this being a
> Protestant dream) no one from Central or South
> America (1964:253).

By 1910, however, almost every country on the face of the
earth would be represented, with the exception of Nepal,
Afghanistan, and Tibet. Otherwise there was practically no
limit to the extent of the missionary enterprise.

REASONS FOR THE WORLDWIDE EXPANSION OF CHRISTIANITY

The Worldwide Expansion of European Peoples

One of the major reasons for the worldwide expansion of
Christianity in the nineteenth century was the worldwide expansion of Western and Northern European peoples--most of whom
were nominal Christians. They explored and subjugated Africa,
completed the conquest of India and Ceylon, blasted open the
doors of China, persuaded the Japanese to admit their merchants
and missionaries, made themselves rulers of the islands of the
Pacific, built new European nations in Australia and New Zeal-
and, and completed their occupation of the Americas. By 1914
all the world was politically subject to European peoples except a few spots in Africa, a few states in Asia, Japan, a
small corner of Southeastern Europe, and the jungles of some of
the larger islands of the South Pacific (Latourette 1970:Vol.4,
13).

This expansion of European peoples powerfully aided the
spread of Christianity. A large portion of the millions who
migrated to the Americas, Australia, New Zealand, and South
Africa held to their ancestral faith. The exploration, the
commerce, and the colonial administration of non-Europeans by
European nations helped pave the way for the missionaries.
Much financial support was given by European colonial administrators to mission schools, not because they were Christian
but because they were schools. Regardless of the reason, this
financial assistance contributed much to the spread of the
Christian faith (Latourette 1970:Vol.4,20).

Mastery of the Physical Environment

Another major reason for the advance of Christianity during
the nineteenth century was the mastery by man of his physical
environment. Railways and steamships carried not only merchants
but also missionaries. Improvements in printing and the advent
of the typewriter made possible the increased publication of
Christian literature, while modern means of transportation fa-
cilitated the distribution of the Sacred Word. The cable, the
telegraph, the improved postal system, and the printing press
provided quick communications between missionaries and their
constituencies back home, facilitating the raising of funds for
the support of missions as well as aiding the dissemination of
the Christian message.

Accumulation of Wealth Due to the Machine Age

Another reason for the rapid advance of the Gospel during
this period was the wealth which mounted so spectacularly because of the products of the machine, making it possible to

finance missions on an unprecedented scale.

It is significant that Christianity spread primarily from those peoples who were most affected by the industrial revolution. It was Protestant Great Britain which took the lead in the industrial revolution and, next to Great Britain, it was the United States, where Protestantism was more prominent than Roman Catholicism, which, through the new machines, expanded most rapidly in population, in territory, and in wealth. And it was from these lands that the majority of the Protestant missionaries came (Latourette 1970:Vol.4,65).

The Prestige of Christianity

Then, too, Christianity acquired a certain amount of prestige, since peoples who were supposedly Christian were the initial possessors of the machines and of the knowledge of the scientific method which made them possible. Because the things that Christianity brought with it were desirable, Christianity was frequently adopted.

Education

A fifth reason for the advancement of the Gospel, especially in Northern Europe and in North America, was the universal primary education made possible by the increase in riches--education which became necessary if people were to take their part in the machine age (Latourette 1970:Vol.4,11). While more and more Europeans were learning to read during the previous three centuries, the literacy rate was greatly accelerated after 1800 (Cipolla 1969:37).

Peace

The relative peace from 1815 to 1914 also assisted the spread of the Christian faith. Because of it, missionaries could travel with comparative safety, funds could be sent expeditiously, new Christian churches could grow without interruption, and fellowship could be maintained and strengthened between the new churches and those which had founded them (Latourette 1970:Vol. 4,19). The era of greatest peace and prosperity and the furthest extension of European imperialism, from 1870 to 1914, was especially favorable for the expansion of the Christian Church (Latourette 1970:Vol.4,177).

Creative Impulse Within Christianity

The remarkable expansion of Christianity in the nineteenth century was not simply the result of a favorable environment. It was due to an upsurging, creative impulse within Christianity itself.

Although there was a great deal of religious scepticism during this period and a growing renunciation of the traditional
faith among the peoples of Western Europe, there was also a ri-
sing tide of vitality within the Christian Churches, both Protestant and Roman Catholic.

WHAT KIND OF CHRISTIANITY WAS IT THAT SPREAD?

The kinds of Protestantism from which the major part of the
expansion took place were those which were most affected by the
Pietist tradition, the Wesleyan movement, and the revivals of
the eighteenth and nineteenth centuries--movements which were
born and perpetuated through prayer, Bible reading, and Bible
preaching (Latourette 1970:Vol.4,65).

HOW DID CHRISTIANITY SPREAD?

Christianity spread primarily, not through the denomination
boards (modalities), but through a whole host of independent
mission societies made up of interested individuals (sodali-
ties), burdened for souls around the world for whom Christ died.
These societies burst upon the scene in the last decade of the
eighteenth century and the early part of the nineteenth century
and continued to multiply during the decades that followed.

The first of these organizations was the Baptist Missionary
Society which had its origin in the purpose of William Carey
(1761-1834). Both his father and grandfather had taught the
village school, so Carey was reared in a family that was familiar with books. He read the Bible regularly and read books of
travel. He was an indefatigable student. His interest in geography and travel was especially aroused when he read the
Voyages of Captain James Cook. The combination of his passion
for geography and his warm religious conviction led to a growing concern for missions. He was also profoundly influenced by
the writings of John Eliot and David Brainerd. He prepared *An
Enquiry into the Obligations of Christians to Use Means for the
Conversion of the Heathen*, in which he suggested feasible steps
for carrying out the Great Commission.

No doubt, this book, as well as one of Carey's sermons, and
his perseverance led to a meeting on October 2, 1792, at which
was organized the Particular Baptist Society for Propagating
the Gospel amongst the Heathen, a name that was soon superseded
by the Baptist Missionary Society.

The organization of this society is usually called the incep-
tion of the modern Protestant foreign mission enterprise. While
this is not quite accurate, Carey and the Baptist Missionary
Society do mark the beginning of a new era. He and the society
which arose in response to his vision and faith were the begin-

ning of an amazing series of Protestant efforts to reach the
entire world with the Gospel of Jesus Christ.

The formation of the Baptist Missionary Society was soon followed by the organization of the London Missionary Society
(1795), the Church Missionary Society (1799), the Religious
Tract Society (1799), the British and Foreign Bible Society
(1804), the Hibernian Church Missionary Society (1814), and the
Wesleyan Methodist Missionary Society (1817). These societies,
together with the older Society for Promoting Christian Knowledge and the Society for the Propagation of the Gospel in
Foreign Parts, were the chief organizations through which English Christianity was spread to non-Western peoples (Latourette
1970:Vol.4,73).

Many similar organizations were founded in Scotland and on
the Continent and in the United States.

EMPHASES OF THE MISSIONARY ENTERPRISE

The Protestantism which spread put much emphasis on education and on the preparation and distribution of Christian literature, especially the Bible.

Bible Translating

It is interesting to note that this Great Century of missionary advance was also a century when the Holy Scriptures were
translated into nearly all of the major languages of Africa,
Asia, and the South Pacific.

At the beginning of the nineteenth century, the Bible had
been translated in whole or in part into not more than seventy
languages (Neill 1964:209). Of the forty languages that had the
entire Bible, all were European or ancient languages except Arabic, Mohican, Tamil (India), and Malay. Of the other languages
that had the entire New Testament, all were European or ancient
languages except Sinhalese (Ceylon), Eskimo (Greenland), Dahn-
kini (India), and Ethiopic (Nida 1972:30).

By 1914 the entire Bible had been translated into 108 more
languages than it had been in the year 1800. One hundred and
twenty-six additional New Testaments had been translated, as
well as Scripture portions in 370 other languages. Of the 108
complete Bibles, 52 were Asian, 23 African, 14 Oceanian, 11
European, 4 North American, and 4 were languages spoken in the
U.S.S.R. Of the 126 New Testaments that appeared for the first
time, 46 were Asian, 41 African, 17 Oceanian, 11 North American,
6 European, 2 South American, and 3 were in the U.S.S.R. (Nida
1972:30-37). A good many of these languages, if not most of
them, had to be reduced to writing by the missionary before the

Scriptures could be translated. By 1914 the Bible had been
translated into languages spoken by ninety percent or more of
the world's inhabitants (Nida 1972:30).

Bible Societies

In 1804 a Welsh Presbyterian approached the Religious Tract
Society (founded in 1799), suggesting that a society was needed
to supply Bibles in Welsh, which were both scarce and expensive.
The excited response was: "If for Wales, why not for the kingdom? Why not for the world?" Soon Granville Sharp was presid-
ing at an important meeting in London where seven hundred
pounds (about thirty-five hundred dollars) was subscribed "for
the wider circulation of the Holy Scriptures without note or
comment", and the British and Foreign Bible Society was born
(Foster 1960:24-25). Within three years, the BFBS formed auxiliaries in Scotland, Ireland, Russia, and Bohemia. (ABS
Record 1973:June-July,9). Within a few years there were a hundred Bible societies in the United States. We shall read more
about these societies later in this chapter.

The British and Foreign Bible Society distributed Scriptures
in the vernacular over much of Europe, from Russia and Scandinavia in the north to Greece and the Iberian peninsula in the
south. It had translations prepared, saw to the printing of
these and existing versions, and employed colporteurs to distribute them. As a result, many were converted to Protestantism, especially in Belgium, France, and in Ireland (Latourette
1970:Vol.4,132).

Sunday Schools

One movement which spread to many lands was the Sunday School
first organized in London in 1780 by Robert Raikes. The original purpose was to give religious and moral instruction to the
poor. At first this involved teaching many of the pupils to
read. One of the early promoters of the enterprise suggested
as an ultimate goal teaching everyone in the world to read the
Bible. The need was clear, and the Sunday School spread rapidly on both sides of the Atlantic and in other lands. In time,
they became the most generally accepted means of giving the
young instruction in Christian principles (Latourette 1970:Vol.
4,38). Through its Sunday Schools, Methodism had an influence
upon the major church quite out of proportion to its own members (Latourette 1970:Vol.4,136).

Student Organizations

Closely allied to the revivals which were frequent during
the eighteenth and nineteenth centuries, and in large measure
an outgrowth of them, were the many organizations which arose

to serve particular groups. Protestant students formed societies for the cultivation of the religious life. In the last
quarter of the nineteenth century and the first quarter of the
twentieth century, student Christian societies rapidly increased in numbers and influence. Largely through the genius of
John R. Mott, they were bound together through the World Student Christian Federation. The movement spread from the United
States to Great Britain, Scandinavia, Germany, France, Switzerland, Holland, Australia, and New Zealand. From these organizations came a large percentage of the church leadership of the
twentieth century (Latourette 1970:Vol.4,35).

CHURCH GROWTH

Europe

In Europe in the nineteenth century, Christianity made some
gains at the expense of the few surviving cults, of Judaism,
and of Islam, but its gains were not as great as they had been
before 1800. The chief achievement of Christianity in Europe
was in holding the nominal Christians to the faith and in shap-
ing European culture. This is quite remarkable in the face of
enormous changes in the social, economic, political, and intellectual structure of that continent. It was able to perpetuate
the faith by organizing religious instruction for the young,
reaching out to special groups, providing opportunities for
worship in new centers of population, and caring for the sick,
the orphans, and the poor (Latourette 1970:Vol.4,173).

It is probable that never before had Christianity displayed
in Europe such tremendous vitality and been such a force in
modifying and molding cultures. In addition, Christianity was
spreading throughout the world, and a very large proportion of
the personnel and funds which made this possible was from Western Europe. Christianity in Europe, in spite of gigantic oppo-
sing forces, was at least retaining its influence and was probably growing in its effect (Latourette 1970:Vol.4,173-174).

United States

In no other nation did the Christian movement of the nineteenth century face an opportunity which more severely tested
it than in the United States. In 1783, the western boundary
of the United States was the Mississippi River, and the south
boundary was the northern line of Florida. By 1914, Florida
had been acquired, and the national domain had been pushed westward to the Pacific, southward to the Rio Grande, and northward
to Point Barrow. The population increased from 5 million in
1800 to 76 million in 1900 and 92 million in 1910 (Latourette
1970:Vol.4,76).

At the beginning of the period conditions did not seem favorable to the spread of Christianity. Religious life was at a
low ebb. And yet, in spite of the enormous growth in the population, in 1914, the proportion of those who were church members was larger than it had been a century earlier.

It had risen from five percent in 1790 to 15.5 percent in
1850 to 35.7 percent in 1900 and 43.4 percent in 1910 (Dorchester 1933:750). In every major group, Christianity won
ground--among the older American stock, on the frontier, among
the immigrants, among the Indians and Negroes, and in rural
areas as well as in the cities (Latourette 1970:Vol.4,177).

Through the initiative of the settlers themselves, through
uncommissioned and unsupported clergymen, and through circuit
riders, Christian churches were organized and nurtured (Latourette 1970:Vol.4,181-191). Another method by which Protestant Christianity spread on the frontier was the revival. Beginning in 1797, New England experienced what has been called
the Second Awakening. Out of it came several of the missionary
societies which were such a prominent feature of the early
nineteenth century. About the same time, revivals began on the
western frontier which were of great assistance in the spread
of Christianity in the new settlements. Camp-meetings, often
attended by thousands of people from a wide area, also played
an important role in the spread of the faith on the frontier.
As a result of these camp-meetings in the first few years of
the century, many churches in the west experienced phenomenal
growth (Latourette 1970:Vol.4,193).

Camp-meetings fell into disuse, but revivals remained a
major means for the spread of Christianity throughout the cen-
tury--on the frontier as well as in the older sections of the
country. From the 1820s until the 1850s, Charles Finney was
the best known of the preachers of revivals. In the second
half of the century, Dwight L. Moody was the most influential
of the itinerant preachers. They were not the only ones. They
were simply the most prominent of hundreds of traveling preachers (Latourette 1970:Vol.4,35).

While much of the spread of Christianity on the frontier was
chiefly by the pioneers themselves, a great deal of the expansion was through societies organized in the older states.
These societies sent missionaries and in other ways aided in
planting and nourishing the churches in the west.

In this home mission effort, the Congregational churches were
in the forefront. Through them many of the first societies were
founded, and through them many outstanding colleges were established. These colleges had a large part in undergirding the
Church of the new frontier with trained leadership (Latourette
1970:Vol.4,203).

In their efforts to win the West, Congregationalists and Presbyterians cooperated through what was known as the Plan of Union, beginning in 1801. This led later (1826) to the formation of the American Home Missionary Society, designed to be an agency for uniting Christians of several denominations in comprehensive planning and action on a nationwide scale. Missionaries sent out by this society were instrumental in founding many colleges in Illinois, Iowa, and throughout the West (Latourette 1970:Vol.4,210-212).

The Baptists were also very active on the frontier. The American Baptist Home Missionary Society sent out fifty missionaries in 1832, the first year of its existence. They also put much emphasis on education and Scripture distribution. Through its colporteurs for the distribution of literature and the organizing of Sunday Schools, it joined in the task of spreading the faith on the frontier (Latourette 1970:Vol.4,216).

Bible Societies. The first English Bible printed in America with approval of the Continental Congress was by Robert Aitken of Philadelphia in 1782. By the latter part of the century, however, English Bibles were being printed in several other cities. Production of Bibles was no longer a problem, but distribution to those who needed the Scriptures, at a price they could afford to pay, became the concern of many religious leaders. The success of the British and Foreign Bible Society in establishing auxiliaries throughout Europe encouraged the organization of the Philadelphia Bible Society in 1808. Within six years, more than one hundred Bible societies were established in the United States with the simple purpose of providing Bibles for the poor (ABS Record 1973:Aug.-Sept.,28-29).

In 1812 the Massachusetts Missionary Society, together with the Connecticut Missionary Society, sent Rev. J. M. Schermerhorn as one of its missionaries to explore the newly developing west and southwest areas of the country. He was accompanied by Mr. Samuel J. Mills who had been instrumental in the founding of the American Board of Commissioners for Foreign Missions (Gibson 1958:4).

The two men spent a full year traveling down the Ohio and Mississippi Rivers, preaching, distributing Scripture, and organizing Bible societies. Again and again the two men found districts where fifty thousand or more people were without an opportunity to hear preaching, and almost entirely without the Bible.

In 1814 the Massachusetts Missionary Society appointed Mr. Mills to make another tour over practically the same territory. From what Mills saw on these journeys, he was convinced that unity of action between the Bible societies was essential.

Through the influence of Mills and Elias Boudinot, president of the New Jersey Bible Society, the American Bible Society was founded in 1816 "...to carry the great work of Disseminating the Gospel of Jesus Christ throughout the habitable world..." (ABS Record 1973:Aug.-Sept.,28-30).

The Society began with practically no funds, but by its fifth anniversary it had distributed nearly 140,000 copies of Scripture in English, French, Spanish, Mohawk, Delaware, and several other languages spoken by immigrants to this country. Scripture portions had also been sent to Sierra Leone in West Africa, to Ceylon, Argentina, and the Sandwich Islands during those early years (Gibson 1958:40-42).

In 1829 the Society entered upon the ambitious project of attempting to supply with a Bible every family in the nation which didn't have one. While at the end of two years it reported that it had not quite reached its goal, it believed that most families in the United States had been provided with Scripture. Since the effort was one which needed to be repeated because of shifts in population, it was undertaken several times. In the fourth of these campaigns (1882-1890), colporteurs were sent to sparsely settled regions. More than six million families were visited, nearly half a million families without a Bible were supplied, and more than eight million copies of the Bible were distributed by sale or gift (Latourette 1970:Vol.4, 219).

Other Christian Literature Distribution. The American Tract Society was founded in 1825. In 1832 it adopted a plan to provide Christian literature to every religiously destitute person or family in the United States. In 1847 it had 267 colporteurs, most of them in the Mississippi Valley. The appointees of the American Home Missionary Society also used large amounts of the tract societies' literature (Latourette 1970:Vol.4,220).

Educational Institutions. These institutions of learning contributed one of the most important means for the propagation of Protestant Christianity on the frontier. Schools, especially high schools, colleges, and seminaries, were necessary if the churches were to have a trained clergy and lay leadership. Schools under Christian auspices could also be communities of earnest and vigorous Christian experience. In student bodies led by teachers with strong religious convictions, many revivals broke out. Many students went out from these campuses transformed and became the backbone of the churches (Latourette 1970: Vol.4,220).

Many colleges were begun by graduates of Yale and Princeton. Throughout the first half of the nineteenth century, each of these two institutions, one Congregational and the other Presbyterian, were visited by revivals, and from them graduates went westward to seek to reproduce the kind of education permeated by warm religious purpose which they had known as students. In 1910 the country had 403 colleges under Protestant auspices (Latourette 1970:Vol.4,221).

The Roman Catholics, who perhaps numbered only 35,000 in 1789 (Latourette 1970:Vol.4,230), grew dramatically throughout the nineteenth century. By 1910 the Roman Catholic Church claimed about 16 million members out of a total U.S. population of 92 million (Latourette 1970:Vol.4,76,255). While much of this growth was due to immigration from Europe, a considerable amount of the increase must also be attributed to their schools.

While the Protestants were putting the emphasis on high schools and higher institutions of learning, the Roman Catholics, although not neglecting higher education, concentrated on developing a vast parochial school system. By 1800, they are said to have had two hundred parish schools, half of them west of the Allegheny Mountains. By 1910, parish schools were reported to have an enrollment of more than 1,230,000 pupils under some 31,000 teachers.

Secondary schools had an enrollment of 75,000. Colleges and universities were also founded. In 1838, fifteen colleges for men were listed, and by 1921 there were 130 universities and colleges. It was this system of schools, making religious instruction an integral part of the education program, to which much of the growth and life of the Church must be ascribed (Latourette 1970:Vol.4,248-250).

Church Growth Among the Blacks. Christianity also spread rapidly among the Blacks during the nineteenth century. Among no other body of non-European people did nineteenth century Christianity make such large numerical gains. All the extensive Protestant missionary work of Europeans and Americans in Asia and Africa from 1815 to 1914 had resulted in no greater numerical gains than had been achieved among the Negroes of the United States in the same period (Latourette 1970:Vol.4,327).

In 1797 the total Negro population in the United States was about 925,000. About sixty thousand of them were members of Protestant churches and another five thousand may have been Roman Catholic. This would mean that slightly more than seven percent of the Negro population were church members in that year--almost exactly the same percentage as among the whites. By 1860, when the total Negro population was 4,441,830, the total number of Negro church members was 520,000--about 11.7 percent. In 1916, the number of Negroes who were church members was reported to be 4.6 million, about 44.2 percent of the total Negro population (Latourette 1970:Vol.4,342,356).

In the spread of Christianity among the Negroes, the chief contribution of white Christianity was in education. From these schools came much of the leadership of the Negro churches and of non-ecclesiastical movements which contributed much to the progress of the race (Latourette 1970:Vol.4,356-357).

The organization which contributed to the founding of some of the most important of the schools for Negroes was the American Missionary Association. It conducted schools from primary grade through institutions of college and university standing. It also maintained theological schools. Under its auspices a number of institutions were begun which became outstanding in the preparation of Black leaders. In 1875 the society was assisting thirty-two schools in the South with an enrollment of over seven thousand, and it estimated that former pupils in its schools were teaching over sixty-four thousand. In 1913 it was aiding sixty-five schools with an enrollment of over twelve thousand students (Latourette 1970:Vol.4,358-359).

Church Growth Among the Indians. Compared with the white westward migration of the white man, or the immigration from Europe, or with the number of Negroes in the United States, the Indian population was not great. In 1837 the Indians in the United States were officially estimated to be about 332,500 (Paxson 1924:284). In 1870 they were reported at 278,000, and in 1890 the national census declared that there were some 248,-000 Indians in the States and another 25,000 in the territory of Alaska (Department of Commerce 1910:10).

The Indians were widely scattered and often in relatively small units. Although there were some Indians in every state, in 1910 Oklahoma contained over one-fourth of them and about half of them were in just four states, namely Oklahoma, New Mexico, Arizona, and South Dakota. Even in these areas they were divided into many tribes. They represented a great variety of languages as well as tribes, and no single mission was able to reach a large number. In many tribes a mission was started and progress was made in establishing congregations and schools, only to have the work disrupted by the forcible removal of the tribe to another part of the country.

Yet, in the face of these obstacles, hundreds of Christian missionaries, both Roman Catholic and Protestant, worked among the Indians. In the course of the nineteenth century, thousands of lives and millions of dollars were devoted to bringing the Gospel to the Indians (Latourette 1970:Vol.4,301).

By 1913 there were said to be 31,815 communicant members of various Protestant churches and another 35,000 adherents. An almost identical number of Indians were reported to be Roman Catholic (Latourette 1970:Vol.4,310,322). About one-third to

one-half of the Indians were at least nominally Christian or
were under Christian influence by 1914.

Church growth among the Indians was truly amazing considering the agony through which the Indian was passing and the dis-
maying difficulties faced by the missionaries who labored among
them. Here was a race in the process of being engulfed by
peoples of an entirely different culture, dislocated from their
ancestral lands, transplanted time and again, treated harshly
by the white man, decimated by diseases and vices to which they
had built up no resistance, repeatedly seeing treaties violated,
preyed upon by greedy officials, and often demoralized by well-
intentioned but poorly directed paternalistic kindness. It is
a wonder that the Indians even survived. But they did survive,
and at least a third of them became Christians. While it is
difficult to say just how much of the growth was the result of
education, it is safe to say that schools and Scripture distribution played an important role.

It is clear that the growth of the Christian Church in the
United States during the nineteenth century--on the frontier as
well as among the immigrants, the Blacks, and the Indians--was
nothing less than phenomenal. It is all the more remarkable
when we remember that Protestant Christianity was also sending
missionaries to all the other continents and to many of the
islands of the sea. The Christianity which had been planted in
colonial days had taken root and flourished in a fashion never
surpassed and seldom equalled in the entire history of Christianity (Latourette 1970:Vol.4,222). Education and Scripture
distribution played a very significant role in this prodigious
growth.

Canada

In British North America during the nineteenth century,
Christianity enjoyed tremendous growth. By 1914, more than
95 percent of Canada's eight million inhabitants were nominal
Christians, about 37 percent Roman Catholic and 63 percent
Protestant (Latourette 1970:Vol.5,4). Much of the growth was
the result of immigration from Great Britain and the United
States and later from the European Continent. It is quite
likely, however, that education played a significant role in the
numerical and spiritual growth of the Church.

Fully as much as in the United States, schools on all levels
from the primary grades to the university level owed their origin to the churches, and much more than in the United States,
they remained under ecclesiastical auspices. As late as 1890
in most provinces the majority of the schools were under the
control of the various denominations, and religious instruction
was included in the curriculum. Even in Ontario, where the
schools were undenominational, prayer and Bible reading were

part of the daily procedure, and members of the clergy were authorized to make arrangements for the teaching of God's Word.
Many colleges were also founded by the various denominations
(Silcox 1933:96-99). Education in Canada was largely the creation of the churches and maintained a Christian emphasis (Latourette 1970:Vol.5,42).

In 1901, Indians, including half-breeds, in the Dominion of
Canada totaled 127,941 (The Canada Year Book 1912:23). Eskimos
numbered another 5,000 (Rogers 1913:125). Three-fourths to
nine-tenths of them were professedly Christian (Latourette 1970:
Vol.5,45). In the Maritime Provinces and in Quebec, nine-tenths
of the Indians were Roman Catholic. In Ontario at least seven-
eighths were Christian and of these, two-thirds were Protestant
and one-third were Roman Catholic. In the West in some areas
practically all were Christian (Latourette 1970:Vol.5,39).
This compares very favorably with the United States where in
1914 considerably less than half of the Indian population had
any formal relationship with the Church (Latourette 1970:Vol.4,
323).

Why is it that a larger percentage of the Indians in Canada
became Christians than in the United States? There could be
any number of reasons for the greater church growth in Canada.
No doubt the fact that the Indians were not so mistreated in
Canada as they had been in the United States had much to do with
it. But perhaps the kind of education that they received also
played a vital part. In the United States, the Federal Government increasingly assumed the burden of Indian schools, and the
education was predominantly secular. In Canada, however,
schools for the Indians were conducted by missionaries (Latourette 1970:Vol.5,38-39).

Greenland

Christianity was first introduced to Greenland by Scandinavian settlers in the tenth century, and it persisted until the
fifteenth century. Then it disappeared with the demise of the
Scandinavian community. The faith was reintroduced in the
eighteenth century by Hans Egede and two bodies, the Danish Lutheran State Church and the Moravians. These missions continued throughout the nineteenth century, by which time almost all
of Greenland's 14,000 inhabitants were professing Christians
(Latourette 1970:Vol.5,46-47).

Largely through the efforts of the missionaries and the
teachers trained under them, most of the Greenlanders could
read and write. Literature in the Eskimo language was prepared.
Samuel Kleinschmidt (1814-1886) devoted most of his life to literary work and, later, to training Greenlanders. Among his major achievements was a new translation of the larger part of
the Bible and the preparation of a grammar of the Eskimo

language. No doubt the Scriptures in the native tongue and the ability of the majority of the Greenlanders to read God's Word for themselves had much to do with the growth of the Church in that land.

Latin America

In colonial days (sixteenth, seventeenth, and eighteenth centuries), Latin America had been a Roman Catholic domain. Other forms of Christianity had not been allowed to enter. The Church of Rome, although dominant, had been passive and dependent upon the Crown for financial support. Its leadership was mainly from Europe. The aborigines, while nominally Roman Catholic, were grossly ignorant. The Church had little or no vitality (Latourette 1970:Vol.5,69). This should not surprise us, for during those three centuries the Bible was almost an unknown book in Latin America. The distribution of Bibles had been forbidden in the colonies, both by the King and by the Pope. The Church of Rome wanted to keep Latin Americans free from the "poison" of the Reformation (Read 1969:38).

When the Spanish and Portuguese yoke was thrown off in the early decades of the nineteenth century, and new nations began their independent careers, they continued to recognize Roman Catholicism as the state religion. But in the 1820s anticlerical opposition developed in several countries, due mostly to the power of the clergy in politics (Latourette 1970:Vol.5, 75). In the latter half of the century, the trend towards religious liberty and the separation of Church and State, so marked in the Western world, made itself strongly felt (Latourette 1970:Vol.5,76).

We hear of no Protestant mission work in Latin America until James Thomson, an agent of the British and Foreign Bible Society and of the Lancastrian Education Society, began work there in 1817 (Read 1969:39). For a brief time he had amazing success. In Buenos Aires he soon had about a hundred Lancastrian schools in operation with the Bible as a textbook. Later he went to Chile and Colombia and Mexico and was highly honored in each place. But in time the higher clergy forbade their members possession of the Bible. The Bible Society in Bogota which had been founded by Thomson was closed. But eventually the ground lost was more than regained (Latourette 1970:Vol.5,77).

In the 1840s an Englishman named Crowe circulated Bibles and Christian tracts in Guatemala and opened a Protestant school in that country, but Roman Catholic opposition brought it to an early end (Crowe 1850:528ff).

During the second half of the century, agents of the British and Foreign Bible Society were particularly active in Brazil,

Argentina, and Chile. Many stories are told of churches and
congregations established solely through the testimony of a
Bible reader who shared with others what he discovered in the
Scriptures. The Holy Spirit worked miraculously through the
printed Word to reveal the living Christ to many people.
Churches sprang up in unusual and unexpected places. Many said
that the pattern was clear: first, the Bible; then, a convert;
then, a church (Read 1969:39).

Many believe that the outstanding growth of the Church in
Brazil is the result of the long-standing emphasis on Bible
distribution and Bible teaching. A pioneer Bible colporteur in
Brazil, F. C. Glass, has this to say:

> In dozens of places where I sold the first
> copies of the Scriptures the people ever saw,
> there are strong Evangelical Churches today....
> It was almost invariably the case that the Bible
> was first in those cases where later came the
> preacher, except in those cases where the colporteur
> being also an evangelist, the Bible and the preacher
> came together. I cannot recall a single case when
> the Bible came second. Speaking from personal
> experience I should therefore say that if you want
> to open up a new area, the first thing to do is
> to send in someone with a Bible (Glass 1943:145).

It was not until the second half of the nineteenth century
that Protestant mission work even began to assume significant
proportions. By then, as we have seen, there was an increase
in religious freedom and political stability. But progress
toward real religious freedom was slow, especially in the
Spanish-speaking North and West coast of the South American
continent. By 1900, statements of religious freedom were on
the books in the various countries of South America, but real
religious liberty lagged decades behind the official pronounce-
ments. Even after 1900 Chile, Colombia, Venezuela, Ecuador,
Bolivia, Uruguay, Paraguay, and Argentina very reluctantly opened their doors to Evangelical missionaries (Read 1969:37).

Permanent Protestant mission work was not begun in Peru until
1891. Continuous evangelical work began in Ecuador in 1896 and
in Bolivia in 1898. In Colombia, permanent work began as early
as 1856 when the Presbyterians gained admission to the country,
but fifty-six years passed before the next Protestant mission,
The Gospel Missionary Union, entered that country (Kane 1971:
466).

There was no continuing Protestant work in Mexico until 1864
and none in Central America until 1882 (Kane 1971:479,487).

It was in Brazil that Protestant missionaries from the United States had the greatest success. Both the British and Foreign Bible Society and the American Bible Society were very active. Numbers of colporteurs traveled throughout the land distributing the Scriptures. Methodists and Presbyterians, Baptists and interdenominational missions entered the field.

In Brazil the Protestant missionaries and church leaders made much of education. Schools, colleges, and seminaries were founded. The most noted was Mackinzie College in Sao Paulo (Braga 1932:76-77).

In 1900, three-fourths of the population of most countries in Latin America was illiterate. Evangelical schools had been instrumental in removing prejudice against Evangelicals. Although they never educated more than a small fraction of the population, these schools were examples of the newest and finest methods of instruction. They were often used as models for new public educational programs. Missionary administrators agreed with Bishop Hendrix, who said, "The time has come to fortify, and to build colleges is to effect fortifications.... A church is no stronger than its institutions of learning" (Tilly 1901:427) (Read 1969:40).

Mission institutions of learning in South America rapidly multiplied as Protestant Churches and missions sought through education to evangelize the upper classes. Latin American leaders, anxious to see education develop, made their task easier. There was such a vacuum in the field of education that it would have been impossible, if not a grievous sin of omission, for the missionaries not to help do something about this neglect that had existed under colonial rule for more than three hundred years. Education was the crying need. And through the educational effort of the missionary enterprise, the Church grew (Read 1969:40).

Even so, there were only 11,376 communicant members of all Protestant churches in Brazil in 1900. But that was more than double the number in all of Spanish-speaking South America where the total was only 5,246. Where there had been religious freedom and continuous mission work for a long period of time, in British and Dutch Guiana, there were 14,376 communicants (Read 1969:36).

By 1916 the total number of Protestant communicants in South America had increased from just under 31,000 in 1900 to 93,337. Well over half of these, 49,623 to be exact, were to be found in Brazil. Central America had 10,442 communicants by 1916, and Mexico had another 22,282. The West Indies which was mostly British or Dutch had a total of 159,642 communicant members of Protestant churches (Read 1969:41).

In proportion to the population, nineteenth century Latin America saw less expansion of Christianity than any other area of comparable size and population except possibly Europe (which was already overwhelmingly Christian in name at the beginning of this period) and parts of the interior of Asia (Latourette 1970:Vol.5,125).

The church did grow, however, in Latin America during the nineteenth century, and Bible reading apparently contributed much toward that growth. But the nineteenth century was mainly a period of pioneering and laying foundations. After 1914, both efforts and fruit were to multiply greatly (Latourette 1970:Vol.5,125).

7

The Great Century
in Africa

At the beginning of the nineteenth century there were very few
Christians in Africa, Asia, or the South Pacific. By the end
of that period there were at least a few Christians in virtually every country of both of those continents and on almost every inhabited island of any size in the Indian Ocean as well as
in the Atlantic and the Pacific. Scriptures were translated into national and minority languages and national church leaders
were trained. Generally speaking, however, the actual number
of converts in Africa and Asia was not great. The nineteenth
century was largely a time of exploration and of laying the
ground work for Christian advance. Churches were planted,
schools were established, literature was prepared in many
tongues. But in most countries, conversions were few indeed.

As we have seen, Christianity reached Africa South of the
Sahara late in the fifteenth century. But for three hundred
years it was found only on the fringes of that Continent. The
Christianity that was introduced was mostly Roman Catholic.
With the decay of Portuguese power in the seventeenth and
eighteenth centuries, it had dwindled and in some places com-
pletly disappeared (Latourette 1970:Vol.5,320). Until the middle of the nineteenth century, Africa remained a dark and mys-
terious continent. Europeans had mapped the entire coastline
by 1850 but the mosquito had kept the white man from penetra-
ting the interior (Neill 1964:305).

In the worldwide expansion of European peoples, white men
made themselves masters of Africa and divided it among them-
selves--the British, the French, the Portuguese, and the Germans
getting the largest share. Protestant missionaries were chief-

ly from Great Britain, the major colonial power. The Roman
Catholic missionaries were mostly from France. By 1914, Roman
Catholics and Protestants had about an equal number of converts
from among the non-European peoples (Latourette 1970:Vol.5,321).

WEST AFRICA

Sierra Leone

Sierra Leone was the first Protestant mission field in tropical Africa. The first missionaries of the Church Missionary
Society arrived in 1804. Methodists began work in 1811 (Olson
1969:15).

The Church Missionary Society rendered an incomparable service to all of West Africa when it founded Fourah Bay College in
Freetown in 1827 (Neill 1964:306) and Annie Walsh School for
Girls in 1847. It is impossible to exaggerate the influence of
these two schools on the educated classes of West Africa (Kane
1971:324). Fourah Bay, throughout the nineteenth century and
after, educated the majority of those Africans who have made the
history of English-speaking West Africa (Neill 1964:306). The
first student to enroll at Fourah Bay was Samuel Adjai Crowther,
a native of Nigeria who was liberated from a slave ship and settled in Freetown along with thousands of others. He later became a pioneer missionary of the Church Missionary Society in his
homeland. He was consecrated bishop in 1864, and gave powerful
leadership to the emerging Church in Nigeria until his death
(c. 1893) (Kane 1971:342-343). He also prepared a grammar and
dictionary in the Yoruba tongue and translated part of the Scriptures into that language (Latourette 1970:Vol.5,437). Under him,
Christianity spread rapidly and he ordained a number of Africans
(Latourette 1970:Vol.5,437). We shall hear more of him later.

Despite a good start in Sierra Leone, in what was almost completely an animistic land in 1804, the expansion of Christianity
in that country and throughout much of West Africa was very slow.
In Sierra Leone, the Creole community which arose from the freed
slaves (ten thousand of them by 1814; forty thousand by 1857)
became completely Christian (Olson 1969:28,31). But only one
tribe has even begun to become Christian to any significant degree, even to this day (Olson 1969:15). The tribes remain pagan,
gradually becoming Muslim by needless default (Olson 1969:15).

The African Churches, after becoming independent of mission
control, have been sealed off in the Creole community or proved
powerless to reproduce among the tribespeople. Much effort has
gone into the multiplication of mission schools in which the
Bible is taught by Christian teachers. Small churches have
usually arisen around these schools, but have not spread to the

various ethnic groups (Olson 1969:16).

The school approach was one of the major reasons for success in Christianizing the liberated Africans because the Church Missionary Society and the Methodists worked among the whole group (Creoles), providing them with sufficient education to help them make the adjustment to the new way of life (Olson 1969:77, 81). The freed slaves were from twenty-two nations and two hundred tribes and spoke a hundred and fifty languages and many dialects. Yet, their common experience of being uprooted and transplanted made them an artificial homogeneous unit.

The school approach was not the only reason for the growth of the Church among the freed slaves. These liberated people wanted the prestige of the African Settlers who had arrived before them from Nova Scotia, Jamaica, and Britain (Olson 1969: 33).

In the 1800s, however, the tribespeople did not want Western education. They had their own. But in time they began to see that a knowledge of English was necessary if they were to live successfully in Freetown. By 1900, many tribespeople wanted their children sent to school.

In the mid-1800s, many tribespeople did not think of a school as a place of education but as an institution which took their children away from them. To them, education (and therefore Christianity) meant losing a potential farm worker. Education made a child unfit for manual labor. The child "scholar" felt that manual labor and village life and his relatives were beneath him. He became detribalized and westernized. It is no wonder that the tribespeople did not want their children to go to school or to accept Christianity (Olson 1969:34).

There were other reasons why the Church in Sierra Leone never grew much in the hinterland during the 1800s:

1) Until the middle of the century, the slave trade and wars confined the missionaries to the coastal area.

2) There were many languages, considered by the missionaries too difficult to learn. Whatever efforts were made to bring the Gospel to these people were through interpreters.

3) The missionaries thought the tribespeople too depraved to ever become Christian. They confused Western civilization with Christianity. They preached to the adults but did not expect them to respond.

4) The Settlers had no desire to win the tribal people. The natives were not looked upon as subjects for conversion but as threats to the existence of the colony.

The unhealthy conditions and the mission's policy which ex-
cluded polygamists from church membership were among other
reasons for the failure of the Church to grow among the tribespeople (Olson 1969:80).

A few educated tribesmen did win some villagers to Christ.
What little success there was among the tribes was due mainly
to these educated tribesmen. But, generally speaking, the higher their education, the more difficult it was for them to mix
socially with the villagers and evangelize them (Olson 1969:40).

Perhaps if these educated tribesmen had taught adults to
read, especially the natural leaders and the new converts,
right in their own village or on their own compound, without
disrupting their work or family life or embarrassing them in
any way, they would have won larger numbers to Christ and
strengthened them in their Christian faith. During the nineteenth century, however, most of the languages of Sierra Leone
had never even been reduced to writing (although by 1853 there
were some Scripture portions in Susu, Temne, Hausa, and Yoruba)
(Olson 1969:81).

But since little work was even attempted among tribal
peoples, especially the adults, by 1914 less than one percent
of the tribal peoples had been led to the Lord. In fact, even
in 1964 only 2.1 percent of them were Christian (Olson 1969:76).

One reason for so little church growth in the interior of
Africa, as was mentioned earlier, was the unhealthful conditions. After twenty years of mission work, only twenty-seven
out of seventy missionaries sent out by the Church Missionary
Society were still alive. This showed the Society the neces-
sity of an indigenous leadership. The first ordinations of
Creole clergy took place in 1852. Thereafter, there was a
steady supply of Creole clergy. By 1860 there were enough
clergymen to staff the entire colony (the thirteen stations
around Freetown) (Olson 1969:80).

The Church Missionary Society had high hopes of using the
Creole clergy to win the liberated Africans from two hundred
tribes of West Africa and that these converted tribespeople
would then evangelize all of Africa (Olson 1969:81).

In 1861 the Church Missionary Society began work among the
Temne in Quiah, just east of the Colony (Freetown). In 1876
this and other work among the Temnes was turned over to the
newly formed Sierra Leone Church Mission. In 1907 the Church
Missionary Society work among the Yalunka was also turned over
to the Sierra Leone Church Mission, but within five years the
Sierra Leone Church Mission withdrew. That same year, 1912,
saw the last of the Sierra Leone Church Mission efforts to evangelize the tribes (Olson 1969:82).

The Methodists also tried using Creoles for evangelizing the tribes of Sierra Leone, but they, too, became disillusioned. They plunged ahead with the evangelization of the Mende, but without using Creole helpers (Olson 1969:106).

Why did the Creole Church fail? Because they were second and third generation Christians, taught to recite parrot-like the Lord's Prayer, the Creed, the Ten Commandments, etc. For most of the Creoles, reading passages from the Bible or saying set prayers in English involves a continuous mental effort in translating English into Krio, his mother tongue. Is it any wonder, then, that many Creoles follow the line of least resistance, and that the teachings of Christianity become an artificial part of their daily lives (Olson 1969:107).

This spiritual vacuum has to be filled with something, and is with the charms and jujus of the "medicine man", and the Creole no longer enjoys spiritual peace of mind or has any spiritual power (Olson 1969:108).

The Creoles, however, are not wholly responsible for their failure to evangelize the tribes. A good share of the blame lies with the policy of the Church Missionary Society.

In 1854, Henry Venn, secretary of the Church Missionary Society in London, had spoken of the euthanasia of a mission, once a church had become self-supporting, self-governing, and self-propagating. This sharp separation between church and mission implied in Venn's policy seems to lack theological foundation. And, as we have read, the first attempt to carry out this policy proved almost wholly disastrous (Neill 1964:260). The establishment of the "Native Pastorate" in Sierra Leone in 1860, with the complete withdrawal of the missionaries from any participation whatsoever in the affairs of the pastorate, inflicted a paralysis upon the Church from which it has never fully recovered (Neill 1964:260).

When the missionaries saw that the Creoles were not succeeding in planting indigenous churches among the tribal peoples, they should have come to their assistance instead of just ignoring them as they did. But perhaps the missionaries felt that they themselves could do no better. And maybe they were right. Maybe they, too, would have failed to produce strong indigenous churches, for in those days, all too often, the missionaries and church leaders confused Christianity with civilization and westernization.

What should the Church Missionary Society have done? Should they have (1) re-established mission work in the interior and forgot the Sierra Leone Church, (2) re-entered, working through

the Creole Church, or (3) left the evangelization of Sierra
Leone to other mission bodies?

Raymond Foster (1961:48-52) advocates the second solution.
He suggests that missionaries from the Anglican communion of
other countries come and help, thus overcoming suspicions of
Great Britain as the former colonial power.

What, you may be asking, has all this to do with literacy
or Bible reading?

In the first place, the Creoles should have been given the
Scriptures in Krio, their mother tongue. In the second place,
literacy is not enough. Before the Creoles were asked to plant
churches among the tribespeople, they should have been taught
cultural anthropology and principles of church growth, and they
should have been instructed in how to reduce a language to writing, how to translate the Scriptures, and how to do effective
literacy work and train the ministry, etc. But, of course, the
science of descriptive linguistics was not so well developed in
those days, and much has been learned in recent years about
church growth and training the ministry by extension. Even so,
the Sierra Leone Church, or any other Creole Church, wishing to
begin missionary work among tribal people, could do a reasonably
good job if the missionaries whom they send were willing to become tribal in their outlook and plant churches without Creole
domination or orientation. In a situation like this, the
Creole is just as much a foreigner as the European missionary,
and his mission is just as cross-cultural (Olson 1969:112).

Before moving on to Liberia, perhaps another word would be in
place concerning the school approach.

Initial growth may be obtained by almost any Mission which
opens schools, hires teachers, and baptizes school children and
other converts. But it is usually a kind of hothouse growth and
does not continue. This approach seals off the general populace.
Nevertheless, a mission may use the school approach and avoid
stagnation by simply using the schools as springboards for vigorous itineration with the purpose of winning families and larger social units to Christ (Olson 1969:196).

Although the Church was planted in all the coastal countries
of West Africa during the nineteenth century, only a very small
percentage of the people became Christian. As late as 1965 only
1.3 percent of Guinea was Christian; Liberia, 12.6 percent; and
Ivory Coast 13 percent. (Wold 1968:14).

Liberia

In 1820 freed slaves from the United States arrived in what is now Liberia, near the present capital, Monrovia. They were Christians and believed themselves called to carry Christianity to Africa (Wold 1968:19). Between 1820 and 1840 some 4,450 Negroes were sent to Liberia by colonization societies, but nearly 2,200 (almost half) of them died, mainly from malaria, dysentery and yellow fever (Wold 1968:20).

From the very beginning the indigenous tribes were hostile and made frequent raids on the freed slaves. If the tribes had not been at war with each other and had united against the colony, it is very doubtful whether the colony could have survived. Vestiges of this hostility still remain today. No doubt this tension is one reason for the slow development of the Churches among the tribes of Liberia.

From the very beginning, Churches recognized the unique opportunity for Protestant missions in Liberia. In 1820 the Baptist Church, Methodist Church, and the Protestant Episcopal Missionary Society were organized on board the ship which carried the first settlers. Many of the settlers were ordained ministers. Mission activity was not only possible in Liberia, but expected and encouraged (Wold 1968:53).

The colonists thought of Liberia as a beachhead for Christianity from which the Gospel could spread to the interior of the continent.

The early missionaries planned also to take the Gospel to the tribes (Wold 1968:54). But the Churches did not follow through. The Baptist, Methodist, Episcopalian, and Presbyterian missionaries all spent their time in the coastal settlements with the colonists (Wold 1968:54). They intended to use the colonists as a stepping stone to the tribes, but they never got beyond the stepping stone.

Liberia, which became an independent nation in 1847, did not actually rule the tribes until after World War I. Travel beyond the limits of the settlements in the early days was éxtremely risky, and living in the interior was out of the question because of the hostility of the natives. A more subtle barrier was the identification of Christianity with civilization. To become a Christian the tribesman had to learn to speak and read English, and this meant going to the foreigners' school. Unfortunately, several denominations have made literacy a requirement for baptism (Wold 1968:57). It was bad enough to make literacy a prerequisite for baptism if this meant literacy in the mother tongue. But since few of the tribal languages were written down in the nineteenth century, this usually meant that the native tribespeople were expected to become literate in English before they could be baptized (Wold 1968:57).

Efforts of the missionaries to learn the tribal languages were sporadic and meager.

In fairness to the early missionaries, it must be said that there was plenty of work to be done among the settlers, as it is estimated that only fourteen to twenty percent of them were Christians when they got off the boats. Most of the settlers, therefore, did not bear faithful witness to their Lord. Settlers who were thought by the tribespeople to be Christians were guilty of all kinds of immorality. Why should anyone want to accept the god of these settlers? (Wold 1968:57-59).

One church--the Episcopal--was successful among the tribal peoples. Some of their early missionaries took the language seriously enough so that by 1839 a Grebo dictionary had been produced, and by 1843 the Gospels of Matthew and Mark had been translated. The mission had strong, continuous leadership in the person of Reverend John, who could speak Grebo and translated portions of the Bible into it. He was followed by another well-trained leader, Samuel David Ferguson, who was consecrated bishop in 1885. During the first ten years of his episcopacy, the Church grew from 419 communicants and thirty preaching stations to 1237 communicants in sixty-three preaching places, not including thirty-five centers across the Cavala River which had been lost to the French (Wold 1968:85).

One of Ferguson's outstanding achievements was the establishment of Cuttington College at Cape Palmas for the training of ministers.

The Lutherans began work in Liberia in 1860, using the school approach. Because of this approach and their small staff in the early years, after sixty years in the country the Church had a baptized membership of only 192, less than ten percent of the total number of students who had gone through the Lutheran schools. Here, as we have read also in Sierra Leone, is evidence that educating the children and neglecting to evangelize the adults will not result in significant church growth. The villagers who had never been to school nor worked for the mission did not even consider Christianity as an option for themselves (Wold 1968:102).

The Prophet Harris. Toward the end of this period, in 1913, one of the most amazing examples of church growth by a people movement in all of Africa took place. It occurred among the peoples of the Ivory Coast and Ghana, all of whom were illiterate, but the man used of God to father this people movement was himself literate and was in possession of some Scripture in his mother tongue, which he was able to read.

William Wade Harris was born of Grebo parents near Cape Palmas, not far from the Ivory Coast border. He attended mission schools and read books which Bishop Auer had translated into Grebo. He also taught in Protestant Episcopal schools for seventeen years, from 1892 to 1909.

In 1913, when he was probably in his sixties, he crossed the Cavala River into the Ivory Coast, carrying a well-worn Bible and a long bamboo staff with a short piece tied across it to form a cross.

Harris had no earthly authority but believed that God had sent him forth. He spoke in pidgin English, which had to be interpreted. His message was simple and direct: "Repent and be baptized!" He proclaimed that there is one God and Savior and that all fetishes and idols are useless and must be destroyed. Converts were to observe Sunday, renounce alcohol, stealing, and adultery. He appealed to them to accept Jesus as their Savior, and he baptized believers right then and there. They were to build churches and wait for white missionaries who would teach them how to obey God's Book. More than 100,000 persons turned from paganism. Little bamboo and thatched churches sprang up in scores of villages where Harris had preached.

In 1914, Harris crossed the border into the Gold Coast (Ghana) and continued his preaching in an area called Appolonia. In fifty-two villages fetishes were burned. About ten thousand Appolonians turned to God. At Harris' suggestion, they asked the Methodists in Axim to send them teachers. Thus in 1914 a Methodist Church was established in Appolonia. After preaching in the Goald Coast for about three months, Harris returned to the Ivory Coast (Southon 1935:47).

In 1915, with World War I raging in Europe, the French Government, fearing any unrest that might lead to an uprising, decided to deport Harris. He was peacefully escorted to the border, some 250 miles from Abidjan, where he had been preaching, and warned not to return to French soil (Johnson and Johnson 1964:16).

Twelve years later, when three English Wesleyan missionaries finally arrived, they found whole groups of villages where fetishism was dead. Their fetishes had been completely swept away and replaced by the Bible, and people were waiting for those who would come and interpret it.

These missionaries gathered more than 45,000 into the churches from the people movement started by Harris (Latourette 1970: Vol.7,222).

One cannot help but wonder what happened to the other 55,000 that had once decided to follow Christ, and how many more might have been won to Christ and remained faithful if they had been given the Scriptures in their own tongue and taught to read, or even if they just had teachers who were able to read God's Word to them regularly.

Nigeria

There is some evidence in ancient art forms that Christianity was known in Nigeria many centuries ago. Historians speculate that Nigeria was originally settled by immigrants from the Mediterranean area who brought Christianity with them. But in time this Christianity completely died out. Why? Again, we can only speculate, but it seems safe to assume that one major reason could be that these immigrants had no Scriptures in their mother tongues.

The first attempt to bring Christianity to Nigeria in modern times was in 1487 when Portuguese missionaries introduced the faith in Benin City and in an area now called Old Warri. They are said to have had three churches in Benin City. The work, however, was short-lived and the converts lapsed into paganism. There may be many reasons for this failure to plant an enduring church. One obvious reason is that the people were never given any Scriptures in their own language (Robinson 1966:269).

As far as we know, Christianity was not introduced to Nigeria again until 1837. From that year until 1842 more than five hundred freed slaves had been returned to Nigeria from Sierra Leone. Many of these were Anglican Christians, and some of them had attended Christian schools (Robinson 1966:37,271). They entered Yoruba country (Southwestern Nigeria) from which they had been taken as slaves. Soon they began to call for pastoral help and, in response to this appeal, the Church Missionary Society sent Henry Townsend and Samuel Crowther to them. When they arrived they found that Thomas Freeman, a Wesleyan Methodist missionary, had preceded them by three months. Both societies soon established churches in the Abeokuta area (Robinson 1966:37). Crowther later (1862) was consecrated bishop and served the church well until his death (c. 1891). The school was his chief method of evangelism (Robinson 1966:276). While emphasizing academic training, however, he depended mostly on middle-aged men barely literate in English and the vernacular--farmers, carpenters, mechanics, masons, etc.--recommended by the Niger Mission Committee as men of proven Christian character, because they commanded more respect with chiefs than the younger, inexperienced, college-trained men. Earlier in this chapter we mentioned the fact that Crowther also prepared a grammar and dictionagy in the Yoruba tongue and translated portions of Scripture into that language (Latourette 1970:Vol.5,437).

The United Presbyterian Church of Scotland was not far behind
the CMS and the Methodists in establishing work in Nigeria. A
former missionary to Jamaica, Hope Wadell, along with several
others, began work in the eastern part of the country in the
Calabar area in 1847. They were later joined by Mary Slessor
who labored in that country for forty years, from 1875 to 1915.
Mary, like Samuel Crowther and so many other pioneer missionaries, made much of schools. She is declared to have said,
"Schools and teachers go with the Gospel. You can't have one
without the other" (Miller 1946:134).

Pinnock wrote in 1917 regarding the direct results from
school work.

> ...Mohammedans and pagans bring their children
> to the missionaries to be educated under Christian
> influence. A notorious medicine man at Ilora, who
> was beyond all hope of conversion to Christianity,
> brought four sons to the native preacher and expressed
> the wish that they might become Christians. His wish
> was granted, for all became followers of Jesus, and
> two of them, James Aloba and David Tade, are today
> students in the seminary at Saki (1917:161).

Education for the youth was provided entirely by mission
societies up to 1899 (Robinson 1966:319). Since the government
was not providing any education for the Nigerians, it would seem
to be a duty of the Church to help these people in this way,
just as much as helping them with their medical and other physical needs. And, of course, the schools were a tremendous door-
opener for the Gospel, and through education the Africans were
able to read the Scriptures for themselves and draw closer to
the Lord. But the Church, in many cases, if not most, spent too
much time, effort, and money on schools and too little effort in
evangelizing the adult population and providing basic education
for them.

There were many very great hindrances to the advance of the
Gospel in Nigeria as there was in all of West Africa'and, indeed
throughout almost the entire continent--hindrances such as slavery and slave traffic, intertribal wars and distrust, difficult
and perilous travel, mission policy regarding polygamy, unhealthful living conditions, and language barriers to mention but a
few (Robinson 1966:277-281). There are more than five hundred
languages and dialects in Nigeria (Grimes 1974:149). None of
these languages had been written down before the white man came,
and very few of them had been reduced to writing before the end
of the nineteenth century (Nida 1972). Because of these and

other obstacles, the total communicant membership of all Protestant denominations in Nigeria by 1900 was a little under six
thousand (Robinson 1966:318). Ninety percent of these Christians were in the southern part of the country (Robinson 1966:
317).

From its beginning in 1842, the Anglican Church has been
ahead of all other denominations in communicant membership in
Nigeria. There are several reasons for this, not the least of
which is the fact that large portions of Scripture were translated from the very beginning of mission work into Yoruba, Ibo,
and other languages. The Church liturgy was also translated,
memorized, and used. Schools were started for the purpose of
teaching the people to read the Bible and other Christian literature. By 1854 the CMS had already produced three thousand literates and imported a printing press to provide them with literature (Robinson 1966:329).

Beginning near the end of the nineteenth century many divisions occurred affecting the growth of all the Churches. Most
of these divisions began within established Churches because
members resented foreign dominance.

Most of these movements are strongly based on literal, yet
uncritical, interpretations of the Bible. The Bible is thus the
point of contact with these movements. Emphasis on Bible teaching and Bible-centeredness in all Churches is the only bond of
Christian unity and is essential to effective evangelism. Broad-
er Bible knowledge leads to better Bible understanding and interpretation. Individual Christians are going to make interpretations of Bible verses, so the better they know the Bible, the
more likely they are to make the correct interpretations. The
only adequate defense against syncretism in these movements is
through Bible study. Traditional Churches can help independent
Churches grow in spiritual understanding and Biblical truth by
offering a thorough Bible-based training program for these
pastors and teachers. These independent Church leaders are open
to help from traditional Churches and, of course, long for rec-
ognition (Robinson 1966:314).

Christianity was introduced to several other countries in
West Africa during the nineteenth century: The Gambia (1821),
Ghana (1828), Cameroun (1842), Togo (1847), and Senegal (1862).
But it is far beyond the scope of this present work to trace the
history of church growth in all of these countries. Suffice it
to say that the conditions under which the missionaries labored
and the results of their efforts were similar to what we have
found in the other countries of West Africa, of which we have
written (Kane 1971:319-348).

SOUTH AFRICA

In 1652 the Dutch East India Company established at the site of Cape Town a "refreshment" station for growing food for its seamen en route to Asia and the East Indies. When the British seized the Cape in 1795, the population numbered twenty-one thousand whites, all of whom were professedly Christian (Latourette 1970:Vol.5,322). The majority of them were members of the Dutch Reformed Church. "There was also a population of slaves, and several hundred of them had been baptized. In the eighteenth century a few converts were made by the Moravian, George Schmidt, among the Hottentots" (Du Plessis 1911:50ff.).

From the time of the British occupation in 1795, British Christians played a leading role in mission work in South Africa. The pioneer society was the London Missionary Society which was founded in the same year that the British occupied the Cape. Their first missionary arrived in Cape Town in 1799.

One of the most famous of LMS missionaries was Robert Moffat (1795-1883) who arrived in South Africa in 1817. In 1820 he settled among the Bechuana at Kuruman and worked among them for forty-eight years. At first, little progress was made, but as soon as he mastered the Tswana language, the attitude of the people toward him completely changed, the seed of the Gospel took root, something like a revival broke out, and the first baptisms took place (Neill 1964:313). Later he analyzed the Tswana language and translated the entire Bible into it, completing the task by 1859. This was quite a feat inasmuch as Moffat had no linguistic training (Neill 1964:313).

More distinguished than Moffat was another LMS missionary, David Livingstone, who arrived in Cape Town in 1840. He won few converts and planted no churches, but through his explorations he perhaps did more than anyone else to open the Continent to the advancement of the Gospel. Moreover, many of the missions which came to Central Africa owed their origin to Livingstone's appeal or to his example (Latourette 1970:Vol.5,349).

Many other missions followed the LMS. The Methodists arrived in 1816 and became the largest group to work among the Bantus. The Presbyterians came two years later, followed by the Paris Evangelical Missionary Society in 1829, the Anglicans in the 1830s, and many others.

By 1911, out of 4,697,152 persons of non-European descent, 1,438,075 were Protestants and 37,212 were Roman Catholic. There were also 69,080 Christians in Basutoland (out of a population of about 402,000). Most of this growth took place after 1860 (Latourette 1970:Vol.5,375-376).

By 1914, about forty percent of all the black and colored Christians and more than half of all the Christians, black and white, south of the Sahara, were in South Africa (Latourette 1970:Vol.5,338).

Among the Blacks, Protestants outnumbered Roman Catholics about two to one in 1914 (Latourette 1970:Vol.5,335).

The rapid progress of Christianity in South Africa was due partly to a concentration of missionary activity in that part of the continent, partly due to white settlement, and partly due to the fact that disintegration of tribal life and old customs had proceeded further than anywhere else. With this disintegration went the tendency to conform to the dominant culture, including Christianity (Latourette 1970:Vol.5,338).

But no doubt much of the growth must be attributed to the large numbers of schools which everywhere were instruments for propagating the faith, to Bible translations, and to the preparation of other Christian literature as a means of spreading Christianity and edifying the believers (Latourette 1970:Vol.5, 375).

The entire New Testament was published in Tswana:Tlapi by 1840, Xhosa by 1846, Sotho by 1855, Zulu by 1865, and in Tsonga and Tswana:Rolong by 1894. These are the major tribal languages of what is now South Africa, Lesotho, Swaziland, and Botswana (Nida 1972:401,436,437,458,469).

A look at the record of Rhodesia gives striking evidence of the energy and rapidity with which Christian agencies penetrated that part of Africa between 1870 and 1914. Beginning in the 1870s, society after society, mostly Protestant, entered, reduced languages to writing, began the preparation of other Christian literature, multiplied schools, and planted churches. We do not have the statistics for 1900 or 1914, but according to the census of 1921, there were 65,000 Protestants and 76,000 Roman Catholics in Rhodesia at that time (Latourette 1970:Vol.5, 390).

To the east of Northern Rhodesia (now Zambia) is Malawi (formerly Nyasaland), one of the more Christian countries in Africa today. About thirty percent of the population profess the faith. Church growth was slow until 1891 when the British began to rule over that country. The coming of order, British prestige, and the faithful work of missionaries combined to produce several people movements to Christ. Schools and churches were multiplied. In 1914, there were 900 schools, 1,618 teachers and 57,000 students. Ten languages were reduced to writing, and a large amount of literature was printed in them. Native Christians carried the faith to neighboring regions and tribes (Latourette 1970:Vol.5,394).

EAST AFRICA

Uganda

In the last third of a century before 1914, there was amazing growth of the Christian Church in Uganda, especially following 1894 with the establishment of British rule and the internal peace which followed. A mass movement to Christianity
began at that time.

When Bishop Alfred Tucker (CMS) arrived in Uganda in 1890,
his flock of baptized believers totaled only about two hundred.
By 1908 it was nearly sixty-three thousand (Latourette 1970:Vol.
5,416). How can we account for such rapid growth. Certainly
it was not just a matter of British rule or the oral proclamation of the Word. The Bible was translated into the vernacular.
An educational system was developed. There were schools for
girls as well as boys. A beginning was made in secondary education. A native staff was trained, composed of teachers, evangelists, and clergy. Hundreds of places of worship were built.
The Baganda people proved eager missionaries, introducing the
faith to neighboring tribes. Within less than a generation,
Protestant Christianity through the Church Missionary Society
had made amazing headway. In 1914 there were more than ninety-
eight thousand baptized Christians in Uganda (Latourette 1970:
Vol.5,416-417). Today more than fifty percent of the people of
Uganda profess Christianity (Kane 1971:384).

Madagascar

One of the greatest illustrations of the power of the written
Word of God comes from Madagascar (now the Malagasy Republic),
about 250 miles east of Mozambique. The London Missionary Society began work on this nine hundred mile long island in the
year 1818. By 1828 the first group of twenty-eight converts was
baptized. In that same year the Gospel of Luke was published,
and by 1830 the entire New Testament appeared in the Malagasy
language. The Old Testament was completed in 1836 (Nida 1972:
269). Everything went well under King Radama, but he died in
1828. He was succeeded by one of his wives, Ranavalona. During
the first few years of her reign, restrictions were made on the
propagation of the Gospel, but not sufficiently to prevent active efforts by missionaries or the acceptance of the faith by
some of the Malagasy. Two churches were formed of the Malagasy
converts, and, as we have read, work continued on the translation of Scripture until 1835 when the entire Bible was completed.
In that very year, however, the queen issued an edict prohibit-
ing Christianity. The Malagasy Scriptures were secretly distributed and hidden before the missionaries were forced to leave
the island in 1836 (Nida 1972:269). Then a bitter persecution

of the Christians began. Scores were killed and thousands were fined, flogged, deprived of their official rank, or sold into slavery. But the Malagasy Christians continued to meet in secret and read the Bible and other Christian books, transcribing them by hand when printed copies ran short (Latourette 1970:Vol. 5,304). Finally, when the queen died in 1861, after twenty-six years of persecution, it was found that there were four times as many Christians as there had been a quarter of a century earlier when the persecution began. The major reason was undoubtedly the possession of the New Testament in Malagasy, on which the Christians had secretly fed their souls (Neill 1964: 319).

8

The Great Century
in Asia

The Great Century also saw the advance of the Gospel into almost
every country of Asia. It is impossible to trace the expansion
of Christianity in every land and to observe the relationship of
Bible reading to the growth of the church. We will, however,
look for that relationship in several countries of the Far East,
especially in India, China, Korea and Japan.

INDIA

In the year 1914 the Christians in India numbered about three
and a half million. About sixty-five percent of them were Roman
Catholics, ten percent were members of the independent Syrian
churches, and about twenty-five percent were Protestants. The
Roman Catholics had quadrupled their membership in a century.
Proportionately the progress of the Protestants had been much
more rapid; since beginning with almost nothing in 1814, they
multiplied themselves eight times over, in the years between
1858 and 1914 (Neill 1970:111-112).

The first British society organized especially for foreign
missionary work, as we have seen, was the Baptist Missionary
Society, and its first and most illustrious missionary was William Carey (1761-1834). He had received his inspiration largely
from the writings of David Brainerd (Mathews 1952:114) and from
the *Voyages* of Captain Cook (Sinker 1953:18).

Carey arrived in India in 1793 and was joined six years later
by Joshua Marshman, a teacher, and William Ward, a printer. Together they were known as the "Serampore Trio".

Carey is best remembered for his role as translator. In a
period of thirty years, six translations of the entire Bible
were completed, Carey himself being responsible for Bengali,
Sanskrit, and Marathi. To these were added twenty-three complete New Testaments as well as Bible portions in ten other
languages. Some of the "languages", however, were no more than
dialects which are no longer spoken. And even though Carey revised the Bengali New Testament eight times, it was unable to
hold its own, and has been replaced by other versions (Neill
1964:263-264).

Other translators were also at work in India. The most notable among them was Henry Martyn, who, like Carey, had received
much of his inspiration from the diary of David Brainerd (Mathews 1952:114). Martyn arrived in Calcutta in 1806 and died in
Persia on his way home to England in 1813 at the age of thirty-
one. In just seven years he had completed the New Testament in
Urdu, a version which still is the basis of that which is in use
today. He had also completed a revision of the Persian Bible
and was well underway on the revision of the Arabic (Neill 1964:
266-267).

In 1813 the English parliament forced the East India Company
to open its territory to mission work. This resulted in many
English missions entering the sub-continent. The Church Missionary Society began work in Madras in 1814. Charles Rhenius,
their first missionary, introduced the teacher-catechist system.
The church was built around the school in each village, and the
school master was also the catechist, responsible to conduct the
Sunday worship services.

While these catechists were not highly educated men, they
grew in knowledge and in Christian character, and in time became
pillars of a great Christian movement. At the time of his death
in 1838 there were Christian groups in nearly three hundred villages over an area of about two thousand square miles (Neill
1970:70). Today there are Christian churches in seven hundred
villages in the Tirunelveli Diocese, thanks largely to the system worked out by Rhenius (Neill 1970:70).

A new period in the history of Indian missions began in 1830
with the arrival of Alexander Duff (1806-1878). It was Duff's
conviction that the time had come to present the Gospel to the
cultured sections of the community through higher education in
English (Neill 1964:274).

He started a school which opened with just five boys, but it
grew to nearly two hundred. Duff's aims were evangelistic as
well as educational. When four young men from one of the higher
castes were baptized, there was a great uproar. The work was

seriously threatened for a time, but gradually it regained the confidence of the public, and the school increased in strength. Duff didn't have many converts. We know of only thirty-three over a period of years. But all of them were of sterling quality, and their descendants became some of the most outstanding Christians in India. Many of them became ordained ministers (Neill 1964:275).

Meanwhile, a constant stream of Scriptures was being issued in many languages (Sinker 1953:30). In 1843, for example, Dr. Herlein of the British and Foreign Bible Society toured all over Bengal and the Ganges country distributing sixty thousand Scripture portions. An average of forty thousand copies of Scripture was distributed annually for the next several years. There were versions for hill tribes and special editions of Testaments for educated Indian students. Missionary journeys were made through villages and jungles and also by boat up the rivers where crowds thronged in order to get a copy of the Sacred Word (Sinker 1953:32).

But then a tragedy occurred which might have easily wiped out the influence of the Scriptures for many years. That it did not do so is due to the spiritual power of the Bible itself. In 1857 the Indian army mutinied, and the sedition spread over a large area. In the looting and destruction that followed, huge supplies of Scriptures were burned or scattered. Books and leaflets were spread far and wide by looters. Some books were found and read by villagers who later asked for a catechist and built themselves a church. In one regiment that fought at the Siege of Delhi, several men were converted by reading some Scriptures they had found in the streets of Delhi (Sinker 1953:33).

After the mutiny, the British Government realized more than ever its responsibility toward the people. The churches became alive to the need for evangelization. There was a demand for the Bible everywhere. By this time Books of the Bible were appearing in the languages of the North in Pashto, Kashmiri, and Tibetan. From a chain of hospitals on the Northwest Frontier, Scripture portions were carried great distances to towns and villages where no Christian could go, but where the Word of God could speak for itself (Sinker 1953:36).

All over India, Books of the Bible were being read. Between 1854 and 1884 the Madras Auxiliary alone circulated over 2.4 million copies of Testaments and Gospels, and all the other auxiliaries combined circulated another two and a quarter million copies. These were in fifteen different languages. A system of colporteurs were ceaselessly on the move in South India, traveling sixty-five thousand miles a year, visiting a thousand towns and villages. As a result there was a steady growth of the

Christian Church throughout the country, along with a desire for
education and a better way of life (Sinker 1953:36-37).

People who read the Bible are changed by the Bible. Between
1858 and 1888 several great persons were born in India whose
lives were changed by reading the Scriptures, and they proceeded
to revolutionize the world in which they lived. One of the most
famous of these was a woman.

Ramabai was a Brahmin, a woman of the highest caste and of
great intelligence. Her father recognized her brilliant mind,
and taught her, as a child, the holy books in Sanskrit which
should not be taught to a woman. For this, he was driven into
the jungle by the edict of some four hundred Hindu priests and
scholars. The family traveled all over India in search of puri-
fication and knowledge. Her parents and her sister starved to
death during a great famine, and Ramabai and her brother made
their way to Calcutta. There she became well known for her unusual gifts. Her powerful exposition of the Hindu Scriptures
compelled Hindu scholars to call her Pandita, or Mistress of
Learning.

Ramabai yearned to help Hindu women who had none of the advantages that she had. She saw the heartbreaking conditions of
their lives, their slavery to men, and the abuses of child marriage and widowhood.

She started a campaign for a higher marriage age and for the
education of women. No one had ever advocated this before, except for a few missionaries. She searched the Hindu Scriptures
in vain for inspiration for this kind of reform. Then she began
to read the Bible, and her search was ended.

She became a Christian, and with the help of friends in England and America, founded a home for widows. It grew into a
garden city for hundreds of needy women and children and included schools, dispensaries, gardens, fields, and industries, where
Christian love was radiated and the Bible was read at family
prayers. She spent the last years of her life translating the
Bible into simple Marathi for the women she knew so well (Sinker
1953:39).

Mass Movements

According to Sherwood Eddy, the various mass movements of the
nineteenth century accounted for eighty percent of the Christians in India (Kane 1971:122). Involved in these mass movements to Christ were hundreds of thousands of Hindu outcasts who
had been denied access to Hindu temples and village wells. Consequently, they had nothing to lose and possibly something to

gain by accepting Christianity (Kane 1971:122). Almost all of
the people who were brought into the church through mass movements were illiterate except in Andhra Pradesch where some of
the higher caste Hindus also came forward after the movement was
well underway (Williams 1975:253).

There were many mass movements throughout the century beginning between 1795 and 1805 when more than five thousand converts were baptized by Christian Schwartz and others in the extreme South. Later, through Charles Rhenius of the Church Missionary Society, about eleven thousand people were added from
the upper class. At least two other mass movements occurred in
the same area under the ministries of the Society for the Propagation of the Gospel and the London Missionary Society.

There were several other mass movements in Telugu country
(now known as Andhra Pradesh). Lutherans saw large mass movements in the coastal area; Anglicans, British Methodists, and
Methodist Episcopals in Hyderabad; and Canadian Baptists and the
London Missionary Society in Northeastern Andhra (Williams)
1975:253).

There were several other large people movements to Christ in
the north hill country among the Oraons, the Mundas, the Hos,
and the Santals, and still others in Central India and in the
Punjab in the northwestern part of the country (Williams 1975:
254).

Perhaps the largest mass movement was one which started in
1859 among the Chamars in Delhi and spread through Uttar Pradesh,
bringing a hundred thousand converts into the Church (Williams
1975:254).

Another mass movement occurred in Northeast India among the
Khasis. After the movement was well underway, the Bible was
translated into the Khasi language, and the movement to Christ
spread throughout the area. Life was transformed and large
churches were established. Today forty-seven percent of the
tribe is Christian. Mass movements also occurred among the many
other hill tribes including the Mizos, the Nagas, the Garos, the
Abors, and the Minis. Some of these had been head hunters (Williams 1975:255).

Most of these mass movements have taken place among the out-
castes, lower castes or tribal peoples following serious economic conditions or famines or oppression from the higher castes.
But it is not correct to say that material or economic gain was
the motive that led people to seek membership in the church in
these movements. Spiritual motives did play a part (Williams
1975:255).

It must be admitted that mass movements have brought some disadvantages to the Church in India. Because of an inadequate training, nominalism has become a major problem. Pagan practices and customs still remained in the lives of large numbers of church members, due mainly to lack of thorough teaching of the Word of God (Williams 1975:258).

For this reason, most of India's Church leaders and many missionaries took a dim view of mass movements. Through much effort, the Indian Christian Church had been raised to a high level of literacy and social acceptance. If it were flooded with thousands of depraved and illiterate people, all that had been accomplished would be undone, and Christianity would be associated to its detriment only with the poorest and least acceptable classes of society.

But Henry Whitehead, bishop of Madras (1899-1923) was convinced that these movements were valid manifestations of the working of the Holy Spirit, and that, although a consecrated Christian life could not be expected of every convert from the beginning, a door was open through which the Church must enter at all costs. He believed, with good reason, that if enough Christian workers could be supplied, thirty million people of the depressed classes could become Christians within a century (Williams 1975:258).

Bishop J. Wascom Pickett says,"To object to mass movements is to place obstacles in the path along which an overwhelming proportion of Indian Christians, including more than eighty percent of those affiliated with Protestant Churches, have come to profess faith in Christ Jesus" (Williams 1975:258).

We agree with Pickett that mass movements have been successful and that much larger success is possible through: (1) ministering to both spiritual and physical needs from the very beginning of the movement, (2) making provision for better Christian leadership, (3) provision of a more adequate program, (4) re-allocation of missionary resources, and (5) interchurch and intermission adjustments to consolidate the effort and avoid any duplication of effort (1933:331-347).

We would especially emphasize the provision of Christian leadership. Trained leaders must be accessible all the time in sufficient numbers--leaders who know the Truth and how to impart it. They must be in thorough sympathy with those whom they serve and willing to identify themselves with them. They must be men who know God and worship Him in Spirit and in Truth. These leaders must come from within the group as soon as possible.

Men and women of the highest educational qualifications should be recruited from the mass movement groups who can live closely with the people they serve. There must be an adequate number of ministers, including pastors, catechists, evangelists, and school teachers. Since the converts themselves are so desperately poor, funds from abroad should be used to provide this leadership until such time that the converts can provide for themselves. The strong ought to bear the burdens of the weak (Romans 15:1).

The hope of establishing a church that is strong enough to assume all responsibility for the support of preachers depends upon strengthening the present staff so that (1) the present Christian groups will be securely grounded in the faith and their economic resources increased and/or (2) other groups will be converted. Wherever an adequate ministry was provided, both these possibilities were realized.

For a more complete treatment of this subject we refer you to J. Waskom Pickett's valuable book, *Christian Mass Movements in India* (1933:331-348).

CHINA

At the beginning of the nineteenth century there were probably between two hundred thousand and two hundred fifty thousand Christians in China, mostly Roman Catholic, but also a small number of Russian Orthodox (Latourette 1970:Vol.6,255). The Roman Catholic Church, however, was on the decline, and there were only a few European priests and bishops scattered throughout the empire. In 1810 there were just thirty-one (Latourette 1970:Vol.6,257).

There was no Protestant mission work in China at all until Robert Morrison arrived in Canton in 1807 and began translating the Scriptures under extremely dangerous and difficult circumstances. To discourage translation of the Scriptures, the Chinese government forbade, under pain of death, the teaching of Chinese to a foreigner. Morrison's teacher always carried poison, and was ready to commit suicide if he should be detected. In spite of the danger, Morrison worked steadily at the task and completed the New Testament by 1814 and the entire Bible by 1823 (Nida 1972:71-72). For nearly thirty years, Morrison's translation served as the basis for other and better versions (Hudspeth 1952:12).

As printed Scriptures became more abundant throughout China, the government decreed the death penalty for any European preparing or disseminating Christian literature and exile to northern Manchuria for any Chinese who were deluded by them (Nida

1972:71). The Imperial edict was posted on every gate in the
walls of the ancient city of Canton (Mathews 1952:173-174).

In spite of these difficulties, attempts were made to circulate the books through Cantonese booksellers. These efforts
were largely unsuccessful, so when Morrison's New Testament was
issued in 1814 it was arranged that his young colleague, the Reverend W. Milne, should visit Java, Malacca, and Penang to circulate the Sacred Word among the many Chinese settlers in those
places. For the next twenty-five years, Malacca and Singapore
were the chief distribution centers for the Chinese Scriptures
(Hudspeth 1952:16-17).

In the 1830s Gutzlaff, Medhurst, and others, sailed in Chinese junks up the coast of China distributing thousands of New
Testaments and Bible portions as far north as Korea. But getting beyond the coast was virtually impossible. All foreign nations were suspect and must be kept out at all costs.

Protestant mission work did not really begin in China proper
until 1842 with the Treaty of Nanking following the Opium War.
This brought an end to the restrictions on the distribution of
God's Word. Also as a result of the war, the island of Hong
Kong was ceded to Great Britain, and five ports, later known as
Treaty Ports, were opened to foreign trade. These were Canton,
Shanghai, Amoy, Foochow, and Ningpo. Shanghai, at that time a
small village, became the headquarters of missionary societies
from all over the world (Kane 1971:214).

Missionaries immediately settled in all of these treaty ports,
and efforts to print and circulate Scripture were intensified.
But the work of distribution was still on a very small scale
(Hudspeth 1952:18).

A second war broke out with Great Britain in 1856 and the work
of distribution almost came to a complete standstill. The war
continued until 1860. But with the coming of peace, ten more
Treaty Ports were opened, the Christian religion was to be tolerated, and missionaries were granted the right to buy land, erect
buildings, and travel and reside in the interior. The Treaty of
Tientsin, which granted these privileges, was the turning point
in the whole missionary enterprise in China (Hudspeth 1952:18-
19). The ten new treaty ports were immediately occupied, and
exploratory trips,involving months of arduous travel, were undertaken in many parts of the empire never before seen by the white
man (Kane 1971:215).

Up to the middle of the nineteenth century all versions of
the Bible were in what is known as the Literary or Wen-li style,
a classical form of expression understood only by well-educated

people. To the average person, the Wen-li language was comparable with what Latin is to English, so that the Wen-li Bible reached only a very small fraction of the people. To remedy this, in the 1850s several missionaries began translating the Scriptures into the vernacular, Mandarin, which extended over about nine-tenths of the country. Between 1857 and 1889 several new translations appeared. Each of these translations had its respective value, and within a few years, the Wen-li Bible was largely replaced. In the family, in the classroom, in the chapel and church services, the Mandarin versions were read with interest and excitement. As Christianity spread and the number of missionaries increased, there developed a widespread desire and an ever-increasing demand to have one unified translation for the whole Protestant Church. But it was not until 1919 that this unified translation, the Union Mandarin Version, was published. This is the version now used by ninety-nine percent of the Protestant Chinese Christians.

In 1860 there were only twenty-five hundred Protestants in all of China and not quite a hundred Protestant missionaries (Hudspeth 1952:19). But as we mentioned earlier, 1860 was the turning point for Protestant missions in China. The period from 1860 to 1900 was a time of rapid expansion. Wherever missionaries went, churches, schools, and hospitals were established. By 1907, Protestant forces comprised a total of ninety-four societies with a total membership of 3,445 missionaries, living in 632 stations, and there were 389 schools of higher learning (Kane 1971:217).

The China Inland Mission, founded by Hudson Taylor in 1865, became by far the largest of all the missions in China, with nine hundred members and four hundred associates, working in fifteen of the eighteen provinces (Kane 1971:215).

During this period there were also three Bible Societies at work and eleven tract societies. Eleven mission presses turned out a steady stream of Christian literature (Kane 1971:216). In 1860, some thirty thousand Scripture portions were circulated. Within ten years, circulation had reached a hundred thousand copies per year throughout seventeen of the eighteen provinces of China. By 1876, a million Testaments had been distributed (Hudspeth 1952:20). This seems like a lot of Scripture, but it was still only one New Testament for every four hundred people in that vast land of four hundred million people (Latourette 1970:Vol.6,253).

By 1899 more than 8,845,000 Bibles, Testaments, and Scripture portions had been distributed throughout the country, perhaps one copy for every one hundred people who had lived and died since the beginning of the Bible Societies' work in China!

In 1900 there was another fanatical outburst of anti-foreign-
ism known as the Boxer Rebellion. One hundred and eighty-nine
Protestant missionaries and their children were killed, and
scores of other missionaries barely escaped to the coast, suffer-
ing severe hardship along the way. This was the largest massa-
cre of missionaries in modern times (Kane 1971:217). It is not
known how many Chinese Christians were put to death at this time
but it would be safe to say that they numbered in the thousands.

When peace was restored, a large number of reforms were made.
An ancient scholastic method was changed into an ever-expanding
modern system, railways began to replace the cart and the mule,
a government postal and telegraph system was introduced, and
newspapers began to appear.

During the decade 1900 to 1910 the church grew faster than
ever before. In fact, if statistics are any criterion, more
progress was made in that decade than in any previous fifty
years (Kane 1971:217).

By 1914 there were 543 high schools with an enrollment of
thirty-three thousand (Kane 1971:218). There were probably
about 1,750,000 Christians in China by that time. About one-
third to one-fourth of these were Protestants (Latourette 1970:
Vol.6,256). These church members were from all ranks of society.
Many Christians, especially Protestants, were well-educated,
bringing into being a leadership which was influential out of
all proportion to the size of the Christian community (Latourette
1970:Vol.6,256). Even so, the fact remains that after nineteen
centuries, China was less than one-half of one percent Christian,
in spite of the intensive efforts made during the Great Century,
especially during the last half of it.

JAPAN

It will be recalled that Roman Catholic missionaries were at
work in Japan from 1549 until they were expelled in the seventeenth century. Church membership reached a peak of half a million by 1615. But before the middle of that century, what had
been regarded as the most promising mission field in Asia was
cruelly suppressed. Except for about ten thousand Christians
discovered some two hundred years later in the Nagasaki area,
the Church was exterminated and the Gospel light extinguished
for two centuries (Chapman 1975:305) (Latourette 1970:Vol.6,376).
We cannot help but wonder what part Christian literature played
during those two hundred years. We know that the Jesuits had
trained preachers, teachers, and catechists, and that they had
also produced a considerable amount of literature.

The first Protestant translator of the Japanese language was
Karl Gutzlaff, who published his translation of the Gospel of

John in 1839. He did this with the help of three shipwrecked
Japanese sailors. Later he attempted to land these men in Japan
but without success (Robertson 1953:17).

Western missionaries were finally allowed to enter Japan in
1859. One of the first to arrive was Dr. James C. Hepburn, who
had already seen service in China. In addition to his medical
work over a period of thirty-three years, Hepburn was an outstanding educator and linguist. He produced an English-Japanese,
Japanese-English lexicon containing forty thousand words and a
Bible dictionary which were a tremendous help to succeeding missionaries. He was also one of the chief translators of the
Bible. Other outstanding missionaries in those early years were
Channing Williams, Samuel Brown, Guido Verbeck, and James Bal-
lagh, all of whom were educators. Verbeck, like Hepburn, was
also a great linguist (Kane 1971:242).

The prospects for Christian mission work in Japan in the
1860s were very poor. Christianity was still a proscribed religion, punishable by death. The treaty of 1858 said nothing
about the residence of missionaries. All that the treaty guaranteed was liberty for Americans to practice their religion on
Japanese soil and to provide appropriate places of worship
(Neill 1964:326). The missionaries were confined to Yokohama
and Nagasaki. For many years they were allowed only to operate
schools and clinics. The missionaries were viewed with suspi-
cion by the government and with hostility and fear by the people.
The first convert, Mototaka Yano, was baptized in 1864. The
first Protestant church in Japan was not organized until 1872,
and then with only eleven members (Kane 1971:243).

The year 1873 was a very crucial one for the success of the
mission, for it was in that year that the government removed the
anti-Christian edicts from all public places. Within a year the
number of missionaries doubled, from twenty-nine to fifty-eight
(Kane 1971:244).

The first translation of the Scriptures actually made in
Japan was Jonathan Goble's translation of St. Matthew, published
in 1871. Goble became the first colporteur in that country. In
1873 he was joined by Nathan Brown, who continued the translation
work while Goble devoted his time to the dissemination of the
books. The remaining parts of the New Testament were completed
in 1879 (Robertson 1953:19). Another translation, that of Hepburn, Brown and Greene, was published about eighteen months later, in 1880. The Old Testament was completed by others in 1887
and was published that same year (Robertson 1953:20). In 1892
the entire Bible in Roman letters was issued by the Bible societies (Robertson 1953:21).

It is interesting to note that in 1883, just three years after the publication of the New Testament translated by Hepburn,
Brown and Greene, a revival broke out in Yokohama during the
week of prayer. It soon spread to Tokyo and to central Japan.
In 1884 it swept through Doshisha College. For several weeks
all classes were suspended and the students gave themselves to
prayer and testimony. All efforts to resume academic work were
useless. At the end of the period, some two hundred students
were baptized. In 1886 a similar revival broke out in Sendai
and spread to Nagoya and Nagasaki (Kane 1971:247).

During these years, the 1880s, there was a steady increase in
the number of missionaries. In one decade the number increased
from 145 to 383. Churches and out-stations increased from 83 to
448 in the same period. In just seven years, church membership
rose from four thousand to thirty thousand.

But in the following decade a negative reaction set in. The
government and the people apparently became alarmed at the growing influence of the Christian religion. Because of political
oppression, church growth almost came to a standstill (Kane
1971:249).

In 1912, however, the government reversed its attitude toward
Christianity, and the political climate during the next fifteen
years was favorable to church growth. And the Church did make
substantial progress. During this time twenty tracts on various
Christian themes were published and distributed in large numbers.
Fifteen hundred Christians in Tokyo alone distributed millions
of pieces of literature. During this time church membership increased from 79,000 to 110,000 and many of the more prominent
Japanese became Christians (Kane 1971:252).

Earlier in this chapter mention was made of Doshisha College.
The manner in which that college was founded makes a very interesting story, and also shows the power of the printed page.
Shimeta Niishima, known better in the West as Joseph Hardy
Neesima, was born and brought up in a family where he had no
opportunity to learn anything about Christianity. When he was
about twenty years of age he stumbled onto a book in Chinese
which consisted of extracts from the Bible. This stirred his
soul, and he was determined to find out more about this illumi-
nating literature. It was during that dark period when Christianity was still a proscribed religion in Japan, and Neesima,
seeing no hope of enlightenment except from foreigners, fled his
country. He made his way to Singapore where he found a copy of
the Scriptures for sale. Against the whole sentiment and tradition of his class, he sold his sword in order to purchase this
Book. Hearing that America was where he could learn most about
this Book, he decided to sail there. On the voyage he read

alone and unaided from that precious Word. At last he came upon
those words which have meant so much to so many people: "God so
loved the world that He gave His only begotten Son, that whoso-
ever believeth on Him should not perish but have everlasting
life." Neesima believed these words and became a child of God
(Mackenzie 1897:79). The year was 1864.

In America Neesima studied at Amherst College and Andover
Theological Seminary. He was baptized and ordained and was accepted by the American Board as a missionary. He returned to
his homeland in 1874 and founded Doshisha (Single Purpose) College in which the Gospel was linked to all that was good in the
ancient tradition (Neill 1964:329). This school became one of
the best known in all of Asia and the strongest Christian university in Japan (Mathews 1952:183). Neesima did more for the
higher education of his countrymen than any other, and throughout his educational labors, he kept in view the evangelization
of his country (Mackenzie 1897:79). And it all started from
reading the Word of Christ, of whom the reader had never heard.

We also heard earlier of Dr. G. F. Verbeck, a brilliant linguist, who was one of the first missionaries into Japan when the
door was reopened in 1859. He was also convinced of the power
of the printed page. He quoted with approval the verdict that
if the choice were ever to be between the Bible without the
teacher or the teacher without the Bible, he would unhesitatingly choose the former. Two of his early converts were brothers
belonging to a noble Japanese family. One of them, on guard to
prevent foreigners entering Japan, found a Dutch New Testament
floating in Nagasaki harbor. Through a Dutch trader he learned
of a Chinese translation and was studying it when Dr. Verbeck
was admitted to Japan in 1861. What Dr. Verbeck then discovered
has been witnessed time and time again in one country after another (North 1938:11).

In 1913 the total Protestant Church membership was a little
under 103,000, and the total Roman Catholic membership was some
66,000. The Russian Orthodox Church numbered about 32,000 (Latourette 1970:Vol.5,378,380,399). Thus, the total number of
Christians in the country at the end of this period was just a
little over 200,000, a very small fraction of one percent of the
population. We should not be surprised at this, since Christianity was hardly introduced to the Japanese people until late in
the nineteenth century.

Even though Christianity was so late in coming to Japan, it
might have made a much greater impact if Buddhism were not so
firmly entrenched and if brutal and immoral white traders, mis-
takenly identified as Christians, had never visited Japanese
shores. Oh, that Christian missionaries had come to Japan in

the first century or at least in the fifth century, before Buddhism had been introduced and before white traders had given Christianity a bad name. If they had, no doubt the status of Christianity in Japan today would be infinitely better.

KOREA

The first Protestant missionaries arrived in Korea in 1885.
Scores of Korean Christians were waiting for baptism. They had
become Christians through secret and dangerous study of the
Gospels which had infiltrated into their country from Manchuria
(Robertson 1954:5). The first New Testament in Korea was published in 1887, just two years after the first Protestant missionaries arrived, but long before this, the Korean Gospels had
been at work.

Today there are far more Christians in Korea than in India or
China or Japan, even though these other countries had the Scriptures before Korea did. The church has grown faster in Korea
than in these other countries. Why is this? Could literacy
have anything to do with it? We know that Korea has a higher
percentage of literacy than China and India. The literacy rate
is probably seventy-five or eighty percent. Japan, on the other
hand, has almost one hundred percent literacy, and yet fewer
than one percent of the Japanese people are Christians. Those
are the statistics today. But it was not always so.

Even as late as 1950, Japan was reported to be eighty percent
illiterate (Demographic Yearbook 1964:698). One cannot help but
wonder what the illiteracy rate was back in the nineteenth century when Protestant missionaries first entered these lands. It
is quite possible that the literacy rate was higher in Korea
than in Japan at that time. For Korea has a phonetic script, invented as far back as 1445, with fourteen consonants and eleven
vowels, well-adapted to represent the phonemes of the Korean language. This was a far simpler writing system than that of Japan
or China. The Koreans also printed books by movable type a hundred years before Gutenberg set up his press in 1452.

There are many instances of people being led to Christ solely
or primarily through reading some portion of Scripture. A shipwrecked Korean merchant helped Dr. John Ross translate the Gospel of Luke on the Manchurian side of the Yalu River, which, by
the way, was a very risky business. If they were caught, both
of them might well have been executed. When the Gospel of Luke
was completed, the merchant applied for baptism, and shortly after this he set out as a colporteur with a few hundred copies of
St. Luke. He returned a few months later with reports that some
men, after reading the Gospel, wanted to be baptized. One day
several men, apparently of good education, arrived in Moukden

where Dr. Ross was so deeply involved in translating and revising. These men were former officials from Seoul who had taken refuge in the Yalu Valley, where they had met the colporteur, read his books, and were converted. Ross determined to make the long and difficult trip to the valley from which these men had come. No sooner had Ross arrived at his destination than the Koreans began coming to the inn where he was staying. They had come to welcome him. About thirty men, former officials who were now well-to-do farmers, and their wives, said they were believers and that they wished to be baptized.

In another valley on the other side of a high mountain pass, nearly a hundred men from sixteen to seventy-two years of age came forward for baptism. Dr. Ross records:

> We were informed--and from what we had seen, we were now prepared to believe anything--that in each of the twenty-eight valleys which lay between us and the Great White Mountain, four hundred miles to the northwest, there were larger or smaller groups of believers waiting to be received into the Church (Robertson 1954:17-18).

The shipwrecked peddler of genseng, a medicine that bestows longevity, had become a peddler of a Book that brought hundreds into a knowledge of eternal life. One of the men who received, read, and believed the Gospel was Saw Sang Yuin. After special training with Dr. Ross, he set off for the capital as a colporteur--a very perilous venture. After one year in Seoul, Mr. Saw wrote to Dr. Ross informing him that there were thirteen converts who wanted to form themselves into a congregation. A year later there were seventy-nine. But Dr. Ross was not able to reach Seoul until 1887, five years after the opening of Korea to the West. By then, after six years of colportage, three hundred men of good standing in the city of Seoul had become believers (Robertson 1954:19).

The first translation of the New Testament was the work of the Reverend John Ross in Manchuria. It was so Chinese in style that revision was soon necessary. A revised New Testament appeared in 1900, another in 1904, and still another in 1906. This latter revision became known as the Korean Authorized Version and had a long and honorable history.

The decade beginning with 1895 was marked by solid church growth. In the year 1900 alone, the year of the first revised New Testament, church membership increased by more than thirty percent (Kane 1971:265).

Bible classes played a major role in the spread of the Gospel

and the growth of the Church. By 1909, in the Northern Presbyterian territory alone, there were some eight hundred Bible
classes with a total attendance of fifty thousand, twice the number of the communicant membership (Shearer 1966:55).

In January, 1907, a great revival broke out in Pyengyang.
For five months prior to that time, both missionaries and national Christians had been meeting daily for prayer, seeking for a
deeper, more satisfying experience of the power of the Holy Spirit. On January 14, the Holy Spirit was poured out upon the sev-
en hundred Christians gathered in Pyengyang from the surrounding
countryside for the annual Bible classes conducted by the missionaries (Kane 1971:267).

The revival spread to Seoul and other cities in Korea and beyond the borders of Korea into Manchuria and China. The 1907
revival made a lasting impression on the Church in Korea. The
spirit of prayer and the passion for piety which have been its
outstanding characteristics for more than half a century can be
directly traced to this source. The year 1907, you will recall,
was just one year after the publication of the revision of the
New Testament that became the Korean Authorized Version.

The foundations of the revival were laid in the Bible training classes. These classes, held throughout the country in both
rural and urban areas, were influential in the life of the
Church. The Reverend W. N. Blair says that more than anything
else, Bible classes accounted for the rapid growth and revival
condition of the Korean Church in those early times (Shearer
1966:55). Since the people of Korea inherited a Confucian respect for good literature and had lived by their classics for
centuries, they eagerly responded to the opportunity to learn
from this ancient, Oriental book, the Bible (Shearer 1966:197).

The Church grew like wildfire in northwestern Korea, but not
so fast in the south. Why the difference? One reason given by
Shearer is that the people of the north, easily attracted to the
Church, were more literate than those of the south (1966:143).
In 1902 a missionary who had held Bible classes in both the
north and the south said that nearly all northerners had studied
Chinese and knew how to study, while those in the south not only
had difficulty in Chinese but could barely read the native Korean script, which is far easier to read than the Chinese characters (1966:143-144).

Missionary itineration was another factor helping to produce
great growth. But how shall we account for churches springing
up where no missionaries even visited? Here is one example
among many:

> Away up in the mountains at the head of a
> little valley, we found a family consisting of
> a man 74 years of age, his four sons and their
> wives, and a daughter and her husband, who were
> Christians. No missionary had ever visited them,
> and a helper but three times. The whole family
> of eleven persons, except one son who was away
> from home, passed a most creditable examination
> and we rejoiced to receive them as catechumens.
> The son-in-law had first heard the Gospel here in
> Pyongyang three years ago and was interested enough
> to buy some Christian books, which he took home and
> which, in turn, led the whole family into believing
> (Shearer 1966:145).

This is the means by which the Korean Church multiplied ahead
of the missionaries. Because of the close-knit web of family
relationships and the interfamily relationship through the clan,
no one wished to make a great step in accepting a new religion
which would break down family ties. A person hearing of the Gospel of Christ, or reading of it from a Bible, would go back to
his own village, talk it over with the members of his family and
clan, and if a positive decision was made, the entire group
often quite naturally became Christians, still holding fast to
its family relationships (Shearer 1966:148).

SUMATRA

Perhaps no church in the Orient has a more remarkable story
than that of the Batak congregations of upland Sumatra. The
earliest attempts to reach these people had not been successful
In 1834 two missionaries tried to enter Batakland, but were
killed and eaten before they had been able to even make a beginning with their mission work (Neill 1964:348).

In 1861 the Rhenish Missionary Society began work among the
Bataks, and the following year they were joined by one of the
most effective missionaries of whom we have any record; namely,
Ludwig Ingwer Nommensen (1834 to 1918). The early years were
difficult, but the situation changed completely with the conversion of several chiefs. The people followed their leaders
almost without hesitation. In 1866 there were fifty-two Christians. In 1876 there were 2,056 believers, and just five years
later there were 7,500. Meanwhile the Scriptures were being
translated into the Batak language. Matthew, Mark, and Acts had
been published by 1867. The entire New Testament was off the
press by 1878, and by 1894 the whole Bible had been completed
(Nida 1972:38). The church continued to grow rapidly, and by
1911 more than 103,000 Bataks had accepted Jesus as their Savior
(Neill 1964:349). Today there is a Christian community of more
than 900,000 people, distributed among almost a thousand churches

(Hoke 1975:287). The Bible, translated into the Batak language
has been the foundation for this unparalleled development (Nida
1952:171-172).

BURMA

While space does not permit even a glance at the missionary
enterprise in every country of Asia during the Great Century, we
must at least take a look at the expansion of Christianity in
one more country where there was a great people movement to
Christ.

Adoniram Judson, who ranks with William Carey, Robert Morrison, David Livingstone, Ludwig Nommensen, and Hudson Taylor, as
one of the greatest missionaries of all time, arrived in Burma
in 1813 when as yet there were no Christians in that country.
He immediately began to study the Burmese language, and although
he suffered severe hardships including nearly two years in pri-
son under the vilest conditions, he completed the translation of
the entire Bible into Burmese by 1834.

> Few men have suffered more or accomplished
> more for the cause of Christ than Adoniram Judson.
> At the time of his death, seven thousand had been
> won to Jesus Christ, and the foundation of the
> Christian church in Burma had been firmly laid
> (Kane 1971:148).

Missions to the Tribes

The vast majority of the Christians in Burma were animistic
tribespeople. The first tribe to be reached for Christ was the
Karens. The first missionary was George Boardman who died in
1831 after only four years in Burma. During this short time, he
was able to lay the foundation of the Karen Church. Closely
associated with him was Ko Tha Byu, a Karen convert who became a
flaming evangelist to his own people and was used of God to begin a great people movement to Christ.

> The Karen movement toward Christianity in
> which Judson, Boardman, and Ko Tha Byu had been
> pioneers continued. Wade reduced the Karen language
> to writing. Literature was prepared, including
> translations of the Bible into the tongues of various
> branches of the Karens....Schools were organized.
> Clergy were trained. The Karens undertook the
> financial support of their churches and schools
> and became more nearly independent of subsidies from
> the outside than almost any other group of Christians
> in southern and eastern Asia (Latourette 1944:Vol.6,231).

The Karens had a tradition which seems to have prepared them for the Gospel. They knew the Creator, and they had a story of the fall through which they had lost the favor of God. They also believed that in the past they had once possessed a sacred book, which their forefathers had carelessly lost. When a preacher came, bearing a Sacred Book and telling them that the God whose anger they had incurred had sent His only Son into the world to pay for their own sins with His own blood, that whoever believes in Him should not perish but have everlasting life, their dreams and hopes had been realized, and Karens came forward by the hundreds to be instructed and baptized. In 1851 there were already more than ten thousand full members of the Church and a Christian community of perhaps thirty thousand (Neill 1964:294-295). By 1921 Christians totaled over 257,000, about two percent of the total population. The overwhelming majority of these were Karens and other tribal peoples who had been animists. Very few Burmese Buddhists responded to the Gospel call.

WRITING SYSTEMS AND THE ADVANCE OF THE GOSPEL

While the Gospel was proclaimed in almost every part of Africa and Asia during the Great Century and several million people were led to Christ, by 1914 Christianity was still a very small minority in these lands. This was especially true in Asia where perhaps 6 or 7 million people were Christians out of a total population of some 900 million. While there is rejoicing in heaven over every sinner who repents and turns to Jesus in true faith, it no doubt also grieves the Holy Spirit as well as every born-again Christian that in 1914 more than 99 percent of Asia was still without Christ and thus without God and without hope (Ephesians 2:12).

There are many reasons that Christianity never became a very dynamic force in Africa and Asia during the Great Century:

1) Considering the size of the populations of most of these lands, very few missionaries were at work.

2) In many languages there was very little Scripture until near the end of the period, and in many languages there was none.

3) There were severe persecutions from time to time.

4) Where there were no persecutions, there were frequently very limiting restrictions.

5) There were controversies in the Christian camp over certain policies.

6) The offenses of white traders, notably the Portuguese, turned the people against the message of the white missionaries.

7) Some areas were very unhealthful places for the white man to live, and large numbers of missionaries either died or had to return to their homeland after only a few weeks or months on the mission field.

The above list could be extended until it were several times its present length, but there is one other factor in particular which we believe may have been very detrimental to the spread of Christianity which we would like to consider at this time. The writing systems of several countries, especially of China, Japan, India, and Ethiopia are among the most difficult in the world.

The development of a full Greek alphabet, about the beginning of the eighth century B.C., expressing single sounds of language by means of consonant and vowel signs, was the last important step in the history of writing. From the Greek period up to the present, nothing new has happened in the inner structural development of writing. Generally speaking, we write consonants and vowels in the same way as the ancient Greeks.

The use of vowel signs and the resulting analysis of writing as an alphabet passed in the course of time from the Greeks to the Semites, thus repaying the debt of the original borrowing. This is the alphabet that subsequently conquered the world. Much as the hundreds of alphabets used throughout the world may differ from each other in appearance, they all have characteristics of outer form, inner structure, or both, which first originated in the small area surrounding the eastern Mediterranean. In fact, if we exclude the various forerunners of writing scattered throughout the world, the small group of writings in eastern Asia which grew out of the Chinese system, and the chiefly syllabic systems introduced in modern times among primitive societies, there is only one system of writing in use today, and that is the alphabet of Semitic-Greek origin.

From the inner structural point of view, the main characteristic of the alphabet is the existence of special signs for both consonants and vowels. As the signs for consonants are used in approximately the same way in all the alphabets of the world, the various types of alphabets can be distinguished only by their use of the vowel signs.

Three Types of Alphabets

Type I, as represented by the Greek alphabet, is the simplest of the three types of alphabets. Vowels are expressed by special signs on equal footing with consonants, as in the writing of the syllable 'ta' by means of the signs 't' plus 'a'. This type of vocalization is characteristic of all the Western writings no matter how much they may differ in outer form: Greek, Latin, Slavonic, etc.

Type II is represented by Syriac, Hebrew, and Arabic. In this type the vowels are indicated by small strokes, dots, or circles, placed either above or below the consonant sign.

Type III, found in the Indic and Ethiopic writings, present some difficult problems. This type of vocalization is very similar to that noted above as Type II with one important difference: while in Type II the vowel marks are written separately, in Type III they are always attached to the respective syllabic signs (Gelb 1952:181-187).

Due to its marginal geographic position in the Old World, China was not affected by foreign invasions to the extent that the Near Eastern areas were. For that reason the evolution of the Chinese writing system progressed through thousands of years undisturbed by foreign influences, resulting finally in a type of writing which suited the needs of a small bureaucratic clique, but was totally inaccessible to ninety percent of the population (Gelb 1952:203).

From the point of view of the theory of writing, the evolution is from a word-syllabic writing through a syllabic writing to an alphabetic writing. From the historical point of view, the development is from the Egyptian writing through the West Semitic writing to the Greek writing (Gelb 1952:205). The Chinese logographic system of writing is similar to that of the ancient Egyptians, and the Japanese writing systems represent the second stage of development, the word-syllabic. The Indic and Ethiopic languages represent the third stage of development, namely alphabetic writing, but as we saw earlier, the most difficult of the three types of alphabets.

Many of the alphabets of India and southeastern Asia turn a single consonant value into a large number of symbols, each of which carries the consonant value plus a separate vowel value, and since the number of possible vowel values in some of these tongues is large, this multiplies the symbols to the point where they become unmanageable and difficult to learn. Tamil, the leading Dravidian language of southern India, has a syllabic script of 312 characters, while other languages of India range up to 500 and even 700 characters (Pei 1949:94).

Reference has already been made to the difficulties of the Chinese language, but perhaps a few more words would be in order here. In all fairness it should be pointed out that the bewil-

dering maze of characters is not quite so bad as it seems to a
person looking at written Chinese for the first time. The rad-
icals, or primary characters, are only 214 in number, and it is
simply a matter of combining them into compound characters, of
which Chinese dictionaries list some forty thousand, but with
only four thousand to eight thousand in general use (although
some of my Chinese friends tell me that ten thousand characters
are required for one to read the Bible). To make things easier,
compound characters often consist of two parts, of which one
conveys the general idea, the other gives a clue to the pronun-
ciation. For example, there is a character for 'horse' (pronounced 'ma' in Mandarin) which originally was a real picture of
a horse. The spoken word for 'mother' is a combination of the
'woman' symbol and the 'horse' symbol, the former indicating
that the word has something to do with the feminine sex, the
latter informing the reader that the word is to be pronounced
somewhat like the word for 'horse' (Pei 1949:376).

Japanese is not related at all to Chinese, but the Japanese
borrowed their writing system from them. Japanese written records begin in the seventh or eighth century of our era, when
Chinese and Korean Buddhist missionaries brought the Chinese
characters to the islands of Japan and put them into use by the
very simple expedient of giving to each character a Japanese-
spoken language value. The pictogram for 'man', for instance,
which is read 'jen' by the Chinese, was read 'hito' instead.
But difficulties soon developed. Unlike Chinese, Japanese is an
inflected language, with case postpositions for nouns and tense
and mood endings for verbs. Written Chinese, relying exclusively upon word order, makes no provision for such variations in a
word. The upshot was that in the ninth century a Japanese Buddhist priest hit upon the clever device of isolating a certain
number of Chinese characters and giving them an invariable phonetic value, to cover all of the possible syllabic combinations
of the Japanese language. If, at this point, the Chinese ideographs had been discarded and the syllabic symbols used exclusively, Japanese would have today a system of writing not too
unlike that of the western languages. Instead, the next step
taken by the Japanese was to combine the new syllabic characters
with the Chinese ideograms, and this method persists to the present day. To render the spoken 'hito no' ('of the man'), the
ideogram for 'man' is used, followed by the syllabic character
that has the invariable phonetic value of 'no'; 'kakimashita'
('wrote') is expressed by the ideogram for 'write' ('kak') followed by the syllabic characters 'ki-ma-shi-ta'.

In both Chinese and Japanese, the adoption of a fully phonetic western alphabet to replace the pictographs and ideographs
has long been under discussion. Communist Chinese language
scholars are at work on a double project, one prong of which

involves the simplification of the written Chinese characters, so that they may be produced with a reduced number of strokes and be easier to read, write, and print; the other prong, involving the complete discarding of the logographic system and its replacement by a modified Latin alphabet, called Latinxua, scientifically constructed and adapted to North Mandarin phonology. Both projects are still in the experimental stage, but both have already given good results from the standpoint of increasing literacy.

The Japanese Romaji movement, older than the Chinese, aims at the use of Roman characters of the conventional variety and is already widely used though a more recent variant, called the Hepburn method, aims at using the Roman characters in such a way that they will correspond even more closely to the Japanese spoken sounds. In both cases, a terrific obstacle is posed by the existing body of Chinese and Japanese literature, which would have to be scrapped and reprinted.

Two Far Eastern languages that are not faced with the problem of phonetization are Korean and Vietnamese. The first, a language sometimes linked with Japanese for what concerns grammatical structure, has long enjoyed a native alphabet of ten vowels and fourteen consonants, known as 'Eunmoon', which is probably one of the most perfect in the world and quite adequate to represent phonetically the sounds of the language.

Vietnamese has possessed since the seventeenth century a Roman script, elaborated by Catholic missionaries and known as 'Quoc-ngu'.

It is interesting to note that these two languages, Korean and Vietnamese, are the two most Christian nations in the Far East, except for the Philippines and now perhaps Indonesia, where the Roman script is also used.

We should hasten to point out, however, that in spite of the difficult writing system in use in Japan, nearly a hundred percent of that nation's inhabitants above school age are literate. Or so it is reported. It would be interesting to find out just how many over fifteen years of age would actually be able to read a newspaper or the Scriptures with understanding.

It is interesting to note that India, with its multiplicity of languages, has always been one of the most illiterate countries. Even as late as 1931 India was 90.9 percent illiterate. Men were 84.7 percent illiterate, and the women, 97.6 percent (UNESCO 1948). Even Japan, as late as 1950, was reported to be 80 percent illiterate (Demographic Yearbook 1964:698). We mentioned earlier that China, in 1950, was also reported to be 80

percent illiterate. One cannot help but wonder what the illiteracy rate was in the days of the early Protestant missionaries
to these countries back in the early nineteenth century. On the
other hand, we know the Hindus have clung to their religion for
over twenty-five hundred years in spite of their illiteracy,
that the Chinese have embraced Buddhism since the first century,
that the Koreans have been Buddhists since the third century A.D.
and the Japanese, since the seventh or eighth century. How did
they embrace these religions, and why is it so difficult to win
them from these religions, when most of the people have never
been able to read their sacred writings? Perhaps it is just for
that very reason, that they regard their scriptures as sacred,
even though they are not able to read them (Pei 1949:206-214).
Oh, that the early Christians had been more obedient to our
Lord's command and had carried the Gospel to China and other
lands in the Far East before the Buddhists arrived, and to
Arabia in the first century; or, at least, before the days of
Muhammad, and had given them the precious Word of Christ in
their own language, and had taught them to read! What a difference there might have been.

9

In Our Time

In the twentieth century, just as in all previous history of the Church, there has been a close relationship between Bible reading and church growth. Hundreds of pages would be required to tell of all the individuals who have been led to Christ solely or primarily through reading, and of all the churches which have come into being as the result of the printed page. This chapter includes just a few of the outstanding and exciting stories of church growth resulting from Bible reading in various parts of the world.

PACIFIC ISLANDS

Philippines

The best known name in the field of literacy is unquestionably that of Dr. Frank C. Laubach who, for more than forty years, was the great friend of the "silent billion".

The story of Laubach's work among the Moros in the Philippines is well known. The Moros were violently prejudiced against the Gospel. For fifteen years Laubach and his fellow missionaries made sporadic attempts to start religious services, but no Moros would come. Then they began teaching them to read. Much to their surprise, dozens, then hundreds, then thousands came to learn to read. Everyone they taught became a friend. The Moros began to come to church services. Even the highest chiefs came. When young Moros joined the church, there was no opposition from anyone, not even from the priests. What had so utterly failed for fifteen years by direct preaching became easy when they began their literacy campaign (Laubach 1950:2).

When the Japanese occupied the Philippine Islands in 1942,
the Rev. Leonardo Dia and his wife withdrew from the city of
Cebu to the mountainous interior of the island and cast their
lot with three small neglected Presbyterian congregations.
These had never had a resident pastor before. For the first few
months the couple visited the scattered homes of Christians in
that rugged country. They found the second generation Christians friendly but largely ignorant of the Bible, though most of
them were literate. At Pastor Dia's urging, three small chapels
were erected in well-hidden locations. Regular worship and instruction began. The pastor had a book on the use of the Bible
in personal evangelism which anchored the main Christian truths
to about a hundred key passages in the New Testament. Instruction consisted in finding these verses in the Bible, explaining
their meaning, and having the passages memorized. As people
learned the passages and their references, and could explain
what they meant, their names were written on the wall of the
chapel. The competition stimulated everyone to learn.

As the members of the congregations learned these verses,
they turned to each other in amazement, exclaiming, "Our religion is true." Then they rushed out to persuade their loved
ones and friends to believe on the Lord Jesus Christ as their
Savior and Lord. In the first six months church membership
doubled. In the next year it doubled again, and other congregations were established.

Dr. Donald McGavran hastens to point out that there were
seven distinct factors which contributed to the churches' growth,
including the faithful and competent pastoring of Reverend Dia.
But the fact that these people were literate and were searching
the Scriptures certainly played a vital role in their spiritual
and numerical growth (1970:18).

The Protestant population of the Philippines grew twice as
fast as the burgeoning general population from 1914 to 1957.
The largest church in the Philippines, which is not the result
of a merger, is the Seventh Day Adventists. One of the very
significant factors in SDA growth has been literature. During
1968 alone they sold $750,000-worth of literature through a
thousand colporteurs. Another factor is their coordinated use
of radio, correspondence courses, campaigns, Sabbath schools,
secular education, medical and relief work. Still another key
is their promotion of home Bible study courses.

Perhaps the most significant factor in SDA success is the
fact that there is only one paid worker for every fifteen to
thirty preaching places. The paid district pastor supervises

these self-supporting lay pastors, visiting any one place perhaps three times a year. This system not only solves the problem of the support of the ministry, but allows the church to
spend more on literature. There is probably no other church
group in the Philippines, or even in all of east Asia, that can
top this literature record (Tolliver 1975:529).

New Guinea

In the interior of New Guinea there is a tribe called Medlpa
numbering about 40,000. A Laubach team prepared literacy lessons and mimeographed 700 copies at Lae on the north coast of
the island. This team of twenty native Christians then flew to
the interior where they were met by 10,000 cannibals of the Medlpa tribe. Each member of the team taught one tribesman until
they had completed the primer. Then there was a graduation ceremony attended by 20,000 tribesmen, half the tribe.

After the diplomas had been distributed, they celebrated all
the rest of the day. Six hundred chiefs held a Council, and the
king of them all told of their decision:

> "This," he said, "is the greatest event in our
> history. You have done more for us than anyone
> who ever lived. You are educating us. We like
> your religion. We have just voted that the entire
> tribe is to be Christian..." (Laubach 1964:53-54).

Indonesia

In what has been called "The Revival of the Century", Indonesia is experiencing a great people movement. A veteran missionary reports:

> We are in the midst of the greatest revival that
> has come to Indonesia in the past 1300 years. In the
> past two years alone, over 250,000 Moslems have been
> won to Christ.

> Literature distribution has been so effective that
> evangelistic teams do not have to seek out those who
> want to find Christ...the people are coming to them.
> Entire villages have been won to Christ. New churches
> are being established inside of a week to a month after
> an invasion of the Gospel. As many as 2,000 converts
> have followed our Lord in baptism in a single service.

> In every area where there is revival, we have found
> that literature has paved the way. The Holy Spirit is
> doing the work through literature, and we are reaping
> the harvest.

Indonesian youth are taking the lead in this
mighty revival. They come together for prayer
between 4:00 and 6:00 in the morning...and then
move out into the villages. At times there may
be up to 90 teams on tour, distributing literature,
testifying, praying for the sick...with each team
seeing as many as 100 conversions per night.

Wherever the witch doctors have held great sway
over the people, these teams have moved in, prayed
in the name of Jesus, and the people have turned from
their demon worship. As a result, the witch doctors
have been run out of town!

In many villages, the prisons have been emptied,
as the people have turned from their wicked ways..."
(BLI, *The Quiet Miracle* n.d.:17-19).

ASIA

India

In 1971 the entire Bible was available in twenty-five of the
languages of India, the New Testament in forty more languages,
and portions in an additional sixty-five (Kane 1971:122). It
should not surprise us too much to find that the Bible is a best
seller in India (Sinker 1953:51) even though only 2.6 percent of
the inhabitants are Christian (Williams 1975:218).

The tragedy is that only 28 percent of India's adults (over
fifteen years of age) are able to read (UNESCO 1964:51). And,
in many of India's 750,000 villages there are hardly any literates at all. To make matters worse, approximately 800 languages
are spoken in the sub-continent, more than 600 of which are without a single Word of Scripture (Williams 1975:223).

Nevertheless, Christian literature has played a vital role,
directly and indirectly, in the advance of the Gospel in India.
During the three year period from 1965 to 1968, nearly fifty-one
million Gospel messages in print were distributed by World Literature Crusade, according to Jack McAlister, president of WLC.
This endeavor drew 460,684 written decisions from Indians, 71
percent of whom were newly converted. McAlister adds that 80
percent of these decisions were by Hindus (ELO Bulletin 1968:
Vol.11,No.4,10).

Bible correspondence courses have also been effective in leading many to Christ (Williams 1975:223); *The Light of Life Bible
Correspondence Course*, prepared in 1949 by Dr. Donald Hillis, is
the most popular. It has been adopted by more than a dozen

missions and has been translated into at least twenty-four languages. By 1967, over a million and a half students had enrolled in the course, eighty-five percent of them non-Christians
(Kane 1971:121).

Formosa

During World War II, an underground Christian movement broke
out among the mountain tribes of Formosa in spite of all efforts
by the Japanese to suppress it. When the missionaries returned
to the island after the war, they found that some seven thousand
of these aborigines, whose forefathers had been head-hunters,
had become Christians. This was the fruit of the work of two
humble, ill-trained workers with only the Bible in their hands
(Chirgwin 1954:86-87).

Laos

This amazing story is from a little tract entitled *The Quiet
Miracle*, published by Bible Literature International. A missionary was driving along a street in the town of Vientiane in Laos
when he saw two Meo tribesmen whom he knew were from an area
that was inaccessible because of Communist guerilla activity.
The missionary picked them up and gave them a ride around town
and then took them to his home. Later that day he led them to
Christ, using the Laotian version of "Heart of Pak". He gave
each of these men a set of four pieces of literature to take
back to their villages, even though one of the men could not
read.

The tribesman who could not read took his booklets to the
village witch doctor who had been educated in a French government school and was the only one in the village who was able to
read. The witch doctor received Christ as he read this literature for the first time. Then he called the entire village together and read the material to them night after night.

Eventually, all fifty-seven adults in that village were converted. They then went out to the eleven surrounding villages
and read the material aloud to the people, and told them what
Christ had done for them.

Six years later, Communist guerilla activity had subsided to
such an extent that the missionary was able to get up into the
area. After three days on horseback, he arrived at the mountainous region. There he found 748 Meo tribespeople who had accepted Christ as their Savior--entirely the result of the Holy Spirit working through literature. All this happened without these
people ever having seen a missionary (n.d.:11-13).

LATIN AMERICA

Ecuador

Today there is a great people movement among the Highland
Quichuas of Ecuador (Klassen 1974:107). Until 1954 there was
not a single baptized believer among the Quichuas of Chimborazo
Province, even though there had been at least one servant of
Christ in that area since 1902, except for about three years,
from 1915 to 1918 (Nickel 1965:43). On April 10, 1954, four
young people were baptized. The church grew slowly but steadily for the next decade, so that by 1964 there were 200 baptized
believers. By 1968 the number of believers had increased to 560
and two years later the total was 1,550. For two years in succession, 1970 and 1971, the church grew by more than eighty percent each year. Although the growth rate was not as spectacular
in the two following years, the church still grew by more than
thirty percent each year, so that by 1973 there was a total of
five thousand baptized believers in Chimborazo Province (Klassen
1974:107).

What made the difference? Why is it that there were only
four baptized believers after fifty-two years of witnessing in
that province, and twenty years later there were five thousand?
Until the decade of the fifties, the evangelical outreach among
the Quichuas in Chimborazo was limited to two centers; the Gospel Missionary Union was located at Caliata, and the Christian
and Missionary Alliance was at Colta. In the late forties and
early fifties, sixteen new GMU missionaries began work among the
Quichuas. Two new stations were opened; one at Pulucate in 1950
and one at El Troje in 1954 (Klassen 1974:98). Meanwhile, the
Gospel Missionary Union acquired the Colta station from C&MA
(Klassen 1974:98).

No doubt the increase in personnel had something to do with
the increased church growth in the years following 1954. But
1954 was also the year that Mrs. Julie Woodward completed her
translation of the New Testament, giving the Quichuas the written Word of Life for the first time.

The decade of 1954 to 1964 was filled with many types of seed
sowing. Baptisms were few, averaging about twenty per year, but
schools and medical aid helped build bridges of communication
and break down prejudices (Klassen 1974:98). This labor of love
undoubtedly contributed to the growth of the church. But what
was the most important contributing factor?

Rev. Henry Klassen, who has worked among the Quichuas of Chimborazo Province since 1952, in a term paper written at Fuller
School of World Mission, enumerates twelve of the factors that

contributed to this people movement to Christ. Of the twelve
factors listed, the first is the Quichua New Testament which
was completed in 1954 (Klassen 1974:112). He also mentions that
the Quichuas were forty percent literate (Klassen 1974:113).

The missionaries at Colta, the central station, named some of
the same factors as did Henry Klassen. The Quichua New Testament was at the top of the list, followed by hymns written and
composed by Quichuas, radio, schools, and clinics, in that order
of importance. Another key factor mentioned was that the Gospel
gives the Indian an "identity", a sense of personal worth that
they never had before (Klassen 1974:114).

Rev. Carl McMindes, the GMU field chairman, agrees with Henry
Klassen and the missionaries at Colta that the Quichua New Tes-
tament was the most important factor in this people movement to
Christ (Klassen 1974:115).

The first translation of the New Testament was a good effort.
It introduced the early leaders to the Word of Christ. But it
did not express itself sufficiently in Quichua culture and
thought pattern. A new translation was clearly needed. In 1969
a new translation was begun under the direction of Gunther
Schulze, a linguist and translator loaned by the United Bible
Societies. Schulze worked with an eight man team that included
several missionaries and key Quichua leaders. In the words of
Jacob Klassen:

> In frank give-and-take sessions, working
> eight to twelve hours a day, the team hammered
> out the functional meaning of the passage as
> originally given, then sought to phrase it in
> Quichua, not as a literal, foreign sounding
> translation, but as a Quichua would say it in
> his thought patterns (Klassen 1974:116).

The reaction of the people to this new translation was "This
is our language. God is speaking to us. God actually loves the
Indian as well as the Spanish" (Klassen 1974:86).

The translation team began working on this translation in
1968. In that year there was an increase in church membership
of sixteen percent. It is interesting to note that the following year, when the Quichua men on that team were really getting
immersed in God's Word, church membership increased by fifty-one
percent. In the following two years, baptized membership rose
by more than eighty percent each year (Klassen 1974:107). While
church growth has not continued to be that spectacular, nevertheless, membership did increase by more than thirty-seven percent
in 1972 and more than thirty percent in 1973. The total member-

ship at the end of 1973 was five thousand, with a total Christian community of some ten thousand souls (Klassen 1974:107).
In a personal interview, Gunther Schulze estimated that the baptized membership today exceeds ten thousand, and that the total
Christian community is at least twenty thousand and increasing
daily (Schulze 1977).

In 1972, having completed the translation of the New Testament in the Colta area, 140 miles south of Quito, the Schulzes
moved to Agato, about 60 miles north of Quito, to begin translating the Scriptures into the local dialect. At least one CMA
missionary had been stationed at Agato since 1914, but in 1969
there were just twenty baptized members (Klassen 1974:130).

A revival began in October 1969 when Evangelism In Depth began its program in Ecuador. Prayer vigils and house to house
visitations resulted in 102 decisions for Christ and thirty-
three baptisms. After EID closed in August 1970, the young
people at Agato continued their witness, outreach, and training.
Five nights a week they met to study the Scriptures. Five of
the young Quichua church leaders also attended the GMU one-week
institutes at Colta, 200 miles to the south. These institutes
were held every two months. Several also attended the six-week
summer Bible institute at the Alliance station at Dos Rios. As
a result of this increased Bible and leadership training, hymn
writing and singing, and house to house visitations, church membership increased from 53 in 1970 to 235 in July 1974 (Klassen
1974:130).

Meanwhile, the translation team was hammering out the new
translation. It was completed in 1975 and the church has been
growing rapidly ever since. Although Gunther Schulze has been
in the United States for the past two years, studying at Fuller
School of World Mission in Pasadena, Ca.,he has kept in close
touch with the workers in Ecuador through correspondence. In a
personal interview he expressed his conviction that there are
now at least five thousand baptized believers in the Otavalo
area (Schulze 1977). It will be very interesting to keep an eye
on this people movement during the next few years as more and
more Quichuas learn to read these Scriptures in their mother
tongue.

Peru

In the early part of this century there was a people movement
to Christ among the Spanish speaking rural folk in Peru. John
Ritchie had arrived in Peru in 1906, and after a few months of
studying Spanish, he accompanied a Bible Society colporteur on
a journey through an isolated area. They visited every house in
each town and village, reading Bible portions to the people and

offering the Scriptures for sale. At that time there was a tremendous thirst for the printed word. The buyer of a book would
frequently sit down at once and begin to read aloud. Many who
could not read would gather around to listen. Ritchie became
convinced that despite a high rate of illiteracy, the way to
evangelize the country was through the printed page (Hamilton
1962:41).

At that time periodicals could be mailed free to any address
within the country. In October 1911, Ritchie began sending out
copies of "El Heraldo". The results of this circulation were
surprising from the start. Letters came from many places including some to which the paper had not been sent, asking for further issues, for books, and at times, for spiritual guidance.

Ritchie followed up contacts as much as possible, visiting a
village for two or three days, bringing a message from God's
Word, and answering questions. He read the answers from the
Scriptures whenever possible. In this way the Gospel was
brought into the people's lives. At the same time, they were
getting a stronger and stronger desire to possess the Book which
answered their questions and comforted them (Hamilton 1962:42).

After each initial visit in a village, the people always asked for a preacher or teacher so that they might have such services regularly, but Ritchie told them that no such person
was available, and they didn't need one. He encouraged them to
meet together each evening, read a lesson from the Bible, and
have prayer together. He suggested that they meet on Sunday and
that one who could read well might read something from the
tracts and papers that would be sent to them, or a sermon from a
book which they could buy.

By 1922 eleven churches had been planted and formed into a
Synod. After a three-day meeting for the delegates, there was a
three-day Convention for all who would come. These three days
were devoted to deepening the spiritual life. After that meeting, evangelistic activity burst out among the village churches.
Many went to neighboring villages preaching, giving out "El
Heraldo" and forming new congregations. Over one period of
three years in the 1920s, a new church was organized every month.
By 1929 there were sixty organized congregations with about
twenty members each. They were not dependent on foreign funds.
They were indigenous in every respect (Hamilton 1962:44-45).

These churches—later called the Iglesia Evangelica Peruana—
numbered about seventy in 1930 with about fourteen hundred full
members (Hamilton 1962:46). They grew by spontaneous expansion,
and they differed conspicuously from the static little "churches"
at most mission stations. This growth was due almost entirely

to the printed page, even though there was a high percentage of
illiteracy in that land.

Bolivia

In 1907 an Aymara-speaking Indian, Señor Camacho, returned
from Chile to his native village near Puno on the Peruvian
shores of Lake Titicaca. He had been educated in a Methodist
school in Chile and upon his return to his home village he started a school for his people. Persecution by the Roman Church
soon followed (Hamilton 1962:46).

In response to his request for a missionary, the Seventh Day
Adventists sent Mr. and Mrs. Stahl to Senor Camacho's aid. The
Stahls arrived in 1907 and were soon swamped with appeals to
establish schools and churches. From one center in 1910 the
SDA movement grew until by 1922 there were ten centers, each of
which was a hub for a surrounding cluster of schools and believers. In 1922 baptized memberships was about a thousand.
By 1930 there were 4,376 full members in southern Peru and 1600
in neighboring Bolivia. For the High Andes this was enormous
and solid growth, and it all came about from a desire to read
and to learn (Hamilton 1962:47).

Panama

In his article, "Literacy: Bridge in Choco Evangelism" in
Practical Anthropology, Jacob Loewen suggests that "the effective Christian witness involves the establishment of a communications bridge". He further proposes that "in pre-literate
societies the teaching of reading can serve as a perpetual communications bridge of inestimable value" (1965:Vol.12,76-84).
His own experiences in working among the Choco Indians in the
Darien of Panama near the Colombian border illustrates the successful use of a literacy program in forming such a bridge.

Loewen and David Wirsche have been associated in a literacy
program among the Choco since 1959. This group of aborigines
surrounded by Spanish speakers had never really been able to
read even though many of them had attended Spanish schools.
They had begun to believe the attitude of those in their community that Indians were too stupid to learn to read.

In the summer of 1959, the two men gathered ten Indians and
began teaching them to read their own language which had been
transcribed as much as possible, following Spanish orthography.
The ten not only learned to read their own language, but Spanish
as well.

In the summer of 1961 and 1962, the literacy program was continued and it "...has not only led to a literacy for many people

but has also become a tool through which churches have been
started--not singularly through missionary effort but rather as
a result of the efforts of the Choco Christians themselves"
(Loewen 1965:Vol.12,81).

The missionary would visit the leaders of a Choco community
to introduce the literacy program. The response would be enthu-
siastic and the leaders would provide housing, food, and moral
support.

The literacy specialist prepared the primer series. He would
show the first primer to a small group of people. As he leafed
through, he noted the responses of the individuals watching,
trying to single out someone who caught on rather quickly. He
would teach the first primer to this individual alone. Then
that individual would be required (under the specialist's supervision and guidance) to teach another individual who had shown
aptitude. The specialist would continue with the first individual through all the seven primers of the series. Then would
follow the first reader, a Bible story book designed to give a
"synopsis of the Scriptural truth".

In 1963 a team of five Choco Christians themselves conducted
a literacy evangelistic campaign among some struggling churches
in a new area. During the two-week campaign, forty people
learned to read, over two dozen accepted Christianity, and
twenty-three were baptized. They also left a trained leader and
an organized functioning church when the campaign was over.

In this way more than 250 Chocos became literate in 1961 and
1963. More than two-thirds of the people learned not from
missionary evangelism and instruction from the outside, but
from their own people.

Loewen summarizes the contributions that literacy made to
Choco evangelism as follows:

1) Government interest was such that they were urged to continue the experiment and asked to help set up similar programs
in other tribes.

2) They were able to establish contact with new people because of offering something the people knew to be in their own
interest.

3) It helped identify those open to learning something new,
whether to learn to read or to learn the Word of Christ.

4) It helped identify those capable of transmitting new ideas.
They became literacy teachers and also Bible study leaders.

5) It conveyed the real message the missionary wanted to convey in the form of simple reading material.

6) Christians were given a convenient way of sharing the Good News with their neighbors.

7) This involved a minimum of equipment, funds, and preparation because the unschooled could teach and witness effectively (1965:84).

Juan Francisco Gonzalez, in a personal interview with the writer, told how he had taught forty-two people to read in the Nazarene Church near the Panama airport over a two year period, from 1973 to 1975, and half of them joined the church. None of them had ever gone to church before. One woman rode forty-five minutes each day on a bus to come to the literacy class. She accepted Christ as her Savior and led her husband to Christ also (Gonzalez 1975).

Mexico

This is perhaps one of the most amazing stories of church growth following a literacy program. In the fall of 1975 the writer had the privilege of a personal interview with Misses Marianna Slocum and Florence Gerdel. They had worked among the Tzeltals of southern Mexico for something like twenty-five years. When they began their work among the Tzeltals, the whole tribe was illiterate and monolingual. It was a very remote and isolated tribe, hostile to outsiders. One believer, the translators' language helper, carried a victrola with two records containing portions of God's Word up and down the mountainsides to those who would listen. By October 1949, there were some eighty believers. Then the Gospel of Mark was completed in Tzeltal and that was a real turning point in the growth of the church. The translators had been teaching reading even before there were any believers. By January of 1950 there were approximately four hundred believers. At that time a pastor of the Presbyterian church came out to collaborate in the work and to take charge. Special campaigns were organized to teach people to read. All of the church leaders were literate and before long there was a core of literate believers. By August 1950, there were fifteen hundred people professing faith in Jesus Christ. As more of the Word was translated, the church continued to grow (Slocum and Gerdel 1975).

The government, too, was interested in having the Tzeltals learn to read their own language. It was Miss Slocum who prepared the primer and trained the first teachers at the request of the National Indian Institute in 1951. This program still is going on.

By 1963 there were approximately eighty-five congregations
and ten thousand believers and the church was continuing to
grow. By 1975 there were some 150 congregations.

There is a Bible Institute established by the Reformed Church
of America where the Word of God is studied in the Tzeltal
language. There also are native authors emerging to write
Christian literature in their native tongue.

Miss Slocum believes that many of the people may have been
won by oral witness, but that having the Scriptures and being
able to read them has enabled them to build the church (1975).

The presence of a church of over eighteen hundred members
among the Chinantec Lalana Indians in Oaxaca, Mexico, is evidence of the power of the Spirit of God and the printed Word.
Dr. and Mrs. Calvin R. Rensch, Wycliffe Bible Translators, went
to live among these Indians in the tropical rain forest eighteen
years ago. When they arrived they were not welcomed. There
were no Christians. Through deeds of love and kindness the
Rensch's soon gained the confidence of the people. But their
first converts, those who helped them translate the Gospel of
Mark, were severely persecuted. In spite of the persecution,
the new Christians continued to witness to others. Long before
the Rensch's had completed the New Testament there were more
than a thousand believers. The Chinantec New Testament was completed early in 1975. By that time there were eighteen hundred
believers. Rensch insists that he never preached but simply
gave them the written Word in their language. The growth of the
church is attributed to the written Word and to the witness of
the first Christians who were converted as they assisted the
translators (Schemper 1975).

Colombia

In 1964 Misses Slocum and Gerdel entered the Paez tribe. Until their arrival, and even for a time afterward, the churches
in the area conducted services in Spanish, using a Paez interpreter for the sermons. The Paez people do not know Spanish
well enough to understand abstract ideas--only well enough to
get along at the market. Many of them were somewhat literate
in Spanish but none in Paez.

Literacy classes were started in 1968, and the first Gospel
was published in 1969. The number of believers in the Christian
and Missionary Alliance Church (the largest church in the tribe)
has grown from approximately eight hundred in 1964 to about
eighteen hundred in 1975 (Slocum and Gerdel 1975).

The C&MA congregations now have singing and Scripture reading
in Paez. Christian literate bilinguals are conducting courses

to teach the illiterates to read Paez because they believe their people need it.

A Paez literacy fund pays full-time workers. Many congregations are taking advantage of the opportunities to get their people literate and the Paez are building their own completely indigenous Bible School to be taught entirely in Paez.

Church growth has been much slower among the Paez where, until recently, people were more illiterate than the Tzeltals who were learning to read from the very beginning of the work. It seems that among the Paez, many accepted Christ upon hearing the Word preached, but soon fell by the wayside because they had no Scriptures on which to feed. Having been church members once and having dropped out, it is difficult for their interest to be rekindled (Slocum and Gerdel 1975).

In 1965 Misses Isabel Kerr and Marie Berg of the Wycliffe Bible Translators began work among the Cuiba people of eastern Colombia, near the Venezuelan border. Their first convert was through oral witnessing, but he never grew spiritually. Their second convert, Weinacu, was born again by reading the Scriptures. He became a very strong witness. Now, there are sixteen believers in the tribe who came to faith either through reading the Word themselves or by hearing the Word read, mostly when the translators were not even in the tribe (Kerr 1975).

Miss Kerr says that those translators who have done no literacy work have few if any converts. One team had been working among the Yucuna people on a Catholic mission compound for twelve years. They were not allowed to do any literacy work (Kerr 1975). There was much oral witnessing, but not a single convert.

El Salvador

In the spring of 1975, Campus Crusade for Christ, known as Alfa y Omega Movimiento in El Salvador, began using Christ-centered primers prepared by the All Nations Literacy Movement. Their goal was to strengthen the Christians and to lead others to Christ while teaching them to read. In a letter dated September 15, 1975, Ladislao Leiva, director of the Movimiento, wrote that by that time fifty-seven people had been led to Christ as a result of this literacy effort, and that all of them had become active members of the church (Leiva 1975).

Brazil

It is difficult to exaggerate the part that the Bible has played in planting and nurturing churches in South America.

Scores and scores of strong evangelical churches in that continent came into existence around a copy of the Word of God. The
Brazilian city of Manaus offers a good illustration. At the
turn of the century a business man in that city bought a wheel-
barrow full of Bibles from a man who came to his shop. He did
not sell them, for that would have brought opposition. He loaned them to anyone who wanted to borrow them. For many years,
these books were the only Christian witness in Manaus. Then the
Bible readers began to meet together, and by 1950 there were
five churches in Manaus, each fully self-supporting, each with
its own national pastor (Chirgwin 1954:81).

One more illustration from Brazil will have to suffice: Many
years ago a colporteur sold a Bible to a farmer. He took it
home and started to read it, but because of his wife's opposition, he gave it up. Later, she changed her mind and they
agreed to read it together. Soon they asked another couple to
join them. In the face of persecution they persisted, and
others joined them. When the colporteur returned, he found 120
people gathered for worship (Chirgwin 1954:102).

Guatemala

For forty years, Protestant mission work had been attempted
through interpreters among the Aguacateco tribe in western Guatemala, and at the end of all that time, there was only one believer. That was Chico, the barber. Chico knew Spanish, but he
was illiterate. Almost all of his fellow tribesmen were monolingual, speaking only their mother tongue which had never been
reduced to writing. Most of the mission work that was attempted
during those forty years was in the Spanish language, so it is
easy to understand why there was so little success. And even
though Chico tried to witness to his fellowmen in their mother
tongue, "...people won't listen to an illiterate preacher". At
least that is true in the Aguacateco tribe, according to Harry
and Lucille McArthur (August 1975).

The McArthurs arrived in Aguacatan and began working with the
Aguacatecos in November 1952, when Chico was the only believer.
These members of Wycliffe Bible Translators began immediately to
learn the Aguacateco language and reduce it to writing with the
help of a monolingual, Chico Kalin. In due time they began
translating the Scriptures, and before long, Chico Kalin was a
child of God.

It wasn't long before others were being won for Christ. By
the time the New Testament was completed in 1975, seventeen
hundred Aguacatecos, about ten percent of the entire tribe, had
accepted Jesus as their personal Savior and Lord. Not all the
growth can be attributed directly to literacy work. Many had

been won for Christ or attracted to Him through personal witnessing and through oral proclamation of the Lord, including a radio program. But all of this radio preaching was done by men who were well versed in the Aguacateco Scriptures (McArthur 1975).

An interesting point brought out by the McArthurs was that those people who don't know how to read equate that ability with spiritual growth. When a literate person sins, they say "Look at him. He sinned, and he even knows how to read" (1975).

Misses Fran Eachus and Ruth Carlson of Wycliffe Bible Translators have been working among the Kekchi Indians, about a hundred miles north of Guatemala City, for many years. In a personal interview with them in 1975 they reported that there were only twenty-five believers in the Cobán area in 1964, after several years of mission work by them, and others. In that year many of the local Kekchis learned to read, and the church began to grow more rapidly, so that by 1975 there were more than six hundred believers meeting in several different villages (Eachus and Carlson 1975).

This same linguistic team also reported on the work in the Chamelco area, south of Cobán. In 1960 fifty believers were taught to read. As a result of the increased witnessing of these new literates, ten new churches sprang up. The mother church now has fifteen hundred members and the ten new churches have between four and five hundred members each (Carlson and Eachus 1975).

Dominican Republic

Perhaps the most convincing evidence of the value of literacy for church growth comes from this country in the Caribbean. In a letter addressed to the Alfalit headquarters in Costa Rica, Rev. Octavio Nadal writes concerning the abundant harvest of souls resulting from the use of this organization's literacy materials over a period of seven years. He says that volunteer literacy workers had personally spoken of Christ to 21,673 people. Of these, 11,312 began coming to church, and 5,173 became active members. Nadal says that they are readers of the Bible, walking in the Light of Christ. They are not just people who raised their hands at a campaign, but are pure believers and active church members. He says that these statistics show that Alfalit is pure evangelism and that this literacy program has been more productive than all the big professional evangelistic campaigns (Nadal 1961:1).

MUSLIM LANDS

In countless cases the mere reading of the Bible has cast a
spell over people. This sometimes happens even in hostile Muslim lands. A Bible Society agent declares that he has often
found a hearing for the Gospel by going boldly into a cafe and
reading aloud a Bible story in colloquial Arabic. He has found
that the story of the Prodigal Son is one of the favorites. The
Parable of the Lost Sheep is another story that is sure to be
listened to, and often purchased (Chirgwin 1954:75).

John Subhan, who later became bishop of the Methodist Church
of North India, had been a loyal Muslim and a strict member of
the Sufi sect. As a boy he attended a Muslim school, studied
the Koran under the direction of the mullahs, and lived in an
entirely Muslim setting. He had no association of any kind with
Christian people. He had never heard any kind of Christian address. But he had read a Gospel. Just one! "It was sufficient,"
he said. "It convinced me, and I decided to become a Christian"
(Chirgwin 1954:70-71).

Iran

Iran is enjoying an atmosphere of increasing religious toler-
ance. Opportunities abound for Christian mission work, especially among the youth. Bible sales have almost tripled in a little
over a decade (International Review of Missions 1967:Vol.1,18).
This is due largely to the almost thirty thousand persons (almost all Muslims) from three hundred cities and towns who are
taking Bible correspondence courses, which, in turn, resulted
from several summers of intensive literature distribution by
Operation Mobilization. International Mission is having difficulty keeping up with demands growing out of this deluge of
Bible students who write in, asking questions, requesting literature, and need follow up (Kane 1971:296).

North Africa

Bible correspondence courses are also in great demand in North
Africa. In 1962 the North Africa Mission initiated a Bible correspondence course in the Gospel of John, and by 1964 something
like twenty thousand Muslims had sent a written request to be
enrolled in the course. When the government learned about this,
it closed the bookstore, which had been the headquarters for the
correspondence course. The mission then moved the operation to
Marseilles, France, where the Bible correspondence courses are
now a part of the Radio School of the Bible. Gospel programs
are beamed into North Africa from three powerful stations, and
listeners are encouraged to write for Bible courses, available
in French, English and Arabic. Each month an average of three
thousand lessons are sent out and two thousand test papers are

corrected. In the first four months of this ministry, over 3500 students sent in a written profession of faith in Christ (Kane 1971:312).

In Morocco the Gospel Missionary Union launched a Bible correspondence course in 1961 and within seven years, forty thousand Muslims, representing every town in that country, had requested courses. Because of this phenomenal success, the GMU missionaries were expelled in 1969. The Bible correspondence course was transferred to Spain, where it continues its work unabated (Kane 1971:318).

Also in Algeria, more and more interest is being shown in the Scriptures. Two Algerian colporteurs sell approximately five hundred books per month on the streets, in market places, and from door to door. Distribution of the Bible increased forty percent in one year, 1968 (Kane 1975:316).

Indonesia

Christian advertisements in Muslim publications are proving an effective tool of evangelism. In a six month period in Indonesia last year 163 new churches were established for former Muslims who accepted Christ in response to the ads (*World Vision* 1976:Vol.21,No.7,22).

AFRICA SOUTH OF THE SAHARA

The Congo

The growth of the church in Wembo Nyama in the Congo is another beautiful example. Laubach literacy workers went there at the invitation of the Methodist mission. They made lessons in the Otetelo language, and mimeographed seven hundred copies. Then they trained 120 members of the church to teach the lessons. Each of those 120 selected one non-Christian illiterate neighbor, brought him to the church one day, and taught him the primer. At the end of each lesson the teacher told a four-minute story about one of the miracles of kindness which Jesus performed, or he would read a miracle story from the Gospels (Laubach 1969: 8-9).

It took just two weeks to finish the primer. Then they had a graduation ceremony at which the 120 new literates were given diplomas for having learned the primer. After this, they began to read the Story of Jesus, and when that was finished, they were able to read Matthew, Mark, Luke and John in their own language. They were now literates, and they were Christians. All of them joined the church! In 1969 one of the largest people movements on earth was going on around the Wembo Nyama region,

and the missionaries who participated in this people movement
say that it began when the 120 church members were trained to
teach the primer and witness for Christ (Laubach 1969:8-9).

Liberia

The years 1947 to 1955 saw rapid growth of the Lutheran
Church in the Totota area of Liberia. The Church grew in one
town after another--from no converts at all in 1947 to 850 in
1955. This was remarkable growth when we consider the fact that
in 1922, after sixty-two years in Liberia, using the school approach, the Lutheran Church baptized membership stood at only
192 (Wold 1968:100,104).

One of the reasons for the rapid growth after 1947 was the
fact that in that year the Evangelical Lutheran Church in Liberia was organized and some of the leaders began to look upon the
Church as their own. By that time, too, the Church was baptizing unschooled villagers--a practice which did not exist before
1947. There were also resident native pastors in some villages,
and there were village evangelists who knew how to plant
churches and did so.

But literacy and Bible translation were also important factors in the growth of the church.

In 1948 Frank Laubach came to Liberia, and a very successful
literacy program was launched. Suddenly hundreds of people were
able to read the Scriptures for themselves, for in that same
year the translation of the Kpelle New Testament was completed.

It was also in 1948 that Dr. Welmers completed his Kpelle
grammar. In 1949 the people in Totota began singing hymns to
native tunes in the worship services (Wold 1968:105-106).

It is impossible to say to what extent each of these factors
contributed to the growth of the church. No doubt all of them
reflect an identification of the church with the people.

In his excellent book, *God's Impatience in Liberia*, Joseph
Wold points out that a good literacy program is important for
the church growth, but that literacy alone is not enough. He
says:

> The excellent literacy program and New Testament
> translations in Kpelle and Loma have set the stage
> for a sound training and solid shepherding of the
> masses of unschooled villagers. But until the Lu-
> therans make hard, bold plans for church planting
> and implement them along sound anthropological lines,
> the literacy program is like a stage set without actors.

The translations are unread scripts, gathering
dust on a shelf (1968:107-108).

Nigeria

One of the most impressive instances of church growth in recent years was that of the Tiv in central Nigeria. This tribe,
numbering a million souls, was occupied by the Christian Reformed Mission. Though mission work began among the Tiv in 1911, it
was not until 1957 that the church was organized with fifteen
hundred members. There seems to be no record of the communicant
membership for that year, but in 1962 the number of communicants
was 4,162. Then, amazingly, membership jumped to 7,352 in 1963!
In 1957 the Sunday morning church attendance was about 24,000.
This figure rose to 105,242 in 1963! Why this tremendous increase? For one thing, we know in 1960 the mission instituted
hundreds of Classes of Religious Instruction (CRI), which were
small schools in which slightly educated and slightly paid workers taught the Bible, reading, writing, and arithmetic, and held
worship services on Sunday for school children as well as for
interested adults. Within three years the Sunday Church attendance at all station churches and CRIs had risen to more than
105,000 (Grimley 1966:103-104; McGavran 1970:218).

AROUND THE WORLD

During World War II, in every country where the Nazis were in
control, men turned increasingly to the Bible. It was a source
of comfort to them, and it strengthened their hearts and stif-
fened their resistance. It helped to keep the Christian faith
alive in those dark days, and it helped to save Europe (Chirgwin 1954:53).

The end of the war did not bring the new interest in Bible
reading to an end. Bible reading has continued to spread and
has made itself felt in various spheres—in the home as well as
in the theological classroom and in the pulpit (Chirgwin 1954:
54).

The most phenomenal development in Bible study and Bible circulation, however, is found among the sects on the outer fringe
of the Protestant world, especially the Pentecostals, the
Seventh Day Adventists, the Jehovah's Witnesses, and certain
other extreme groups. These denominations came into existence
largely as a reaction against the neglect of the Bible, and they
are now growing at a phenomenal rate and moving out into every
part of the world. These denominations insist that all their
members shall take an active role in evangelism and they give a
central place to the Bible.

An illustration of their activity is seen in a recent evangelistic campaign organized by the Pentecostals in Chile. The campaign made a profound impression upon the whole country and was
marked by Bible sales that broke all records. It is this branch
of the Church that is buying and circulating the Bible in record
numbers, and it is this branch that is said to be growing more
rapidly than any other. They may not interpret the Bible the
way we do, and they may be more inclined than most of us to
bring their own ideas into it than to try to discover what the
Biblical writers really meant to say. But the fact remains that
these sects are probably doing more Bible reading and Bible distributing than any other section of the Christian Church, and
they are the ones which are growing the fastest (Chirgwin 1954:
55; Wagner 1973:15-27).

By way of contrast, it is interesting to note that the Eastern Orthodox Church is quite stagnant. Perhaps it is because
this Church has its main strength in countries such as those of
Eastern Europe and the Near East, where the illiteracy rate has
always been rather high. We know, too, that the Orthodox Church
has rarely encouraged even its literate members to read the
Bible for themselves. The Bible is read in public worship, but
in spite of the respect paid to it, its reading takes second
place to the recital of the liturgy. Some patriarchs and bishops
are beginning to take a new interest in the Bible, but that is
not yet true of the Orthodox clergy and people as a whole (Chirgwin 1954:57).

SUMMARY

There is no end to the stories that can be told of individuals
coming to faith in Christ solely from reading the Scriptures.
And there is no end to the stories that can be told of entire
churches coming into existence where there was just one Bible
and one literate person. Many books have already been written
on this subject, and a good many of them are listed in this
bibliography. The Bible Societies and various organizations engaged in the distribution of Christian literature can also supply countless stories of the impact of the printed page on the
readers of the Word of Life.

In the twentieth century and all through its history, whenever
the Church has seriously sought to win people to Christ and
equip them to win others, it has used the Bible as its main in-
strument. The times when the Church has gone to its evangelistic task with the open Bible have been the times when it has won
its greatest victories. The Sword of the Spirit has been the
cutting-edge of its advance (Chirgwin 1954:64).

In the words of F. R. Barry, in his book, *The Relevance of Christianity*:

> Nearly all the renewals and moral reforms
> within Christianity have sprung from the re-
> discovery of Scripture, and especially the
> Synoptic Gospels. The moment Christianity loses
> touch with the inspiration of the New Testament,
> it tends to sink to a sub-Christian level, and
> its moral witness is weakened or obscured (Barry
> 1932:40).

This chapter has also shown that thousands of individuals and entire tribes have become responsive to the Gospel or even active church members as a result of a church-sponsored literacy program, taught by witnessing Christians who loved them and sacrificially gave of their time and talent to help them.

10

Conclusion

We have seen that down through the centuries the church was strongest when the leadership was literate and when the church membership was also able to read God's Word and encouraged to do so, as in the early centuries of the Christian era (Chapter 2). We saw that during the Middle Ages, when there was almost total illiteracy among the laity on the European Continent, the church was very corrupt and filled with superstition (Chapters 3 and 4). History has also shown us that where the laity had the Scriptures in their mother tongue, the church not only endured persecution, but even multiplied in the face of such opposition and the absence of missionaries, as in Madagascar during the nineteenth century (Chapter 7).

In Chapter 9 we saw that literacy campaigns have opened many doors for the Gospel--doors to countries, doors to various ethnic groups, and doors to individual hearts. It was shown also that many people have been led to Christ solely or primarily through reading and that new literates have often led large numbers to their Savior.

But history also shows us that literacy in itself is no guarantee of church growth. Japan, for example, is ninety-nine percent literate but less than one percent Christian. The vast majority of the people in Northern Europe and in the United States and Canada are able to read, and yet only a small percentage of them could be classified as committed Christians. Literacy does not assure church growth; it can even be a hinderance.

DISADVANTAGES OF LITERACY

Communism

Karl Marx (1818-1883) and his followers have been literate people. That is, the leaders have been literate and they have taught all of the people in the Soviet Union (or at least ninety-nine percent of them) to read, so that they could more easily perpetuate their atheistic teachings. In about 1960 they spent $6,000,000,000 (six billion dollars), two dollars for every man, woman, and child on the face of the earth at that time, on literature in order to win the world to their cause.

Atheistic communism has made effective use of the printed page all over the world. In Madras, India, for instance, we have a striking example of the effectiveness of literature in the rapid growth of communism among industrial workers. Around any mill or factory during the mid-day rest hour, groups of fifty to one hundred workmen can be seen seated around one of their fellowmen who is reading aloud from a communist book or magazine. Russia is held up as a workers' paradise, and strikes are advocated as steps toward a social revolution which will establish the "rule of the proletariat" in India. A steady stream of books, magazines, and handbills has produced a complete change in the outlook and mentality of the Indian industrial worker (Warren 1938:513). Such stories can be multiplied over and over again.

Apocryphal Writings

Mention was made earlier of the apocryphal writings which were written between the first and third centuries B.C. and which were included in the Septuagint. These were never recognized by the Jews as part of the Hebrew Scriptures (Metzger 1965: 35). They were never quoted by Jesus, nor anywhere else in the New Testament (Jackson 1949:214). However, when the Bible was translated into Latin in the second century A.D., its Old Testament was translated not from the Hebrew Old Testament, but the Greek Septuagint version of the Old Testament. From the Septuagint these Apocryphal books were carried over into the Latin translation, and from there, into the Latin Vulgate (Encyclopedia Britannica 1973:s.v.), which became the Bible of Western Europe for a thousand years, and is used in the Church of Rome until this day (Herklots 1957:53). The attitude of the Reformers toward the Apocrypha was determined by the use made of these writings by the Roman Church in support of such doctrines as salvation by works, the merits of the saints, purgatory, and intercession for the dead (Russell 1960:90). But the Roman Catholic Church, in the Council of Trent in A.D. 1546, declared these books to be canonical (Encyclopedia Britannica 1973:s.v.), and they are still in the Douay Version (Roman Catholic Bible) (Jackson 1949:215). Thus these damnable heresies have been perpetuated.

New Testament Apocryphal Books

These were spurious Gospels, Acts of the Apostles, and Epistles which began to appear in the second century. They were forgeries and were recognized as such from the start. They were deliberate attempts to fill the gaps of the New Testament story of Jesus in order to perpetuate heretical ideas. There were at least fifty of the spurious "Gospels", and many "Acts" and "Epistles". The large number of these forged writings made it necessary for the early Church to distinguish between them and the true Word of God. It is said that Mohammed got some of his ideas about Christianity from these books. They are also the origin of some of the teachings of the Roman Catholic Church (Jackson 1949:Vol.1,225-226). When the canon of the New Testament was fixed and the apocryphal books became outlawed, they ceased to be read. Unfortunately, from their fables sprang sacred legends, which were kept alive in the church during the Middle Ages as "ecclesiastical tradition". And this was often used in the development of its dogma (Jackson 1949:Vol.1,225).

The Latin Vulgate

We have seen that the Vulgate included the apocryphal books of the Old Testament, and because of these writings, many false doctrines crept into the Church of Rome. The Vulgate was also the parent version of all the early pre-Reformation vernacular Scriptures, such as Wycliffe's translation into English.

Jerome (329-420). Jerome was the most learned scholar of his day, and he was a very devout man. Nevertheless his translation had at least two very serious mistakes. Perhaps the worst mistake was in the translation of the word "repent". The Vulgate says "Do penance". This corruption of the thought has been the source of endless error in the Roman Church. Instead of an internal process, it makes repentance an external process (Boyd 1933:64).

Another serious error which we find in the Vulgate is the mistranslation of the Greek word "presbuteros" which means "elder". This work appears sixty-two times in the New Testament, and is translated "elder" or "ancient" in the Vulgate on fifty-six of these occurrences. However, on six occasions the word "presbuteros" has been deliberately translated as "priest", evidently to perpetuate a false teaching. It is translated "priest", for example, in James 5:14 which should read "Is any among you sick? Let him call for the elders of the church, and let them pray

over him..." (RSV). But the Vulgate reads "Let him call for the
priests..." The Greek word for priest is "hiereus" which looks
nothing like "presbuteros", so this was not just an innocent mistake.

The other passages in which "presbuteros" is translated
"priest", are the following: Acts 14:23 "And when they had appointed 'priests' for them in every church..."; Acts 15:2 "...
Paul and Barnabus...were appointed to go up to Jerusalem to the
apostles and the 'priests'..."; I Timothy 5:17 "Let the 'priests'
who rule well be considered worthy of double honor..."; I Tim.
5:19 "Never admit any charge against a 'priest'..."; and Titus
1:5 "This is why I left you in Crete, that you might...appoint
'priests' in every town..." (Young 1955:293).

Other False Teachings

It was literate people who invented the doctrines of purgatory, the immaculate conception of Mary, Mary as mediator and
intercessor with God, and papal infallibility (Qualben 1955:379).
Pope Pius IX (1846-1878) published his "Syllabus of Errors"
which refuted (1) freedom of conscience, (2) freedom of the
press, (3) Protestantism, (4) Bible societies, (5) civil marriage, (6) separation of church and state, and (7) religious
toleration (Qualben 1955:379).

The Humanists

These people were literate who found joy in the literature
and art of pre-Christian Rome and Greece. One kind of humanism
found its goal in exuberant appreciation of life in this present
world. These men of the Renaissance were self-confident, trust-
ing in man rather than God. Some were very religious but many
were content to pay lip service to the faith and regarded man
as the competent architect of his own future. They looked with
disdain on the schoolmen and scholasticism (Latourette 1965:148).

A number of Humanists of Central and Southern Europe began to
register their intellectual objections to various doctrines of
the Church and especially to the belief in the divinity of
Christ. This led to Unitarianism. In 1579 Faustus Socini organized a Unitarian community known as the Polish Brethren. His
activities soon extended to Transylvania which became the great
stronghold of the Unitarians (Qualben 1955:334-335). They
taught that all religious teaching must be tested by human
reason. The doctrine of the Trinity and the divinity of Christ
were contrary to reason and must therefore be denied (Latourette
1953:795).

Liberal Theologians in the Protestant Church

Theologians like David Frederick Strauss (1808-1874) deny the historical validity of many of the Gospel narratives (Qualben 1955:400). Down through the nineteenth century and down to the present time there are countless liberals and "moderates" who are very well educated, denying the virgin birth of Christ, his resurrection, and just about all of the fundamental teachings of Christianity, twisting the Scriptures to their own destruction (2 Peter 3:16).

Harvard University

The liberals who took over Harvard University were very literate people. They asserted that human nature is essentially good and that salvation is insured by developing the good in man. These liberals included men like Ralph Waldo Emerson, Henry W. Longfellow, and William H. Taft, president of the United States from 1908 to 1912 (Qualben 1955:472).

The Koran

The Koran is a strange jumble of facts and fables, laws and legends, full of historical errors and superstition, but in it there is just enough truth--truth borrowed from previous Revelations, yet cast in another mold--as to divert attention from the need for more (Glover 1962:30).

False Cults

Some of the fastest growing denominations in the world today are those that deny the Lord that bought them, such as the Jehovah's Witnesses and the Mormons. These people, especially the Jehovah's Witnesses, spend vast amounts of money on literature. The Jehovah's Witnesses have the largest press in the world. Every twenty-four hours they produce so much literature that it could make a pile higher than the Empire State Building.

We could go on and on pointing out the dangers of literacy. Like fire, it can be used for destructive purposes as well as for good. But we believe that history has shown that the advantages of literacy for church growth far outweigh the disadvantages. Let us now consider some of these advantages.

ADVANTAGES OF LITERACY

Literacy Work Can Open Doors for the Gospel

Door to the Country. The illiteracy rate in many countries of Africa and Asia is very high. In many countries not more

than ten percent of the population can read and write. Maps
showing poverty and disease coincide with maps showing illiteracy (See figures 1,2,and 3). Illiterates have the shortest life
expectancy, the most sickness, the lowest economic living scale,
and the least food (Espenshade 1975:51,59,63).

When poverty, disease, hunger, and illiteracy go hand in hand
together, they breed the unrest and resentment that threaten a
stable society. They are the conditions out of which revolution
and war develop. Illiteracy is a major obstacle to economic development and a threat to peace.

Literacy can influence development in a number of ways. It
is an essential aid in the improvement of agriculture and public
health, in the development of skills for industry, in an intelligent adjustment to changing society, in responsible participation in political affairs, and in the enrichment of cultural and
spiritual life.

Government leaders are well aware that literacy is a key to
economic and social development. Therefore, when missionaries
or anyone else comes with an offer to teach people to read,
doors otherwise shut to missionaries have been flung wide open.
This was the case, for example, when the Wycliffe Bible Translators entered Mexico in 1935. If they had come with the avowed
intention of preaching the Gospel only, they would not have been
given permission to enter the country. But because their purpose was to reduce languages to writing and teach people to read
and to provide them with helpful literature, they were welcomed
into that country, and they have been there ever since (Steven
and Hefley 1972:20,24).

From my own experience I know that in 1960 the Lutheran
Church - Missouri Synod had been trying for eighteen months to
raise its quota in Nigeria from thirty-five workers to forty-
five without success. Meanwhile, the Wycliffe Bible Translators
with their offer to do language analysis and literacy work and
provide literature of high moral value, including the Scriptures,
were allowed to bring as many as seventy-five new workers into
the country--all that they had requested (Bendor-Samuel 1961).

Door to the Tribe. Missionaries have often gained entrance
into a country only to run up against a stone wall when trying
to gain entrance into one of the tribes. In Chapter 9 we read
how literacy work broke down the barriers for Frank Laubach and
his co-workers in the Philippines, so that they were allowed to
work among the Moros who, until literacy work began, were violently opposed to the Gospel.

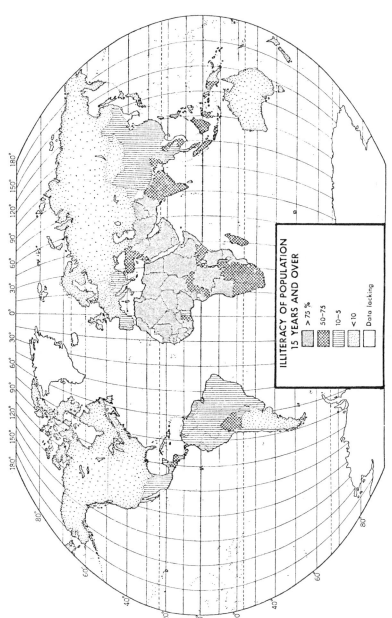

Figure 1. Percentage of Illiterate People Fifteen Years of Age and Older.

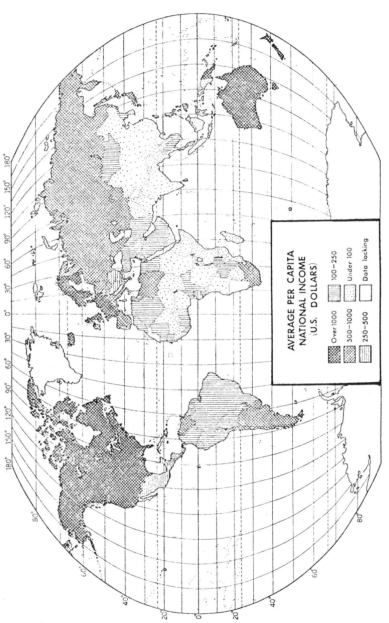

Figure 2. Average Per Capita National Incomes.

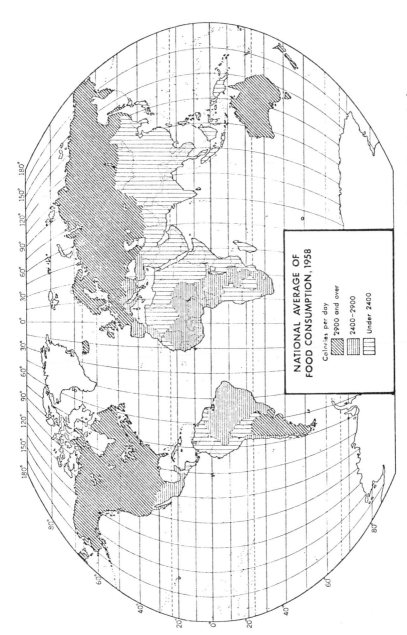

Figure 3. National Average of Food Consumption (Caloric Intake).

NATIONAL AVERAGE OF
FOOD CONSUMPTION, 1958

Calories per day

2900 and over
2400–2900
Under 2400

One of the most remarkable instances of receptivity in recent
years was that manifested by the Tiv in central Nigeria. This
tribe of about one and a half million was occupied by the Christian Reformed Church. There had been a Christian witness in
that tribe for twenty-five years. In 1960 the Church consisted
of 7,352 communicant members, in and around the several mission
stations. Out among the Tiv villages, the mission had instituted hundreds of classes of religious instruction, which in
effect were small schools, too elementary to receive grants in
aid. In these schools, workers who had very little training and
received a minimal amount of pay, taught the Scriptures, reading,
writing, and arithmetic during the week, and conducted worship
services on Sundays for the school children and for adults who
might be interested. By 1963 the Sunday church attendance at
station and village churches was up to 105,242--more than fourteen times the number of communicants just three years earlier
(Grimley 1966:103-104).

Door to the Individual Heart. If we talk about the love of
Christ but do not demonstrate that love, we are "as sounding
brass or a tinkling cymbal" (1 Corinthians 13:1). On the other
hand, when the individual missionary or other literacy worker
shows his love for people by teaching them to read, when he wins
respect for what he does, he may soon find that he is also respected for what he believes. Certainly, if he is not respected
for his actions, he will not be respected for his faith (Mason
1967:38).

Literacy Education Provides an Outlet for Meaningful Service

In his book, *Reaching the Silent Billion*, David Mason writes:

> New converts always want something to do. Chris-
> tianity encourages participation and involvement.
> The Bible says we should be doers and not hearers
> only. Without an outlet for meaningful service, the
> individual, the church, and the denomination will
> wither on the vine. Adult literacy education has
> proven itself...as an instrument for assimilating
> new members and invigorating old ones. Therefore,
> when the need for literacy outside the church and
> the need for rejuvenation within the church exist
> in the same community, an Each One Teach One program
> (literacy) can help solve both problems.

> If the indigenous church is to be robust, its
> laity as well as its clergy must be committed to the
> task. Whether the literacy teaching is carried out
> as a humanitarian service or as a means of communicat-
> ing the Gospel, it can invigorate the church sponsor-
> ing the work (1967:33-36).

People Can Be Led to Christ While They are Learning to Read

Teaching people to read gives the teacher an excellent opportunity to witness for Christ, an opportunity with every lesson
he teaches. In the very first lesson, the teacher can ask:

> Do you know why I am teaching you to read?
> It is because Jesus is our leader. Jesus healed
> all kinds of sickness and disease. He made the
> deaf people to hear and the blind to see. Jesus
> loves you and wants to help you. You, in a way,
> are also blind, because you cannot read. Jesus
> wants you to be able to read so you can read about
> Him and all the wonderful things He has done for
> you.

The teacher can then go on to explain that Jesus came into
the world to save sinners, that He died for us and rose again
and ascended into heaven to prepare a place for us, that whoever
believes in Him will have everlasting life.

Every day the lesson can begin and end with prayer, and every
day the teacher can tell a short story about Jesus. If the
primers are Christ-centered, which we strongly recommend, then
the student learns about Jesus as he learns to read, and by the
time he has completed the primer, he can read the Scriptures.
The primer thus becomes an evangelistic tool, as well as a literacy tool, in the hands of the new literate.

We saw in the last chapter how large numbers of people in El
Salvador and in the Dominican Republic came to faith in Christ
and became active church members through the literacy program.

How Ability to Read Can Help Church Members

Growth in Grace and Knowledge of their Savior. This increase
in grace and knowledge enables Christians to comfort and edify
one another. It helps them to more diligently teach their own
children, to withstand all the wiles of the devil, and to be
more confident and thus more effective witnesses for Christ.

This is well illustrated in the story of the Reverend Dia and
his wife in the Philippines, referred to in Chapter 9. As
people learned Bible passages, they realized their religion was
true, and they rushed out to persuade their loved ones to become
believers. In six months the membership doubled, and in the following year, it doubled again. Other congregations were also
established.

Literacy was not the only factor that contributed to the
growth of this church. But the fact that they were able to read

the Word for themselves seems to have played an important part
in convincing them of the truth of the message which, in turn,
enabled them to convince their loved ones to accept Christ as
their Savior too (McGavran 1970:18).

Prevention of False Teaching in the Church. We know of no
permanent indigenous church that did not have the Scriptures in
its own language and at least one church leader who was able to
read those Scriptures or who had committed to memory a large
amount of Scripture. In either case, whether that church leader
had memorized a large amount of Scripture or was able to read
the Scriptures, or both, if no one else in the congregation were
literate, no one would know if the church leader was preaching
and teaching the truth or not. The more laymen in the congregation who are able to read, the less opportunity there will be
for false teachings to be propagated. We have already seen
(Chapters 3 and 4) what happened in the Middle Ages when laymen
had no access to the Scriptures and could not have read the
precious Word if they had it in their hand. Those were truly
Dark Ages, filled with fear and superstition when men were mis-
led to look upon Christ as a stern judge rather than as a loving
Savior, and put their trust in their own works and in the
prayers to Mary and the saints, and in relics rather than in Him
who died for them and rose again.

It is also important for the laymen to be able to read the
Bible so they will not be deceived by false teachers who approach them from outside the church, who come to them in sheep's
clothing, but inwardly are ravening wolves (Matthew 7:15).
Sooner or later, these false teachers appear, and rather than
try to win the non-Christians to their particular persuasion,
they prey upon the Christians and try to lead them out of their
church into that of the false cult. Possession of the Bible and
the ability to read it for himself will help the layman to know
false teaching when he hears it, so that he will not be led
astray.

*Training Strong National Church Leaders and Building a Strong
National Missionary Church.* There are more heathen in the world
today than ever before. In fact, the number of heathen in the
the world today is greater than the entire world population of
1960 and three times greater than the global population of 1830.
Asia alone has more non-Christians (two billion) than there were
people in the entire world before 1930.

If the church is going to make any significant impact on the
peoples of Asia, hundreds of thousands of national workers must
be trained. But Asia is largely illiterate. About 50 percent
of the entire adult population of that vast continent can neither read nor write. Seventy-two percent of India's adult

population (over fifteen years of age) cannot read. Nepal is more than ninety percent blind to the printed page. Pakistan, Bangladesh, and most of the countries of Southwest Asia are at least eighty percent illiterate. Some ethnic groups are totally illiterate since their mother tongue has never even been reduced to writing. Many other ethnic groups have some Scripture in their language, but the translation is often in need of revision. Even where good translations exist, in many ethnic groups there are few who are able to read.

To win Asia to Christ, we must train all the national workers we can possibly train, and we must train them as fast as we possibly can. But before they can be trained, in many areas, they will first have to be taught to read. Most of these workers will probably have to be trained through Bible and leadership extension courses. But whether they are trained through extension courses or in residence schools, they will be trained better if they are literate.

Scripture Reading

A Functional Substitute, Utilized for Spiritual Gain. When a tribesman accepts Christ, whether in Africa or South America or Asia, if all his spiritual and social needs are not met, sociological voids or vacuums are created. Bible reading, as well as memorizing Scripture, singing Christian songs, dramatizing Bible stories, and listening to spring-driven cassette players in a village are all excellent functional substitutes. This fulfills the need of social intercourse, while avoiding the temptations of the cantinas (Klassen 1974:88).

Helping to Avoid Syncretism. Wherever the Gospel is proclaimed there is always a danger that some of the people, if not all of them, will cling to their old gods and beliefs while professing to be Christian.

In Guatemala, for example, the Christo-pagan believes in two gods. He believes in the Christian God and the traditional Dios Mundo, the owner of the world. Before the Roman Catholics arrived, the "god of the dead" was the son of the moon and the sun. It was not difficult, therefore, to identify the crucified Christ with the traditional "god of the dead". Since the missionaries referred to God as the "God of Heaven", the pagan identified Him with the sun. It followed, then, that Mary should be identified with the moon deity—the symbol of fertility.

The Catholic custom of giving saints' names to persons, places, shrines, and churches was also compatible with pre-Columbian paganism, for the *dueños* (wicked spirits) of the Indians also had their assigned images and shrines. Thus, a mere trans-

ference of names was all that was necessary for a Christo-pagan
blending (Luzbetak 1970:243).

It is easy to understand how this syncretism came about. We
have seen that the Catholic Church has always been opposed (until recently, at least) to the translation of Scriptures into
the vernacular and to the reading of Scripture by the laity wherever it was available to them in their own language. If the
early Catholic missionaries had learned the culture and the language of these various Indian tribes and produced dynamic equivalence translations of Scripture for them, and thoroughly instructed them in God's Word, no doubt, much, if not all, of this
syncretism could have been avoided.

Helping to Avoid Materialism. When people are lifted up from
their abject poverty to a "higher standard of living" through
literacy and basic education, there is the danger that they will
become more interested in the things of this world and set their
affections on them rather than on the things above. If the missionaries, however, are not materialistic themselves, and if
they thoroughly instruct the people in God's Word, this danger
is minimized. Teaching the Word (including Bible reading in
church and in the home) and living the Word is what transforms
individuals and cultures, resulting in spiritual and numerical
growth.

Some may doubt that Bible reading helps avoid materialism,
pointing out that so many church members in the United States
are so materialistic. However, it is very doubtful that these
materialistic church members are serious students of God's Word,
for His Word does transform lives. Peter writes "Like newborn
babes, long for the pure spiritual milk, that by it you may grow
up to salvation" (1 Peter 2:2,RSV). The Apostle Paul writes
"All Scripture is inspired by God and is profitable for teaching,
for reproof, for correction, and for training in righteousness,
that the man of God may be complete, equipped for every good
work (2 Timothy 3:16,17). The Apostle John writes in his first
epistle, "Do not love the world or the things in the world. If
anyone loves the world, love for the Father is not in him" (2:15).
James writes in similar words, "Do you not know that friendship
with the world is enmity with God? Therefore whoever wishes to
be a friend of the world makes himself an enemy of God (4:4).
The Scriptures are full of warnings against covetousness and
worldliness (Matt. 6:19-34; 1 Tim. 6:6-10; Luke 9:23-25;12:15-21;
John 6:27; 1 Tim. 6:18-19; Romans 12:1,2; Hebrews 13:5; Eph. 5:
3-5; Col. 3:1,2; 1 John 3:16-17 can be cited to mention but a
few). People cannot read such admonitions daily and observe the
self-sacrificing life of Jesus and Paul without being influenced
thereby.

Importance for All Christians, Especially for Spiritual Leaders. The spiritual life of the Christian worker is the most vital element in his character and influence. He or she is supposed to be "God's person, in God's place, doing God's work, in God's way, and for God's glory". If, therefore, he is to be God's servant in any true sense at all, he must be a person who walks closely with the Lord. This is because the worker himself is the greatest factor in evangelism. His deep underlying convictions have more to do in evangelization than the mere methods adopted. What the worker says and does is extremely important, but what he is, is even more important (Brown 1907:177).

Spirituality is necessary to the Christian worker's own happiness as well as to the success of his work. No man can be happy or largely useful in the Lord's work unless he is inspired by considerations that render him, like Paul, comparatively indifferent to merely physical and temporal conditions.

No initial Christian experience can carry one through life, especially in a hostile mission field. Like the manna sent to the Israelites, the soul's food must be gathered fresh every day. Unceasing effort is necessary. In the spiritual realm, as in the physical realm, things do not grow by themselves. They must be watched and cultivated.

These cautions are necessary because the knowledge that one is a spiritual guide to others involves subtle dangers to himself. The mission field is often a place of spiritual tragedy. There, men often live away from the holy influences of Christian society, and there is always the danger that what is fine in us will grow coarse (Brown 1907:107).

The helps to the spiritual life are therefore of vital importance for the Christian leader and to those he would win to Christ, and for those whom he would comfort, edify and inspire. One of these helps, of course, is Bible study. The Christian leader is supposed to have a good knowledge of the Bible. He can never know it well enough. It is not sufficient to have a general familiarity with Scriptural places and events. One should have a knowledge of the Bible's deepest spiritual truths and be able to make a personal appropriation of them. The Bible is God's direct message to men. How can we know the will of God unless we understand that message?

The ambassador for Christ will find his Bible indispensable to his own comfort. It will bring to him guidance in every perplexity, strength in every weakness, resources for every emergency.

And, of course, the messenger of Christ needs the Bible for
his work. His job is not to put forth his own ideas, but the
knowledge of salvation and godly living that he has found in the
Bible. His warnings against sin, his accounts of God's love,
his authoritative declaration as to what man ought to do, must
all rest upon Scripture. St. Paul exhorts all Christians to
"put on the whole armor of God"--truth, righteousness, the Gospel of peace, faith, salvation, and the sword of the Spirit
(Ephesians 6:11,13-17). Every one of these coverings is the
Word of God, or is vitally dependent upon His Word. The Christian must put on this armor if he is to be victorious! He is in
a better position to put it on and keep it on if he knows how to
read and does read the precious Word every day and meditate upon
it day and night.

FUTURE USE OF LITERATURE IN WORLD EVANGELIZATION

China

In no country has there been a greater reverence for literature than in China (Broomhall 1934:1). Respect for the printed
page is almost a religion to the Chinese, and the man of letters
holds the rank in society. Societies exist for the rescue of
the printed page from desecration and there are many shrines for
the burning of loose sheets, lest they be trampled underfoot.

Before the Communist take-over in 1949, foreign language students were anxious to get hold of anything printed in English,
and the students' interest clearly centered in four main themes:
the existence and nature of God; the relation between science
and religion; the nature of the post-war world; how to find meaning in life.

What an opportunity for Christian literature! Most university students could read the books and magazines and pamphlets in
English, if only they could get them (Smalley 1944:296-297).

India

In India the Bible is a best seller and the only book so
widely translated (Sinker 1952:50). There is no lack of reverence for the Bible or for the person of Christ, but Christians
are watched and criticized, and their divisions deplored and
condemned. Division is the greatest drawback of the Christian
Church in India, and the Bible is the one uniting force which
all the different churches have in common (Sinker 1952:50).

Bible correspondence courses have been effective in bringing
many to Christ. The Light of Life Bible Correspondence School
which promotes Bible study in twenty-four languages of India had

more than one and a half million enrolled in 1967, eighty-five
percent of whom were non-Christians (Kane 1971:121).

From 1964 to 1978 World Literature Crusade has delivered
280 million booklets in 23 major Indian languages; and, there
has been 3.4 million written responses. Founder and President Jack McAlister said the World Literature Crusade now has
a fulltime staff of more than 1,000. Their pioneer crusaders
have walked or bicycled more than 8 million miles to deliver
the Gospel to Indian homes.

In India today there are a number of extraordinary opportunities for the Bible. There is the fact of religious
freedom under the Constitution which removes by law all restrictions and embargoes against the Bible. There are increasing numbers of literates each year. More recent data
than that used in figure 1 reflects from 60-80% literacy among
the "over 15" population in India. In fact, World Literature
Crusade noted that in Bangladesh, among the impressionable
8 to 15-year-olds, 80% are able to read. There is also the
challenge of thousands of spiritually displaced persons--
Hindus in Pakistan and Muslims in India--cut off from their
co-religionists in either country and looking for a spiritual
home which the state in which they live cannot give them.
There are millions of intelligent people in both states who
find the old religions empty and who are hungry for an adequate spiritual life. We must rush in to fill the vacuum with
the Word of Eternal Life, lest we be guilty of a great sin of
omission.

Pakistan

Christian commandos are taking the Bible out into Eastern
Sind where many caste Hindus are still living peacefully in
this Muslim State. Whole villages have been deeply interested through adult literacy campaigns and audio-visual aids,
and have asked to become Christians. Among Muslims also
there is a genuine interest in the Bible (Kane 1971:121).

The Muslim World

Among Muslims there is an increasing demand for Christian
literature (Sanders 1944:209). We read in Chapter 9 that
thousands upon thousands of Muslims in Iran and North Africa
were enrolled in Bible correspondence courses.

Christian literature is valuable not only as a supplement
to the direct preaching of the Gospel, but often as a substitute to these basic forms of evangelism. The work of missionaries and even of national evangelists is often confined

to definite centers, but literature has penetrated to every
nook and corner of the country (Wysham 1937:57).

The evangelistic value of literature has been great in an
indirect way--by disarming prejudice and preparing the human
heart for the direct Gospel message.

A young Zoroastrian had never had contact with any Christian
until the day when he was converted by reading a tattered tract
which had been thrown into a corner by an uninterested relative
(Wysham 1937:58). Iran, like many Moslem lands, has for centuries thought that it knew all about Christianity, but most
of its ideas were warped and twisted. It is not virgin soil
for Gospel seed, but is already sown thickly with brambles.
Much of this error is deeply embedded in the religious and
other literature of centuries. To rid the minds of the Iranian
people of ancient prejudices and superstitions about Christianity is a herculean task that can be accomplished only by a
widespread distribution of Christian literature.

A government censor in Iran refused to authorize the publishing of two books on the grounds that they were Christian propa-
ganda and harmful to Islam. When challenged to pick out the
objectionable passages for deletion, he floundered a bit, then
blurted out: "The trouble with these books is not in any
special passage, but that everyone who reads them wants to
become a Christian" (Wysham 1937:59).

It is almost unheard of for a person to refuse a tract or
fail to read it when accepted. Christian literature has made
a secure place for itself in every phase of evangelistic work
in Iran (1937:60). Villagers are eager for reading matter and
those who are literate read books and tracts to others for
months after the evangelist has gone.

"In asking Christians, who had formerly been Moslems, what
first attracted their attention to Christ and what finally
brought about their conversion, I discovered that in a large
majority of cases, the Bible had much to do with the process"
writes J. Christy Wilson in *The Moslem World*.

He states objections to the Bible:--(1) that it has been
abrogated by the Koran, (2) that it has been changed and corrupted by Christians, and (3) that Christ took the genuine New
Testament back with Him to heaven--are not heard as often these
days as in times past (Wilson 1937:237).

The Spirit has used, to bring about the conversion of people,
such various passages as: Isaiah 42:3, Zech. 13, Luke 4:18,19
and Romans. It is the Word of God that saves, not man's word.

We must, therefore, present the Bible to the Moslems under the direction of the real Author, the Holy Spirit.

It is a healthy and humbling experience for one of us, who has been preaching for years in the world of Islam, to ask fifty or a hundred converts what led them to Christ, and note how few were brought by preaching (Wilson 1937:240).

Samuel M. Zwemer, who was a scholar, preacher, writer, evangelist, and apologist throughout the world of Christian missions to Muslims, has this to say about the effectiveness of literature:

> No other agency can penetrate so deeply, abide so persistently, witness so daringly, and influence so irresistibly as the printed page (Read Magazine 1970:Vol.5,No.1:1).

Practically all literate people in the Muslim World have the Bible in their mother tongue! Now, all we have to do is teach them to read (Wilson 1937:239)!

Japan

John R. Mott once said "The Bible is the best missionary." One of the outstanding missionaries to Japan in the nineteenth century, Dr. G. F. Verbeck, agrees with him. He said "If the choice were ever to be between the Bible without the teacher or the teacher without the Bible, I would unhesitatingly choose the former" (Robertson 1953:7).

The New Testament is the best seller in Japan. In 1952, although there were only about half a million baptized believers in that country, the Japan Bible Society had been selling more than half a million New Testaments every year for the past seven years (1953:37).

From 1945 to 1972 the Japan Bible Society distributed more than seventy million Scriptures--Bibles, New Testaments and portions of them. In 1970 alone, nearly nine million copies of Scripture were distributed, ranking Japan second only to the United States in Scripture circulation (Hammond 1975:335).

There is even a demand for Bibles in Greek, German, English, Chinese, French, Latin and Russian, all pointing to the inquisitiveness of the Japanese people (Robertson 1953:13).

Evangelical Christians will certainly want to capitalize on this love for the printed Word of God. Perhaps what is needed in Japan, more than preachers, are more Japanese Christian writers.

THE CHALLENGE

In all of the Asiatic countries, literature and teachers are highly respected. If the Christian Church accepts the challenge to teach people to read and provides literature that grips their souls, we may be able to penetrate the political, cultural, and other barriers that have walled off some two billion people from the Truth that sets men free.

But there is a dearth of national Christian writers in most Asiatic lands. Thousands of them must be trained to write for all age levels on a variety of subjects. This, we believe, is one of the greatest needs in Asia (as well as in Africa and Latin America), and perhaps one of the best ways to lead multitudes to Christ and thoroughly instruct them in His Word. Only writers from within their culture will be able to effectively speak to their hearts.

Where can we find the writers and how can they be trained? And where can we find the literacy workers to teach hundreds of millions in India, Africa and the Muslim world to read? How can we train enough pastors and evangelists when even a million more would mean only one more worker for every 2300 non-Christians in Asia. These and many related questions are answered in a companion volume by my wife, Lois Watkins, that is entitled *The Strategic Use of Literacy and Literature in World Evangelization.*

SUMMARY

Throughout history the Written Word of God has proven itself powerful in evangelism and in building the Christian Church. This should come as no surprise to us, for God Himself has given us His promise regarding the potency of His Word. He says:

> So shall my word be that goes forth from my mouth; it shall not return unto me empty, but it shall accomplish that which I purpose, and prosper in the thing for which I sent it (Isaiah 55:11,RSV).

Paul, in his letter to the Romans, stated:

> For I am not ashamed of the gospel: it is the power of God for salvation to every one who has faith, to the Jew first and also to the Greek (Romans 1:16, RSV).

We believe that the power of the Written Word is just as great or even greater than the Spoken Word, even if that Spoken

Word came from one risen from the dead. In Luke 16, in the story of the rich man and Lazarus, the rich man lifted up his eyes in hell and pleaded:

> "Then I beg you, father, to send him to my father's house, for I have five brothers, so that he may warn them, lest they also come into this place of torment." But Abraham said, "They have Moses and the prophets; let them hear them." And he said, "No, father Abraham; but if some one goes to them from the dead, they will repent." He said to him, "If they do not hear Moses and the prophets, neither will they be convinced if some one should rise from the dead" (Luke 16:27-31, RSV).

On another occasion Jesus referred to the writings of Moses, claiming them to be as powerful as His own spoken words:

> Do not think that I shall accuse you to the Father; it is Moses who accuses you, on whom you set your hope. If you believed Moses, you would believe me, for he wrote of me. But if you do not believe his writings, how will you believe my words? (John 5:45-47, RSV).

But people will believe what Moses wrote. Multitudes will believe not only the written words of Moses, but also the words of Matthew, Mark, Luke, John, Paul and Peter, and all the other writers of Scripture, if they are just given an opportuhity to read the precious Word for themselves. Meanwhile, we must use every church growth principle and every form of communication that God has given us to make disciples of all nations.

APPENDIX

Scripture References to Bible Reading and the Power of the Written Word

In Deuteronomy 6:6-9, Moses writes by inspiration of God, saying

> And you must think constantly about these
> commandments I am giving you today. You must
> teach them to your children and talk about them
> when you are at home or out for a walk; at bedtime
> and the first thing in the morning. Tie them on
> your finger, wear them on your forehead, and write
> them on the doorposts of your house (Living Bible).

God later spoke similar words to the children of Israel
through His servant Joshua, saying:

> Constantly remind the people about these
> laws, and you yourself must think about them
> every day and every night so that you will be
> sure to obey all of them. For only then will
> you succeed (Joshua 1:8, Living Bible).

While these words, like those above, cannot be taken as a
command that every person be literate, they imply at least that
for spiritual growth the leadership had to be literate, including the leadership of each household.

In the first Psalm we read:

> Oh, the joys of those who do not follow evil
> men's advice, who do not hang around with sinners,
> scoffing at the things of God: But they delight

in doing everything God wants them to, and
day and night are always meditating on his
laws and thinking about ways to follow him
more closely (Psalm 1:1-2, Living Bible).

How much easier it is to know that Word of God and to
meditate therein, if one is able to read it over and over and
over again.

In 1 Timothy 4:13 the Apostle Paul reminds the young minister
Timothy to devote attention to "the public reading of the
Scriptures" (New English Bible). The exhortation apparently
is to read the Scriptures loudly and clearly and with expression.

In his second letter to Timothy, the Apostle Paul reminds the
young minister:

...from early childhood you have been familiar
with the sacred writings which have power to make
you wise and lead you to salvation through faith
in Christ Jesus. Every inspired Scripture has its
use for teaching the truth and refuting error, or
for reformation of manners and discipline in right
living, so that the man who belongs to God may be
efficient and equipped for good work of every kind
(2 Timothy 3:15-17,NEB).

The written Word of God is powerful, as powerful as a message
from one risen from the dead. In Luke 16, in the story of the
rich man and Lazarus, the rich man lifted up his eyes in hell,
and pleaded:

"Will you send him to my father's house, where I
have five brothers, to warn them, so that they
too may not come to this place of torment?" But
Abraham said, "They have Moses and the prophets;
let them listen to them." "No, father Abraham,"
he replied, "but if someone from the dead visits
them, they will repent." Abraham answered, "If
they do not listen to Moses and the prophets,
they will pay no heed even if someone should rise
from the dead" (Luke 16:27-31, NEB).

In John 5:45-47 Jesus told the Jews:

If you believed Moses you would believe what
I tell you, for it was about me that he wrote. But
if you do not believe what he wrote, how are you to
believe what I say? (NEB)

The author of the fourth Gospel writes:

>   ...these are written that you may believe
>   that Jesus is the Christ, the Son of God, and
>   that believing you may have life in His name
>   (John 20:31, RSV).

In his first epistle, John writes:

>   I write this to you who believe in the name
>   of the Son of God that you may know that you
>   have eternal life   (1 John 5:13, RSV).

The Bible records three of Satan's attacks upon Jesus, and every time Jesus defeated Satan, saying, "It is written..." (Matthew 4:1-11; Luke 4:1-13).

We see, then, that the written Word of God can be used to convert; it can be used with as much impact as a message from one risen from the dead, or from Christ Himself. It gives assurance of salvation, and it is profitable for doctrine, for reproof, for correction, and for instruction in righteousness. And it can be used to defeat the devil.

Glossary

Church Growth: In this dissertation, refers not to the physical growth of the nominal church, but to the spiritual and physical growth of the truly born-again believers in Jesus Christ--the true Christian Church.

Dynamic Equivalence Translation: This is a translation that (1) sounds natural to the receptors and (2) has an impact upon them equivalent to that experienced by the original readers of the original writings in the original language (Kraft 1973:277).

Indigenous Church: Not only a church that is self-supporting, self-governing, and self-propagating, but one that has its own form of church government, its own music, its own order of service, its own methods of communicating the Gospel, its own architecture and art forms, etc. In short, everything about it is indigenous.

Literacy: In this dissertation, refers to "functional literacy" the ability to read the newspaper and the Bible with comprehension, to fill out application forms, to follow printed instructions, and the like. A person is literate when he can understand anything in print that he can understand when communicated orally.

Bibliography

ABEL, J.F. and BOND, N.J.
    1929 *Illiteracy in the Several Countries of the World.*
         Washington, D.C., U.S.Dept.of Interior, Bur.of Educ.

ABERLY, John
    1945 *An Outline of Missions.* Philadelphia, Muhlenberg Press.

ADDISON, James Thayer
    1936 *The Medieval Missionary: A Study of the Conversion of Europe.* New York, International Missionary Council.

ALLEN, Roland
    1972 *Missionary Methods, St. Paul's or Ours?* Grand Rapids, Mich., Wm.B.Eerdmans Publishing Co.

AMERICAN BIBLE SOCIETY RECORD
    1972-1975 Vols. 117 through 120. New York, American Bible Society.

    1973 "In Every Tongue and Nation" Part 3, Vol.118,No.6,pp.7-9. New York, American Bible Society.

    1973 "In Every Tongue and Nation" Part 4, Vol.118,No.7,pp. 27-31. New York, American Bible Society.

BAHUA, Pedro
    1975 Personal Interview, Quito, Ecuador, September 22.

BAINTON, Roland H.
    1950 *Here I Stand: A Life of Martin Luther.* New York,
          Abingdon-Cokesbury Press.

    1962 *The Medieval Church.* Princeton, N.J., D. Van Nostrand
          Co., Inc.

    1964 *The Horizon History of Christianity.* New York,
          American Heritage Publishing Company.

BALDSON, J.P.V.D.
    1969 *Life and Leisure in Ancient Rome.* New York, McGraw-
          Hill Book Company.

BAMBERGER, Bernard J.
    1957 *The Story of Judaism.* New York, The Union of American
          Hebrew Congregations.

BARCLAY, William
    1959 *The Master's Men. Character Sketches of the Disciples.*
          New York, Abingdon Press.

BARRETT, David
    1970 "A.D. 2000: 350 Million Christians in Africa", *Inter-
          national Review of Missions,* Vol.59, January,pp.39-54.

BARRY, Frank Russell
    1932 *The Relevance of Christianity.* London, Nisbet & Co.

BEACH, Harlan P.
    n.d. *The Cross in the Land of the Trident.* New York,
          Fleming H.Revell.

BEACH, Harlan P. & FAHS, Charles H.
    1925 *World Missionary Atlas.* New York, Institute of Social
          and Religious Research.

BEDFORD, F.J.
    1952 *The Bible in East Africa.* London, British and Foreign
          Society.

BENAISSA, Taik
    1975 Personal Interview, Lomalinda, Colombia, September 5.

BENDER-SAMUEL, John
    1961 Personal Interview, Yahe, Ogoja Province, Nigeria,
          August 3.

BENNETT, Charles
    1968 *Tinder in Tabasco.* Grand Rapids, Wm.B.Eerdmans Pub. Co.

BIBLE LITERATURE INTERNATIONAL
  n.d. *The Quiet Miracle*. Columbus, Ohio, Bible Literature
        International.

BLISS, Edwin Munsell
  n.d. *The Missionary Enterprise*. New York, Fleming H. Revell
        Co.

  1891 *The Encyclopedia of Missions* (ed.,2 vols.) New York,
        Funk and Wagnalls.

  1897 *A Concise History of Missions*. New York, Fleming H.
        Revell Co.

BLOUNT, Turner
  1976 Personal Interview, Huntington Beach, Ca., March 25.

BOAK, Arthur E.R. and SINNIGEN, Wm.G.
  1965 *A History of Rome to A.D. 565*. New York, The Macmillan
        Company.

BOUQUET, A.C.
  1953 *Everyday Life in New Testament Times*. New York,
        Charles Scribner's Sons.

BORMAN, Bud and Bobbie
  1975 Personal Interview, Limón Cocha, Ecuador, September 15.

BOYD, Frank M.
  1933 *God's Wonderful Book: The Origin, Lineage and
        Influence of the Bible*. Springfield, Mo., Gospel
        Publishing House.

BOYD, James Oscar
  1937 "The Bible in the Balkans", *Muslim World*, Vol.27,pp.
        251-253.

BRAGA, E. and GRUBB, K.G.
  1932 *The Republic of Brazil: A Survey of the Religious
        Situation*. London, World Dominion Press.

BRATTON, Fred Gladstone
  1959 *A History of the Bible*. Boston, Beacon Press.

BROOMHALL, Marshall
  1934 *The Bible in China*. London, British and Foreign Bible
        Society.

BROWN, Arthur J.
  1907 *The Foreign Missionary*. New York, Fleming H. Revell Co.

BROWNE, Benjamin P.
1952 *Christian Journalism for Today.* Philadelphia,Pa. The Judson Press.

BULLOCH, James
1963 *The Life of the Celtic Church.* Edinburgh, Saint Andrew Press.

BURNS, Donald and Nadine
1975 Personal Interview, Quito, Ecuador, September 21.

CABLE, Mildred and FRENCH, Francesca
1947 *The Bible in Mission Lands.* London, Fleming H. Revell Co.

CANTON, William
n.d. *A History of the British and Foreign Bible Society.* London, British & Foreign Bible Society.

CARCOPINO, Jerome
1940 *Daily Life in Ancient Rome.* New Haven, Yale University Press.

CARRICK, John Charles
1908 *Wycliffe and the Lollards.* Edinburg, T and T Clark.

CARR-SAUNDERS, A.M.
1936 *World Population.* London, Oxford at the Clarendon Press.

CHANDLER, Tertius and FOX, Gerald
1974 *3000 Years of Urban Growth.* New York, Academic Press.

CHANG, Lit-sen
1970 *A Strategy of Mission in the Orient.* Philadelphia, Presbyterian and Reformed Publishing Co.

CHAPMAN, Gordon H.
1975 "Japan: A Brief Christian History" in Donald Hoke (ed.)

CHIRGWIN, A.M.
1954 *The Bible in World Evangelism.* New York, Friendship Press.

1954 *A Book in His Hand.* London, United Bible Societies.

CIPOLLA, Carlo M.
1969 *Literacy and Development in the West.* Baltimore, Penguin Books.

CLAIBORNE, Robert
1974 *The Birth of Writing*. New York, Time-Life Books.

CLARKE, C.P.S.
1959 *A Short History of the Christian Church*. London,
Longmans.

COHEN, Paul A.
1963 *China and Christianity*. Cambridge, Mass., Harvard
University Press.

COOK, Bruce
1976 "Picture Communication in Barili" in *Interlit*, Vol.13,
No.1,pp.6-7,16. Elgin, Ill., David C. Cook Foundation
News.

COOK, Eulalia
1975 Personal Interview, Alfalit Office, Alajuela, Costa
Rica, September 28.

COOK, Harold R.
1954 *An Introduction to the Study of Christian Missions*.
Chicago, Moody Press.

1959 *Missionary Life and Work*. Chicago, Moody Press.

1963 *Strategy of Missions*. Chicago, Moody Press.

1971 *Historic Patterns of Church Growth*. Chicago, Moody
Press.

COOKSEY, J.J.
n.d. *The Land of the Vanished Church*. London, World
Dominion Press.

COWAN, George
1976 Personal Interview, Huntington Beach, Ca., March 25.

CRAGG, Kenneth
1964 *The Call of the Minaret*. New York, Oxford University
Press.

CROWE, Frederick
1850 *The Gospel in Central America; Containing a Sketch of
the Country, Physical and Geographical--Historical and
Political--Moral and Religious: A History of the
Baptist Mission in British Honduras and of the Introduction of the Bible into the Spanish American Republic of
Guatemala*. London, Charles Gilpin.

DANA, H.E.
  1937 *The New Testament World.* Nashville, Broadman Press.

DAVIES, J.Roderick
  1939 "Literature Evangelism in Brazil." *World Dominion,*
        Vol.XVII,No.3,July.

DAVIS, John D.
  1956 *Dictionary of the Bible.* Grand Rapids, Baker Book
        House.

DEANESLY, Margaret
  1959 *The Significance of the Lollard Bible.* London, The
        Athlone Press, University of London.

DEMOGRAPHIC YEARBOOK
  1964 New York, UNESCO.

DIRINGER, David
  1948 *The Alphabet, A Key to the History of Mankind.* New
        York, Philosophical Library.

  1962 *Writing.* London, Thames and Hudson.

DOBSCHUTZ, Ernst von
  1914 *The Influence of the Bible on Civilisation.* New York,
        Frederick Ungar Publishing Co.

DODD, C.H.
  1947 *The Bible Today.* New York, The Macmillan Company.

DORCHESTER, Daniel
  1933 *Christianity in the U. S. from the First Settlement to
        the Present Time.* New York, Hunt and Eaton.

DOUGLAS, J.D. (ed.)
  1962 *The New Bible Dictionary.* Grand Rapids, Wm.B.Eerdmans
        Co.

  1974 *The New International Dictionary of the Christian
        Church.* Grand Rapids, Mich., Zondervan Publishing Co.

DRUMMOND, Richard Henry
  1971 *A History of Christianity in Japan.* Grand Rapids, Wm.
        B.Eerdmans Co.

Du PLESSIS, J.
  1911 *A History of Christian Missions in South Africa.*
        London, Longmans, Green and Company.

DURANT, Will
1944 *Caesar and Christ.* New York, Simon and Schuster.

DWIGHT, Henry Otis, TUPPER, H. Allen and BLISS, Edwin M. (eds.)
1910 *The Encyclopedia of Missions.* New York, Funk and
Wagnalls Co.

EACHUS, Frances and CARLSON, Ruth
1975 Personal Interview, San Cristobal, Guatemala, August 6.

EDERSHEIM, Alfred
1953 *The Life and Times of Jesus the Messiah.* New York,
Longmans, Green and Company.

EDMAN, V.Raymond
1949 *The Light in Dark Ages.* Wheaton, Ill., Van Kampen
Press.

ERNST, Morris L. and POSNER, Judith A. (eds.)
1967 *Comparative International Almanac.* New York, Macmillan
and Company.

ESPENSHADE, Edward B. Jr. (ed.)
1975 *Goode's World Atlas*, 14th edition. Chicago, Rand
McNally & Co.

EVANGELICAL LITERATURE OVERSEAS
1968 *Bulletin,* Vol.II,No.4,p.10. Wheaton, Evangelical
Literature Overseas.

FOSTER, John
1960 *To All Nations.* London, Lutterworth Press.

FOSTER, Raymond
1961 *The Sierra Leone Church.* London, Society for Promoting
Christian Knowledge.

FRANCIS, J.de
1950 *Nationalism and Language Reform in China.* Princeton,
Princeton University Press.

FREDERICK, Paul William H.
1957 *John Wyclif and the First English Bible.* Fremont,Neb.,
Central Lutheran Theological Seminary.

FREITAG, Anton (ed.)
1963 *The 20th Century Atlas of the Christian World.* New
York, Hawthorne Books Inc.

FRENCH, W.E.
   1946 *The Gospel in India.* London, The Carey Press.

GAEBELEON, Frank E.
   1936 *Down through the Ages, The Story of the King James
         Bible.* New York, "Our Hope".

GAUSTAD, Edwin Scott
   1962 *Historical Atlas of Religion in America.* New York,
         Harper and Row, Publishers.

GELB, I.J.
   1952 *A Study of Writing.* Chicago, University of Chicago
         Press.

GIBBON, Edward
   1960 *Decline and Fall of the Roman Empire.* New York,
         Harcourt, Brace and Company.

GIBSON, John M.
   1958 *Soldiers of the Word. The Story of the American Bible
         Society.* New York, Philosophical Library.

GLASS, Frederick C.
   1943 *Adventures with the Bible in Brazil.* New York,
         Loizeaux Brothers, Bible Truth Depot.

GLOVER, Robert Hall and KANE, J.Herbert
   1960 *The Progress of World Wide Missions.* New York, Harper
         and Brothers.

GOLDEN, Hilda
   1968 "Literacy", *International Encyclopedia of Social
         Sciences*, New York, Macmillan and Free Press.

GONZALES, Juan
   1975 Personal Interview, Panama City, Panama, September 2.

GOODRICH, L. Carrington
   1963 *A Short History of the Chinese People.* New York,
         Harper and Row, Publishers.

GOODSPEED, Edgar J.
   1957 *The Twelve: The Story of Christ's Apostles.*
         Philadelphia, The John C. Winston Co.

GOODY, J.R.
   1968 *Literacy in Traditional Societies.* Cambridge,
         Cambridge University Press.

GRANT, C.M.
n.d. *Between the Testaments.* London, Fleming H. Revell Co.

GRAVES, Frank P.
1909 *A History of Education Before the Middle Ages.* New York, The Macmillan Company.

GREEN, J.R.
1879 *A Short History of the English People.* New York, Harper and Brothers.

GREENWAY, Roger S.
1973 *An Urban Strategy for Latin America.* Grand Rapids, Baker Book House.

GREGG, David
1908 *Between the Testaments.* New York, Funk and Wagnalls Company.

GRIFFEN, Paul F. (ed.)
1969 *Geography of Population.* Palo Alto, Ca., Fearon Publs.

GRIMES, Barbara F. (ed.)
1974 *Ethnologue,* Huntington Beach, Ca., Wycliffe Bible Translators, Inc.

GRIMLEY, John B. and ROBINSON, Gordon E.
1966 *Church Growth in Central and Southern Nigeria.* Grand Rapids, Wm.B.Edrdmans Publishing Co.

HALVERSON, Marian
1966 *Supervisors' Guide.* Nairobi, Kenya, East African Literature Bureau.

HAMILTON, Keith
1962 *Church Growth in the High Andes.* Lucknow, India, Lucknow Publishing House.

HAMMOND, Alvin D.
1975 "Japan's Postwar Renaissance" in Donald Hoke (ed.).

HARNACK, Adolph
1907-1925 *New Testament Studies,*Vol.V. London, Williams.

HASTINGS, James (ed.)
1963 *Dictionary of the Bible.* Rev.ed.by Frederick C. Grant and H.H. Rawley, New York, Charles Scribner's Sons.

HAWKES, Jacquetta and WOOLLEY, Leonard
1963 *Prehistory and the Beginnings of Civilization.* New
York, Harper and Row, Publishers.

HAYWARD, Harold D.
1933 "Chinese-Moslem Literature". *Muslim World,*Vol.23,
p.356.

HENNE, David
1975 Personal Interview, Chichicastenango, Guatemala, October 20.

HERKLOTS, H.G.G.
1950 *A Fresh Approach to the New Testament.* New York,
Abingdon-Cokesbury.

1957 *How Our Bible Came To Us, Its Texts and Versions.* New
York, Oxford University Press.

HEWITT, Gordon
1949 *Let the People Read. A Short History for the United
Society for Christian Literature.* London, Lutterworth
Press.

HOKE, Donald E. (ed.)
1975 *The Church in Asia.* Chicago, Moody Press.

HOLY BIBLE
1946 *Revised Standard Version.* Cleveland, Ohio, The World
Publishing Company.

HU, Chang-tu
1960 *China, Its People, Its Society, Its Culture.* New
Haven, H.R.A.F. Press.

HUDSPETH, W.H.
1952 *The Bible in China.* London, British and Foreign Bible
Society.

INTERNATIONAL REVIEW OF MISSIONS
1967 "Survey of the Year 1965-1966". ASIA, Vol.I,pp.3-21.

JACKSON, Samuel M. (ed.)
1958 *Schaff-Herzog Encyclopedia of Religious Knowledge.*
Vol.II. Grand Rapids, Baker Book House.

JEFFRIES, Sir Charles Joseph
1967 *Illiteracy, A World Problem.* New York, F.A. Praeger.

JOHNSON, Carl E.
  1969 *How in the World?* Old Tappan,N.J., Fleming H. Revell Co.

JOHNSON, Raymond and JOHNSON, Lu Verne
  1964 "Church Growth in the Ivory Coast". An unpublished manuscript, School of World Missions, Fuller Theological Seminary, Pasadena, Ca.

KANE, J.Herbert
  1971 *A Global View of Christian Missions*. Grand Rapids, Baker Book House.

  1975 *The Making of a Missionary*. Grand Rapids, Baker Book House.

KATZNER, Kenneth
  1975 *The Languages of the World*. New York, Funk and Wagnalls.

KERR, Isabel and BERG, Marie
  1975 Personal Interview, Lomalinda, Colombia, September 6.

KEYES, Nelson Beecher
  1959 *Story of the Bible World*. New York, C.S. Hammond and Company.

KILGOUR, R.
  1939 *The Bible Throughout the World*. London, World Dominion Press.

KLASSEN, Jacob Peter
  1974 "Fire on the Paramo". Unpublished master's thesis, Fuller Theological Seminary, Pasadena, Ca.

KONDO, Victor and KONDO, Riena
  1975 Personal Interview, Lomalinda, Colombia, September 7.

KRAFT, Charles
  1973 "Christianity and Culture". Unpublished manuscript, Fuller Theological Seminary, Pasadena, Ca.

KWAST, Lloyd E.
  1971 *The Discipling of West Cameroon*. Grand Rapids, Wm.B. Eerdmans Publishing Co.

LARA, Aguilar
  1975 Personal Interview, Mexico City, Mexico, November 8.

LATOURETTE, Kenneth Scott
  1946 *A Short History of the Far East*. New York, The
        Macmillan Company.

  1946 *The Development of China*. Boston, Houghton-Mifflin Co.

  1947 *The History of Japan*. New York, The Macmillan Co.

  1953 *A History of Christianity*. New York, Harper and Row,
        Publishers.

  1958–1962 *Christianity in a Revolutionary Age*. 5 Vols.,
        New York, Harper & Bros.

  1964 *China*. Englewood Cliffs, N.J., Prentice-Hall, Inc.

  1965 *Christianity Through the Ages*. New York, Harper & Row,
        Publishers.

  1970 *A History of the Expansion of Christianity*. 7 Vols.,
        Zondervan CEP ed., Grand Rapids, Zondervan Publishing
        House.

LAUBACH, Frank C.
  1950 *Literacy as Evangelism*. New York, Foreign Mission
        Conference of North America.

  1964 *How to Teach One and Win One for Christ*. Grand Rapids,
        Zondervan Publishing House.

  1969 *Christian, Save Your World*. Syracuse, N.Y., Laubach
        Literacy, Inc.

  1970 *Forty Years with the Silent Billion*. Old Tappan, N.J.,
        Fleming H. Revell Co.

LAUBACH, Frank C. and LAUBACH, Robert S.
  1960 *Toward World Literacy*. Syracuse, N.Y., Syracuse
        University Press.

LAUBACH, Robert S.
  1976 Letter to the author, February 6.

LEIVA, Ladislau
  1975 Letter to the author, August 20.

LINDSELL, Harold
  1955 *Missionary Principles and Practice*. Westwood, N.J.,
        Fleming H. Revell Co.

LOEWEN, Jacob
  1964 "Literacy: Bridge to Choco Evangelism". *Practical Anthropology*, Vol.12,pp.76-84.

LUZBETAK, Louis J.
  1970 *The Church and Cultures*. South Pasadena, Calif., William Carey Library (1975).

MACGREGOR, Geddes
  1959 *The Bible in the Making*. London, John Murray.

MACKAY, John Alexander
  1935 *That Other America*. New York, Friendship Press.

MACKENZIE, W. Douglas
  1897 *Christianity and the Progress of Man*. New York, Fleming H. Revell Co.

MARTIN, W.A.P.
  1881 *The Chinese, Their Education, Philosophy, and Letters*. New York, Harper & Bros., Publishers.

MASON, David E.
  1966 *Apostle to the Illiterates*. Grand Rapids, Mich., Zondervan Publishing Co.

  1967 *Reaching the Silent Billion: The Opportunity of Literacy Missions*. Grand Rapids, Mich., Zondervan Publishing House.

MASON, Joseph
  1976 Letter to the author, February 6.

MATHEWS, Basil
  1938 *The Church Takes Root in India*. New York, Friendship Press.

  1945 *Unfolding Drama in Southeast Asia*. London, Edinburgh House Press.

  1951 *Forward Through the Ages*. New York, Friendship Press.

  1952 *Disciples of All Nations*. London, Oxford Press

MATHEWS, Shailer
  1933 *New Testament Times in Palestine*. New York, Macmillan and Company.

McARTHUR, Harry and Lucille
  1975 Personal Interview, Guatemala City, Guatemala, Aug. 10.

McCUNE, Shannon
    1966   *Korea: Land of Broken Calm.*   Princeton, N.J.,
          D. Van Nostrand.

McGAVRAN, Donald
    1955   *The Bridges of God.*   New York, Friendship Press.

    1970   *Understanding Church Growth.*   Grand Rapids, Mich.,
          Wm.B.Eerdmans Publishing Company.

McGAVRAN, Grace
    1947   *Stories of the Book of Books.*   New York, Friendship
          Press.

McNEILL, John Thomas
    1974   *The Celtic Churches: A History A.D. 200 to 1200.*
          Chicago, Ill., University of Chicago Press.

MEDARY, Marjorie
    1954   *Each One, Teach One: Frank Laubach, Friend of Millions.*
          New York, Longmans Green.

METZGER, Bruce M.
    1965   *The New Testament, Its Background, Growth, and Content.*
          Nashville, Tenn., Abingdon Press.

MILLER, Basil
    1946   *Mary Slessor, Heroine of Calabar.*   Grand Rapids, Mich.,
          Zondervan Publishing House.

MOENNICH, Martha L.
    1950   *World Missions.*   Grand Rapids, Mich., Zondervan Pub-
          lishing House.

MONTGOMERY, Helen Barrett
    1920   *The Bible and Missions.*   West Medford, Mass., The
          Central Committee on the United Study of Foreign
          Missions.

MOORE, George F.
    1946   *Judaism in the First Centuries of the Christian Era.*
          The Age of the Tannaim.   Vol.1.   Cambridge, Mass.,
          Harvard University Press.

MORRIS, C.H.
    1954   *The Bible in Brazil.*   London, British and Foreign Bible
          Society.

MOULE, A.C.
    1930   *Christians in China before the Year 1550.*   London,
          Society for the Promulgation of the Gospel.

MOULE, Arthur Evans
    1911 *Half a Century in China*. New York, Hodder and
          Stoughton.

NADAL, Octavio
    1971 Report to Alfalit Headquarters on Work in the Domini-
          can Republic, March 18.

NEILL, Stephen
    1952 *The Christian Society*. New York, Harper & Bros.

    1964 *A History of Christian Missions*. Baltimore, Penguin
          Books, Inc.

    1970 *A Story of the Christian Church in India and Pakistan*.
          Grand Rapids, Mich., Wm.B.Eerdmans Publishing Co.

NEILL, Stephen, ANDERSON, Gerald, and GOODWIN, John (eds.)
    1971 *Concise Dictionary of the Christian World Mission*.
          Nashville, Abingdon Press.

NEVIUS, John L.
    1958 *Planting and Development of Missionary Churches*.
          Pusan, Korea, The Presbyterian and Reformed Publishing
          Company.

NEW ENCYCLOPAEDIA BRITANNICA
    1973 15th ed., 30 Vols. London, Wm. Benton, Publisher.

NICKEL, Benjamin J.
    n.d. *Along the Quichua Trail*. Missouri, Smithville Gospel
          Missionary Union.

NIDA, Eugene A.
    1952 *God's Word in Man's Language*. South Pasadena, Calif.,
          William Carey Library (1973).

    1960 *Message and Mission*. South Pasadena, Calif.,
          William Carey Library (1972).

    1972 *The Book of a Thousand Tongues*. Rev. ed., New York,
          United Bible Societies.

NORMAN, Ross (ed.)
    1961 *Life Pictorial Atlas*. New York, Time, Inc.

NORTH, Eric M. (ed.)
    1938 *The Book of a Thousand Tongues*. New York, American
          Bible Society.

OGG, Oscar
1948   *The 26 Letters.*   New York, Thomas Y. Crowell Co.

OH, Chae Kyung (ed.)
1958   *Handbook of Korea.*   New York, Pageant Press.

OLSON, Gilbert
1967   "Sierra Leone Africa - A Bold Plan", *Church Growth Bulletin*, Vol.IV,No.1,September.

1969   *Church Growth in Sierra Leone.*   Grand Rapids, Mich., Wm.B.Eerdmans Publishing Co.

ORR, J. Edwin
1965   *The Light of the Nations.*   Grand Rapids, Mich., Wm.B. Eerdmans Publishing Co.

OXFORD ECONOMIC ATLAS OF THE WORLD
1965   3rd ed. London, Oxford University Press.

PADWICK, C.E.
1938   "The Madras Meeting and Literature". *International Review of Missions*, Vol.28, Oct., pp.501-507.

PALMER, Donald C.
1974   *Explosion of People Evangelism.*   Chicago, Ill., Moody Press.

PARKER, Joseph I.
1938   *Interpretive Statistical Survey of the World Mission of the Christian Church.*   New York, International Missionary Council.

PATTERSON, George
1975   Personal Interview, La Ceiba, Honduras, October 4.

PAXSON, Frederich
1924   *History of the American Frontier 1763-1893.*   Boston, Houghton Mifflin Co.

PEI, Mario
1949   *The Story of Language.*   Philadelphia, J.B. Lippencott.

PERNOUD, Regine
1950   *The Glory of the Medieval World.*   London, Dennis Dobson.

PFEIFFER, Charles F.
1959   *Between the Testaments.*   Grand Rapids, Baker Book House.

PICKETT, J. Waskom
    1933 *Christian Mass Movements in India.* 2nd Indian ed.,
    Lucknow, Lucknow Publishing House.

PINNOCK, S.G.
    1917 *The Romance of Missions in Nigeria.* Richmond, Va.,
    Education Department, Foreign Mission Board, S.B.C.

PLATT, W.J.
    1934 *An African Prophet.* London, n.p.

PROSNER, Rebecca
    1966 *The Romance Languages: A Linguistic Introduction.*
    Garden City, N.J., Doubleday and Co., Inc.

PUDIATE, Rochunga
    1976 Letter to the author, February 16.

QUALBEN, Lars P.
    1955 *A History of the Christian Church.* New York, Thomas
    Nelson & Sons.

READ MAGAZINE
    1970 "Pictorial Material in the Education of Illiterates."
    Vol.5, No.1, Jan., pp.11-12. Ukarumpa EHD, Papua New
    Guinea, Summer Institute of Linguistics.

READ, Wm.R. and MONTERROSO,V.M. and JOHNSON, H.A.
    1969 *Latin American Church Growth.* Grand Rapids, Mich.,
    Wm.B.Eerdmans Publishing Co.

RICE, Robert F.
    1972 "Literacy Opens Closed Doors," reprint, *Interlit*, June.

ROBERTSON, E.H.
    1963 *The Bible in the Local Church.* New York, Associated
    Press.

ROBERTSON, J.C.F.
    1953 *The Bible in Japan.* London, British and Foreign Bible
    Society.

    1954 *The Bible in Korea.* London, British and Foreign Bible
    Society.

ROBINSON, H. Wheeler
    1940 *The Bible in Its Ancient and English Versions.* London,
    Oxford Press.

ROBINSON, Gordon E.
  1966 *Church Growth in Southern Nigeria.*   Grand Rapids, Mich.
        Wm.B.Eerdmans Publishing Co.

ROGERS, Edgar
  1913 *Canada's Greatest Need.*   Westminster, Society for the
        Propagation of the Gospel in Foreign Parts.

RUSSELL, D.S.
  1960 *Between the Testaments.*   Philadelphia, Muhlenberg
        Press.

RYCROFT, W. Stanley
  1942 *On This Foundation.*   New York, Friendship Press.

SAINT, Rachel
  1975 Personal Interview, Limón Cocha, Ecuador, September 15.

SALES, Jane M.
  1971 *The Planting of the Churches in South Africa.*   Grand
        Rapids, Wm.B.Eerdmans Publishing Co.

SANDERS, E.
  1944 "The Nile Mission Press." *Muslim World*, Vol.34,
        pp.209-213.

SARGENT, Mary
  1975 Personal Interview, Limon Cocha, Ecuador, September 16.

SAVAGE, John
  1939 "The Printed Page as a Pioneer." *World Dominion*, Vol.
        XVII, No.1, Jan., pp. 36-40.

SCHAFF, Philip
  1910 *History of the Christian Church*, Vol.I.   New York,
        Charles Scribner's Sons.

SCHEMPER, Chester
  1975 "He Put a New Song in Their Mouths." *The Sower*, Vol.
        XXIV, No.3, June.

SCHULZE, Gunther
  1977 Personal Interview, Pasadena, Ca., March 22.

SCHWARZ, W.
  1955 *Principles and Problems of Biblical Translation.*
        Cambridge, University Press.

SCHURER, Emil
  1901 *History of the Jewish People.*   Vol.II, Edinburgh, T.
        and T. Clark.

SHACKLOCK, Floyd
    1967 *World Literacy Manual*. New York, Committee on World
          Literacy and Christian Literature.

SHEARER, Roy E.
    1966 *Wildfire: Church Growth in Korea*. Grand Rapids, Mich.
          Wm.B.Eerdmans Publishing Co.

SILCOX, Claris Edwin
    1933 *Church Union in Canada, Its Causes and Consequences*.
          New York, Institute of Social and Religious Research.

SIMONSON, Bengt K.
    1965 *The Way of the Word*. New York, The Committee on World
          Literacy and Christian Literature.

SINKER, Margaret
    1953 *The Bible in India, Pakistan, and Ceylon*. London,
          British and Foreign Bible Society.

SLOCUM, Marianna and GERDEL, Florence
    1975 Personal Interview, Lomalinda, Colombia, September 5.

SMALLEY, B.
    1952 *The Study of the Bible in the Middle Ages*. Oxford,
          Blackwell.

SMALLEY, Frank A.
    1944 "Christian Literature in China." *International Review
          of Missions*, Vol.33, July, pp.296-303.

SMALLEY, William S. (ed.)
    1974 *Readings in Missionary Anthropology*. South Pasadena,
          Calif., William Carey Library.

SMITH, Asbury
    1958 *The Twelve Christ Chose*. New York, Harper & Bros.

SMITH, Bill
    1975 Personal Interview, Totonicapán, Guatemala, October 19.

SMITH, George
    1897 *A Short History of Christian Missions*. Edinburgh, T.
          and T. Clark.

SOLTAU, T.Stanley
    1966 *Missions at the Crossroads*. Grand Rapids, Mich.,
          Baker Book House.

SOUTHON, Arthur E.
    1935 *Gold Coast Methodism*. London, Cargate Press.

STANDARD EDUCATION CORPORATION
  1975 *New Standard Encyclopedia,* 1975 ed.,s.v.,"Alexandrian
        Library."

STEVEN, Hugh
  1970 *Manuel.* Old Tappan, N.J., Fleming H. Revell Co.

SULLIVAN, Helen
  1933 "Literacy and Illiteracy." *Encyclopedia of Social
        Sciences,* Vol.9. New York, Macmillan and Free Press.

SWEAZEY, George E.
  1953 *Effective Evangelism.* New York, Harper & Bros., Publs.

SWEETMAN, J.W.
  1953 *The Bible in Islam.* London, British and Foreign Bible
        Society.

TENNEY, Merrill C.
  1953 *The New Testament.* Grand Rapids, Mich., Wm.B.Eerdmans
        Publishing Co.

THIESSEN, Henry Clarence
  1943 *Introduction to the New Testament.* Grand Rapids, Mich.
        Wm.B.Eerdmans Publishing Co.

THOMPSON, James W.
  1966 *The Literacy of the Laity in the Middle Ages.*
        Berkeley, Calif., University of California Press.

TILLY, E.A.
  1901 "Brazil: A Survey of the Field." Methodist Episcopal
        Church South, *General Missionary Conference of the
        Methodist Church in the South.*

TIME MAGAZINE
  1975 December 22.

TIPPET, Alan R.
  1967 *Solomon Islands Christianity.* South Pasadena, Calif.,
        William Carey Library (1975).

  1971 *People Movements in Southern Polynesia.* Chicago,
        Moody Press.

  1973 *Verdict Theology in Missionary Theory.* South Pasadena,
        Calif., William Carey Library.

TITUS, Murray T.
  1943 "Christian Literature for Moslems in India." *Muslim
        World,* Vol.33, pp.187-190.

TOLLIVER, Ralph
1975 "The Philippines" in Donald Hoke (ed.)

TURNER, Glen and Jeannie
1975 Personal Interview, Limón Cocha, Ecuador, Sept. 16.

UNESCO
1948 *Statistical Yearbook.* Paris, UNESCO.

1952 *Basic Facts and Figures.* Paris, UNESCO.

1957 *World Illiteracy at Mid-Century.* Paris, UNESCO.

1964 *Statistical Yearbook.* Paris, UNESCO.

1970 *Statistical Yearbook.* Paris, UNESCO.

1972 *Literacy 1969-71.* Paris, UNESCO.

1973 *Statistical Yearbook.* Paris, UNESCO.

URE, Ruth
1946 *The Highway of Print.* New York, Friendship Press.

UNITED STATES DEPARTMENT OF COMMERCE, BUREAU OF THE CENSUS
1930 *Religious Bodies: 1926.* 2 Vol. Washington, U.S.
Gov't. Printing Office.

VAN HORNE, Marion
1970 *Give the Children Wings.* New York, Committee on World
Literacy and Christian Literature.

VARGAS, Kenneth
1975 Personal Interview, Managua, Nicaragua, October 2.

WAGNER, C. Peter
1973 *Look Out! The Pentecostals Are Coming.* Carol Stream,
Ill., Creation House.

WAKATOMA, Pius
1972 "Africa Needs a Robust Literature." *Interlit,* Vol.9,
No.1, March, p.13. Elgin,Ill., David C. Cook Foundation News.

WALLIS, Ethel Emily
1959 *Two Thousand Tongues to Go.* New York, Harper & Row,
Publishers.

WARREN, W.H.
1938 "The Madras Meeting of Christian Literature in India."
International Review of Missions, Vol.28, Oct., pp.
508-517.

WATKINS, Lois
    1978 *The Strategic Use of Literacy and Literature in World
          Evangelization.* S. Pasadena, Ca., William Carey Library.

WEINS, Marlene
    1975 Personal Interview, San Cristóbal, Verapaz, Guatemala,
          August 6.

WEST, Andrew Fleming
    1912 *Alcuin and the Rise of the Christian Schools.* New
          York, AMS Press.

WESTCOTT, Brooke Foss
    1864 *The Bible in the Church.* London, Macmillan and Co.

WILLIAMS, Theodore
    1975 "India a Seething Subcontinent" in Donald Hoke (ed.).

WILSON, Christy
    1937 "The Bible and Moslems." *The Moslem World*, Vol.27,
          July, pp.237-250.

WOLD, Joseph C.
    1966 "Now to Father a People Movement." *Church Growth
          Bulletin*, Vol.III,No.1,September.

    1968 *God's Impatience in Liberia.* Grand Rapids, Mich.,
          Wm.B.Eerdmans Publishing Co.

WORLD VISION
    1977 "Globe at a Glance." Vol.21,No.7,July,p.22.

WRONG, Margaret
    1944 "Literacy and Literature for African Peoples."
          International Review of Missions, Vol.33,April,pp
          pp.193-199.

WYSHAM, William N.
    1937 "The Use of Literature in Evangelism." *Muslim World*,
          Vol.27,pp.56-64.

YANAGITA, Tomonobu
    1957 *A Short History of Christianity in Japan.* Sendai,
          Japan Seisho Tosho Kankokai.

YOUNG, Robert
    1955 *Analytical Concordance to the Bible.* Grand Rapids,
          Wm.B.Eerdmans Publishing Co.

YUTANG, Lin
    1935 *My Country and My People.* New York, John Day.

Index

Aachen, 45
Abor people, 117
Academies, theological, 6
Acquinas, Thomas, 54
Aedesius, 29
Afghanistan, 27
Africa, 12,30,48,74: Division
 of, by European nations, 97;
 Exploration of, 97; Mission
 work in, between A.D. 1500
 and A.D. 1800, 74; south of
 the Sahara, 12,97,110,154-6.
 See also East Africa, North
 Africa, South Africa, West
 Africa, *and various count-
 ries*
Aguacateco, 151
Aidan, 41,43
Aitken, Robert, 87
Aix-la-Chapelle. *See* Aachen
Albertus Magnus, 54
Albigenses, 58
Alcuin, 45
Aldhelm, 39
Alemanni, 42
Alexander the Great, 3,7-8
Alexander of Hales, 54
Alexandria, 5,8,17-21,23,29-
 30,50: catechetical school of,
 30; center of Christianity, 8;
 intellectual capital, 8;
 library of, 8; literacy in,
 at time of Christ, 11
Alfalit, 152

Alfa y Omega Movimiento, 150
Algeria, 154
Alfred the Great, 36
All Nations Literacy Movement,
 150
Alopen, 50
Alphabet: Armenian, 29; Cyrilic
 or Slavic, 47; development
 of, 132-3; Indic, 133; Irish,
 32; Zyryan, 57. *See also*
 Writing systems
Ambrose, 20
American Baptist Home Mission-
 ary Society, 87
American Home Missionary Soc-
 iety, 87-8
American Missionary Associa-
 tion, 90
American Bible Society, 88,95
American Board of Commiss-
 ioners for Foreign Missions,
 87
American Home Missionary Soc-
 iety, 87
American Tract Society, organ-
 ized, 88
Amharic, 30
Amoneburg, 44
Andelm, 46
Angles, 41-42
Anglican Church: in India,
 117; in Nigeria, 108
Anglican Missions, 109
Anglo-Saxon, 25,39,41-42

211

New Testament: writing & circulation of, 14-16; use of, in evangelism, 15-16,24-25. *See also* Bible translations, Bible reading, Bible distribution
Nigeria, 106-08,156
Ninian, 31
Nommensen, Ludwig Ingwer, 129
North Africa, 153
North African Mission, 153
Northumbria, 41,43
Norway, 57
Nova Scotia, 99
Nunneries, 44
Nyasaland. *See* Malawi

Old Testament: commonly read in apostolic times, 21-23; evangelistic use of, 24; translation of, 9-10. *See also* Septuagint
Olga, 48
On the Division of Nature, 46
Operation Mobilization, 153
Opium Wars, 120
Oraon people, 117
Origen, 17,19,24,30
Orthodox Church, 57-58
Otetelo tribe, 154
Oxford University, 65,70

Pacific islands, 137-140,154
Paez Indians (Colombia), 149-50
Paez language (Colombia), Bible translation, 149
Pakistan, 175
Palestine, 3,7: schools of, 6, 11,30
Panama, 146-48
Pantaenus, 30,32
Papacy: rise of, 46; attitude toward missions, 63; toward Bible reading & translations, 56
Paper, manufacture of, 62
Paraguay, 73
Paris Evangelical Missionary Society, 72, 109
Parochial schools, 89
Pashto, Bible translation, 115
Patrick, 31-32,39
Paul, Apostle, writings of, 22
Pentecostals, 156
People movements: in Ecuador,

142-43; in Ghana, 105; in Ivory Coast, 104; in Peru, 144-45; in the Congo, 154
Pepin the Short, 36
Pergamon, 8
Persecution of Christians, 60; in Bolivia, 146; in China, 119,122; in Japan, 77,122; in Madagascar, 111-12; in Mexico, 149; in Russia, 48; of Hus, 60; of Lollards, 60
Persia(n), 30,33,50; language, revision of Bible in, 114
Peru, 94,144
Peshitta, 26
Peter, The First and *Second Epistles of*, 16
Philadelphia Bible Society, 87
Philippines, 137-38
Philo, 4
Phoenicia, 28
Pickett, J. Wascom, 119
Picts, 31, 40-41
Pietism, 67,69
Pilgrims, 68
Pilgrim's Progress, 18
Pius IX, Pope, 162
Plan of Union, 87
Plutschau, Heinrich, 76
Polo, Marco, 63
Polo, Nicolo, 63
Polycarp, 17-19
Polygamy, 100,107
Polytheistic peoples: church growth among, 58
Portuguese: in Africa, 72,74; in Brazil, 73,93; in India, 75; in Nigeria, 106
Presbyterians: in early United States missions, 87; in Liberia, 103; in Nigeria, 107; in South America, 109; in the Philippines, 138
Princeton University, 88-89
Printing: prior to Reformation, 62; invention of, 62; introduction in China, 51; relationship of, to Bible translation, 62
Protestant church membership: in China, 119-22; in India, 113; in Japan, 125; in Latin America, 95; in Rhodesia, 110; in South Africa, 109-10; in the Philippines, 138; in the West Indies, 95
Protestant Episcopal Missionary

Morris Watkins was born in 1923 and grew up in the Los Angeles area. He graduated from Concordia Teacher's College in Seward, Nebraska, now married to Lois Bargman. He taught in Lutheran schools in Iowa and Nebraska before receiving a call to Nigeria, where he taught in the Lutheran High School and the Lutheran Teacher Training Center.

In 1953 the family returned to California, where he worked as a teacher and principal. He then attended Concordia Theological Seminary in Springfield, Illinois, graduating in 1959, and the family returned to Nigeria where he started the Lutheran Bible Institute in Ogaja Province and served as principal there for three years. After further study during furlough in 1962, he became Director of Literature and Literacy for the Lutheran Church of Nigeria.

In 1964 he and his wife founded the Lutheran Bible Translators and he served as Executive Director for eight years. They also founded the All Nations Literacy Movement in the spring of 1972, of which he still serves as president.

BOOKS BY THE
WILLIAM CAREY LIBRARY

STRATEGY OF MISSION

Chur   paper,
25   **DATE DUE**

Com   rles J.
 Me
The (edited
 by
Cruci   et al.,
 $7
Evan   win L.
 Fri
Evang   84 pp.
The I $2.95
 pap
A Mar   44 pp.
Missio   Daniel
 C.
Readir   edited
 by N

AREA

Christi   rmed
 App   ander
 Werf
Church
The De   iouth
 Pacifi
Indones   , Jr.,
 $6.95
New M   aking
Baptis~ ~y vvilliam L. Wagner, $8.95 paper, 368 pp.

Toward Continuous Mission: Strategizing for the Evangelization of Bolivia by
W. Douglas Smith, $4.95 paper, 208 pp.

APPLIED ANTHROPOLOGY

Becoming Bilingual: A Guide to Language Learning by Donald Larson and
William A. Smalley, $5.95x paper, 426 pp.

Christopaganism or Indigenous Christianity? edited by Tetsunao Yamamori
and Charles R. Taber, $5.95 paper, 242 pp.

The Church and Cultures: Applied Anthropology for the Religious Worker by
Louis J. Luzbetak, $5.95x paper, 448 pp.

Customs and Cultures: Anthropology for Christian Missions by Eugene A. Nida,
$3.95 paper, 322 pp.

Message and Mission: The Communication of the Christian Faith by Eugene
A. Nida, $3.95x paper, 254 pp.

Tips on Taping: Language Recording in the Social Sciences by Wayne and
Lonna Dickerson, $4.95x paper, 208 pp.